The Meta Incognita Project
Contributions to Field Studies

edited by
Stephen Alsford

Mercury Series
Directorate Paper No. 6

published by the
Canadian Museum of Civilization
in collaboration with the
Arctic Studies Center,
Smithsonian Museum of Natural History

with the authorization of the
Meta Incognita Project Steering Committee

© Canadian Museum of Civilization 1993

Canadian Cataloguing in Publication Data

Main entry under title:

The Meta Incognita project: contributions to field studies

(Mercury series, ISSN 0316-1854)
(Directorate paper / Canadian Museum of Civilization; no. 6)
Includes an abstract in French.
Issued in collaboration with the Arctic Studies Center, Smithsonian Museum of Natural History.
ISBN 0-660-14010-1

1. Inuit — Northwest Territories — Frobisher Bay — Antiquities.
2. Frobisher Bay (N.W.T.) — Antiquities.
3. Arctic Regions — Northwest Territories — Frobisher Bay — Discovery and exploration.
I. Alsford, Stephen, 1952–
II. Canadian Museum of Civilization.
III. Arctic Studies Center (U.S.)
IV. Title.
V. Series.
VI. Series : Directorate paper / Canadian Museum of Civilization; no. 6.

E99.E7M47 1992   971.9'95
C93-099432-9

Printed and bound in Canada

Published by
Canadian Museum of Civilization
100 Laurier Street
P.O. Box 3100, Station B
Hull, Quebec
J8X 4H2

Cover photo:
A Skirmish with the Eskimo, by John White. *Courtesy of the Trustees of the British Museum*

Paper Coordinator: Stephen Alsford

Production Coordinator: Lise Rochefort

Cover Design: Francine Boucher

Canada

OBJECT OF THE MERCURY SERIES

The Mercury Series is designed to permit the rapid dissemination of information pertaining to the disciplines in which the Canadian Museum of Civilization is active. Considered an important reference by the scientific community, the Mercury Series comprises over three hundred specialized publications on Canada's history and prehistory.

Because of its specialized audience, the series consists largely of monographs published in the language of the author.

In the interest of making information available quickly, normal production procedures have been abbreviated. As a result, grammatical and typographical errors may occur. Your indulgence is requested.

Titles in the Mercury Series can be obtained by writing to:

Mail Order Services
Publishing Division
Canadian Museum of Civilization
100 Laurier Street
P.O. Box 3100, Station B
Hull, Quebec
J8X 4H2

BUT DE LA COLLECTION MERCURE

La collection Mercure vise à diffuser rapidement le résultat de travaux dans les disciplines qui relèvent des sphères d'activités du Musée canadien des civilisations. Considérée comme un apport important dans la communauté scientifique, la collection Mercure présente plus de trois cents publications spécialisées portant sur l'héritage canadien préhistorique et historique.

Comme la collection s'adresse à un public spécialisé celle-ci est constituée essentiellement de monographies publiées dans la langue des auteurs.

Pour assurer la prompte distribution des exemplaires imprimés, les étapes de l'édition ont été abrégées. En conséquence, certaines coquilles ou fautes de grammaire peuvent subsister : c'est pourquoi nous réclamons votre indulgence.

Vous pouvez vous procurer la liste des titres parus dans la collection Mercure en écrivant au :

Service des commandes postales
Division de l'édition
Musée canadien des civilisations
100, rue Laurier
C.P. 3100, succursale B
Hull (Québec)
J8X 4H2

ABSTRACT

The Meta Incognita Project investigates Martin Frobisher's Arctic expeditions of 1576-78 (which included the first English attempt to establish a colony in Canada and to mine its mineral resources) and their effects on the culture of the Inuit he encountered. The project is also aimed at ensuring the long-term protection of the historic sites associated with these expeditions. Although the voyages are well documented in contemporary official records and personal accounts, this evidence presents only the Elizabethan perspective and leaves unanswered intriguing questions, such as why Frobisher and his backers believed there was gold in ore that was actually worthless. The project seeks a fuller understanding of this episode in the history of European exploration of the New World through archaeological data, Inuit oral history, and further archival studies.

This progress report, focusing particularly, but not exclusively, on field investigations conducted in 1991 and on the analytical work supporting them, comprises papers by Canadian and American archaeologists, anthropologists and geologists, as well as other scientists engaged in the project. Besides the preliminary findings from their work, the papers present an introduction to the historical context and to the problems and questions facing researchers.

RÉSUMÉ

Le projet Meta Incognita se penche sur les expéditions de Martin Frobisher dans l'Arctique, entre 1576 et 1578, qui comprennent une première tentative de l'Angleterre pour établir une colonie au Canada et pour en explorer les ressources minières. Le projet étudie aussi l'influence de ces événements sur la culture des Inuit que les voyageurs ont croisés. Il se propose également d'assurer la protection à long terme des sites historiques concernés. Bien que des documents officiels de l'époque et des relations de voyageurs livrent de bonnes informations sur ces expéditions, ils se situent néanmoins dans une perspective élisabéthaine et laissent de côté des questions litigieuses, comme celle de savoir pourquoi Frobisher et ses bailleurs ont cru que du minerai sans valeur pouvait contenir de l'or. Le projet tente de mieux comprendre cet épisode de l'exploration européenne du Nouveau Monde grâce à des données archéologiques, à l'histoire orale des Inuit et à de nouvelles enquêtes dans les archives.

Ce rapport traite, d'une manière particulière mais non exclusive, des recherches menées sur le terrain en 1991 et des analyses qu'elles ont engendrées. Les auteurs, qui collaborent au projet, sont d'origine canadienne et américaine et œuvrent dans les domaines de l'archéologie, de l'anthropologie, de la géologie ou d'autres disciplines scientifiques. En plus de présenter les résultats provisoires de leurs travaux, ils situent les expéditions dans leur contexte historique et dressent la liste des problèmes et questions qu'ils se posent.

iv

CONTENTS

LIST OF TABLES

LIST OF FIGURES

Introduction

It was just over one hundred and thirty years ago that American explorer Charles Francis Hall, probing the Baffin Island region in the belief he might find survivors of the ill-fated Franklin expedition, with some excitement deduced - by comparing oral information supplied by local Inuit with what he had read of Sir Martin Frobisher's Arctic expeditions of 1576-78 - that he had come across the North American terminus of those expeditions. That terminus was a small and desolate island off the coast of the Baffin Island peninsula now named after Hall. The island had no identity for the Inuit other than their association of it with the white-skinned visitors, and had been named accordingly; Hall transcribed the name as "Kod-lu-narn".

Consequent to Frobisher's explorations, the region in which Kodlunarn Island was situated was named (by Queen Elizabeth I) "Meta Incognita", the unknown shore, representing as it did for the English the boundary of certain knowledge of the region's geography. "Meta Incognita" was at that time applied to the lands stretching along either side of what was optimistically named "Frobisshers Streights", a thoroughfare (it was hoped) between the northern Atlantic and the seas surrounding fabled Cathay, but subsequently proving to be a bay.

Frobisher's expeditions are similarly perceived as a "dead end". Notwithstanding the initial commemorative praise his exploits won from Elizabethan poets, even before he reached England on his return in 1578 it had been realized that a severe disappointment was in store. The original intent of the first voyage, to find a Northwest Passage, had been deflected by the discovery of a mysterious "black ore" which, it came to be believed, bore gold and silver. A new smelting works was even built in England specifically to handle the anticipated bonanza of precious ore to be excavated by Frobisher. On the latter two voyages, now backed by a consortium of England's most notable merchants, financiers, and political leaders (including the Queen herself), serious exploration took a back seat to mining; perhaps unfortunately, since the results of exploration might have been more beneficial. Frobisher discovered no route through to Cathay. The hundreds of tons of ore, arduously hand-mined and loaded into the holds of his ships, were found to be virtually worthless. A plan to establish a colony on Kodlunarn was abortive. Efforts to develop friendly relations with local Inuit (seen as a source of geographical and geological knowledge), from promising beginnings, quickly turned sour.

If the expeditions now receive relatively little attention from scholars, and tend to be viewed as a footnote to the historical mainstream of European maritime exploration, it is in part because they failed in the terms indicated above. Yet also because the voyages are among the most thoroughly documented of that era: notably in the chronicles compiled by Frobisher's captains, George Best and Edward Fenton, but also in accounts by several lesser participants in one or other of the voyages, and in a range of other documents whose survival owes something to the requirements of evidence for the litigation following the financial failure of the venture. Historians have perhaps felt that the Frobisher episode in the story of northern exploration was well enough understood from the known and well-exploited archival sources.

Nonetheless, there remain a number of question-marks surrounding the expeditions, not least because of the secrecy imposed over certain aspects of operations by the English authorities and Frobisher himself. The "black ore" was not fool's gold, nor did it contain even the amount of gold normally found in most ores. Why, then, did some assays suggest that the ore was rich in precious metals, and why did the sponsors of the expeditions allow themselves to be persuaded (in the face of contrary evidence) by those assays? Why did further assays on Kodlunarn apparently fail to alter Frobisher's conviction on the nature of the ore? How were the mining and assaying operations actually carried out (something on which documentary sources have little to say)? What are the precise whereabouts of the mines, furnaces, and other sites referred to in the contemporary accounts? What was the fate of several English crewmen who went missing during Frobisher's stays on Kodlunarn? What effects did the infusion of European materials rare in the Arctic (e.g. metals, tiles) have on the socio-economic development of Inuit society? These are questions which the written records alone cannot answer.

For over a century after Hall's discovery the Frobisher sites on Kodlunarn, remote and isolated, received only a handful of brief investigative visits from archaeologists. Interest intensified after 1981, the year Dr. William Fitzhugh of the Smithsonian Institution (repository of the Hall archives and remains of part of his Arctic collections) assembled a team of American and Canadian researchers to explore Kodlunarn and examine questions such as those noted above. As part of his ongoing survey work in the Arctic, he and his team examined Kodlunarn again, and also neighbouring Frobisher and Inuit sites, in the summer of 1990. At the same time, a small group of Canadian archaeologists went to Kodlunarn to make their own preliminary assessment.

In 1964 Kodlunarn had been declared, by the National Historic Sites and Monuments Board of Canada, a site of national historic importance, worthy of preservation and investigation; although the designation had no immediate consequences in either area. With the increased interest of archaeologists in the site by 1990, indicators that growing public awareness of the site (the latter in part a consequence of the former) would encourage group tourism or more casual souvenir-hunting there, and a growing consciousness of the fragility of the island's natural and historical resources, it was felt that Canada should take the lead in directing any research programme. The island's resources, although unspectacular, are also non-renewable; they present an historical landscape not so greatly changed from a few years after Frobisher's final departure (once the main thrust of Inuit scavenging had likely taken its toll). It was therefore felt incumbent on Canadian authorities to ensure that the need for long-term preservation of the site was met. An inter-institutional Steering Committee was set up to articulate goals for research activities, to coordinate independent research initiatives, to ensure the communication of findings, and to pave the way for the long-term protection and management of Kodlunarn and other Frobisher-related sites. The Steering Committee was authorized, by the Government of the Northwest Territories, to act in an advisory capacity with regard to the granting of research permits pertaining to those sites.

In the summer of 1991 the Steering Committee, with funding from a variety of sources including the institutions involved, grants, and private donations, fielded a two-pronged expedition; its aim was to gather information necessary for planning the future of the Frobisher sites. Under the leadership of Dr. Robert McGhee, assisted by Dr. James Tuck and Dr. Réginald Auger, one part of the team worked on Kodlunarn, conducting a careful surface survey and using modest test excavations and non-intrusive methods to examine selected site features. Led by Dr. Fitzhugh, assisted by Lynda Gullason and Anne Henshaw, a second group surveyed other sites in Frobisher Bay and commenced archaeological excavations at the historic Inuit sites of Kuyait and Kamaiyuk, expected to yield Frobisher artifacts. Dr. Donald Hogarth divided his time between the two branches of the team, assessing the threat of erosion to Kodlunarn, and seeking to identify Frobisher sites off-Kodlunarn.

After consulting with the researchers who had participated in this expedition, as well as those supporting them with laboratory analysis of recovered materials, and after much consideration of the findings from 1991 and earlier years, as well as of other factors, the Steering Committee issued (1992) a position paper making the following recommendations:

* That Kodlunarn is a unique site, significant in Canadian history, and that Canada must therefore continue to take a leading responsibility for the Frobisher sites and related research efforts.

* That the chief priority is to ensure the protection and preservation of the historical resources.

* That research interests are valid (if secondary) but that, to avoid unnecessary disturbance of the heritage landscape, any future archaeological work would need to be problem-focused and conservation-conscious.

* And that federal and territorial agencies with mandated interest in the *in situ* historic resources, or the lands on which they stand, should begin cooperatively

planning for the long-term management (preservation, development, and interpretation) needs of Kodlunarn and associated sites.

Pending the realization of the latter recommendation, towards which significant progress has very recently been made, no further work on Kodlunarn was undertaken in 1991, although it continued off-site.

Archaeology is not the sole research method employed; the Meta Incognita Project is not only international in character, it is also multidisciplinary. An Archival Research Task Force, chaired by Sir Ian Gourlay and involving British scholars expert in relevant fields, has been set up in the United Kingdom to explore (principally) documentary and cartographic sources of information, it being felt that there remain untapped or under-exploited resources here; the National Archives of Canada is offering such assistance as it is able in this area of Project operations. While archival materials inevitably present a European perspective on the Frobisher expeditions, counterbalance may be found in archaeological evidence and in that of Inuit oral history. Hall's investigation showed that knowledge of Frobisher's visits had survived in Inuit collective memory for almost three centuries. Dr. Susan Rowley has discovered that they still survive today, and hopes to probe deeper than did Hall (who was, initially, preoccupied with getting information about Franklin).

This collection of papers is essentially a progress report on work conducted by Project researchers (excepting the Archival Task Force, only just underway), with particular but not exclusive emphasis on the results of investigations undertaken in 1991. The volume stems from the goal of the Meta Incognita Project Steering Committee to make accessible the results of research, and is issued under the auspices of the Steering Committee, whose membership presently comprises: Dr. T.H.B. Symons, Vanier Professor of Trent University (chair); Dr. George F. MacDonald, Executive Director of the Canadian Museum of Civilization; Dr. Christina Cameron, Director General of National Historic Parks and Sites; Dr. Charles Arnold, Director of the Prince of Wales Northern Heritage Centre; Dr. Douglas Stenton of Arctic College (Iqaluit); Dr. Donald Clark, Chief of the Archaeological Survey of Canada; and the Committee's Coordinator, Dr. William E. Taylor, Director Emeritus of the Canadian Museum of Civilization, who played an important role in coordinating the 1991 field work reported in this volume. This publication is a collaborative effort of the Canadian Museum of Civilization and the Smithsonian's National Museum of Natural History (Arctic Studies Center). Thanks are due to Dr. Fitzhugh, the Center's Director, not only for arranging financial support to help make this volume possible, but also for coordinating the preparation and provision (to the editor) of papers by some of his colleagues.

The Meta Incognita Project is international in more than just the identity of its participants. The Frobisher expeditions are of historical significance to Canada, Britain, and the United States. The 1578 expedition remains one of the largest *ever* sent to the

Canadian Arctic; and Kodlunarn holds the oldest English archaeological sites on the North American continent, representing the first English attempt to settle there. For the United States, the expeditions are part of the much larger story of maritime exploration leading to European colonization of the New World. For Britain they are pertinent to the history of Elizabethan navigation, entrepreneurial venturing, and mining; they helped stimulate not only the search for a Northwest Passage, but also the notion that new wealth might be closer to home than Cathay, in the New World itself.

For Canada, on whose soil the Frobisher sites stand, the significance is naturally even greater. The foundations of Canada's claim to sovereignty in the Arctic Archipelago may be traced back to the early English explorers, perhaps Frobisher most of all. His 1578 expedition included the first concrete plan to establish an English foothold in Canada, with the aim of exploiting its rich natural resources (some not so rich as others!) in commercial ventures. If successful, it would have been a further and more definitive "token of possession", consonant with Sir Humphrey Gilbert's proposal (1566, published 1576) for colonizing North America, with George Best's expressed belief that the Arctic could support habitation by Europeans, and with Queen Elizabeth's inclusion of Meta Incognita in a formal claim (made after Frobisher's second voyage) of territories "discovered" by her sea-captains. It was not to be, although Frobisher's example was soon after followed more successfully by Gilbert and Raleigh in more southerly climes.

Nor can we ignore the Frobisher expeditions' significance to Canada in terms of the early contact between native and non-native cultures. The heritage of Inuit Canadians is no less important than that of Canadians of European descent. The voyages helped introduce Europeans to the concept of a people who had fashioned a somewhat different way of life to their own, in the harsh environment of the north. And for the Inuit the encounter opened new vistas, presenting a source of material wealth to which they had little or no previous access.

As a report of a project "in progress" the various papers in this volume reflect the divergent opinions that almost inevitably exist within any area of research in its early phases; detailed study and analysis of much of the material found to date by archaeologists remains to be done. The differences are sometimes concerned with approach (such as the question of balancing preservation and research needs), sometimes with interpretations of the evidence. For instance, was the Ship's Trench actually used for building or repairing boats? Was an iron arrowhead found on an Inuit site fashioned from Frobisher material? To what extent, and at what rate, is erosion occurring on Kodlunarn? Questions such as these remain to be resolved. Some may never be. But new sources of information *will* come to light in the course of the Meta Incognita Project. Recently a further Frobisher bloom turned up (misidentified) in the Robert E. Peary collections of the American Museum of Natural History; the search for the missing Hall collections of artifacts from Frobisher sites (at least, that portion deposited in England) has not yet been given up. And a descendant of Martin Frobisher has been identified - although it is a long-shot that the family might retain private papers of interest. All areas of research can be expected to contribute something new to what is already known of the Frobisher voyages.

In that sense, *Meta Incognita* serves as a metaphor for the boundaries of our knowledge, constantly expanded through research: for the unknown terrain we have yet to explore in order to reach a fuller understanding of Frobisher's Arctic expeditions and their ramifications for the Inuit of southeastern Baffin Island.

This book, contributing to that research, is dedicated to Gloria Shulman, Mary Simpson, and Margaret Hess, in gratitude for their support of the Meta Incognita Project.

Stephen Alsford
Secretary, Meta Incognita Project Steering Committee

An Archaeological Assessment of Qallunaaq Island

Robert McGhee
Archaeological Survey of Canada
Canadian Museum of Civilization

James A. Tuck
Archaeology Unit
Memorial University of Newfoundland

RÉSUMÉ

En 1990, le Musée canadien des civilisations a évalué les vestiges archéologiques sur l'île Kodlunarn. Le présent article décrit l'état de conservation apparent des éléments suivants : deux importantes mines, six structures industrielles, deux grandes caches, plusieurs cercles de tentes, deux supposées pierres tombales, un édicule de maçonnerie, et d'autres objets associés aux expéditions de Martin Frobisher. On a estimé que la valeur de l'île comme lieu historique dépasse son potentiel archéologique. Parmi les recommandations faites, citons-en deux : restreindre l'accès de l'île aux touristes; imposer un moratoire sur les projets archéologiques ou tout autre développement sur l'île.

ABSTRACT

An assessment of the archaeological remains on Kodlunarn Island was carried out in 1990 by the Canadian Museum of Civilization. This paper describes the surface appearance of two major mine features, six industrial structures, two large caches, several tent rings, two possible gravestones, a small masonry building, and other features associated with the Frobisher expeditions. The value of the island as an historical landscape was judged to be greater than its potential for archaeological research. Recommendations include restriction of access to tourists, and a moratorium on archaeological or site development projects.

Introduction

Qallunaaq (Kodlunarn) Island is a small and very barren islet, lying approximately 500 m off the northeastern coast of Frobisher Bay (62°49'N, 65°26'W). Its *inutituut* name means "White Man's Island" and commemorates the fact that over four hundred years ago, this small scrap of rock and gravel was the headquarters of the first major European mining endeavor in North America.

In 1577, Martin Frobisher's second expedition to the Arctic discovered that this tiny island contained a vein of black rock which was thought to be gold-bearing ore. They named it "the Countess of Warwick's Island" and there established their first mine and associated shore facilities. During Frobisher's third and largest expedition, in 1578, Countess of Warwick Island was not only the centre of mining activity, but was the site where Frobisher and his backers planned to establish the first English colony in the New World. Fortunately for the intended colonists, the scheme was abandoned when construction materials were lost in a ship sunk by ice. Before abandoning the island, the English planted peas and grain "to prove the fruitfulnesse of the soyle against the next yeare", and buried the timber and supplies which had been brought for the use of the colony [Stefansson 1938, 1:116].

The location of Frobisher's enterprise was lost to European history for almost three centuries, although it survived in the oral histories of the Frobisher Bay Inuit. In 1861, these Inuit brought the explorer Charles Francis Hall to Qallunaaq Island, and Hall [1865] recognized the archaeological remains there as the site of Frobisher's mine. Hall collected relics of the Frobisher expeditions, which he sent to the Smithsonian Institution and the Royal Geographical Society; unfortunately, almost all of these artifacts have since been lost [Stefansson 1938, 2:240-4].

Because of Qallunaaq Island's isolated location, and the consequent expense of reaching the area, the Frobisher sites have been neglected by both archaeologists and heritage managers. Before 1990, it had been visited by only three small archaeological parties: Duncan Strong of the 1927 Rawson-MacMillan Expedition from the Field Museum [Stefansson 1938, 2:245-47]; Walter Kenyon of the Royal Ontario Museum in 1974 [Kenyon 1975]; and William Fitzhugh of the Smithsonian Institution in 1981 [Fitzhugh 1981]. None of these groups spent more than a few days on the island, and their investigations were limited to mapping, surface collecting, and digging a few small test-pits.

The 1990 Assessment

In the summer of 1990, the Canadian Museum of Civilization undertook a brief assessment of the extent and condition of the archaeological remains on Qallunaaq Island. The field party consisted of Charles D. Arnold (Prince of Wales Northern Heritage Centre), Robert McGhee (Canadian Museum of Civilization) and James Tuck (Memorial University of Newfoundland). The assessment and recording of the condition of Frobisher-related sites was completed in three days of calm weather and brilliant sunshine. During much of the work, the party was accompanied by William Fitzhugh (Smithsonian Institution) and Réginald Auger (Université Laval).

Qallunaaq Island is surrounded by vertical seacliffs 5 to 7 m high; one can scramble to the island surface in only a few localities. The portion of the island above the cliffs measures approximately seven hectares in extent; at low tide, a strip of foreshore measuring approximately two hectares is exposed below the cliffs. The southern two-thirds of the island is a jumble of rock outcrops and boulder-fields, reaching an elevation of approximately 20 m above the level of high tide. A more gentle topography is found in the northeastern section of the island, which comprises an undulating gravel-covered plain surrounding small knolls formed by rock outcrops. The majority of remains relating to sixteenth century English activities are concentrated in this area.

The entire area of the island was walked over and viewed several times. All of the features noted previously by Hall, Kenyon, and Fitzhugh were relocated and examined. Several other features, some of which had been noted from a study of aerial photography, were located on the ground and the locations of features were marked on enlarged airphotos. Most of the small test pits made by Kenyon and Fitzhugh were reopened, in order to assess the depth and nature of deposits, but no new test pits were made. An inventory and brief description of the various archaeological features observed on the island is presented below:

"Ship's Trench": (*Fig. 1 #19; Figs. 3-5*)

This large notch-like feature is cut through the cliffs, midway along the northern coast of the island. It is about 25 m long and 5 m wide, and slants upward from the high tide line to the surface of the island. At the lower end it is 3 m deep, and the apparent depth is increased by the large mounds of spoil piled on the surface of the island at either side. The trench is not perpendicular to the shore, but meets the coast at an angle of approximately 60°, apparently following the strike of an ore vein. Along the eastern wall of the trench, a thin layer of ore has been peeled from the surface of a harder rock face, which clearly bears the scars of hand-mining (*Fig. 5*).

The Ship's Trench was probably the first mine opened by the Frobisher party in 1577. It also likely served as a ramp to provide access from the beach to the island surface, which at the top of the Ship's Trench lies at an elevation of about 8 m above high tide. It has also been suggested, on the basis of Inuit stories told to Hall [1865], that the Trench was used as a slipway for the construction or repair of ships. More probably, the feature was used to cache supplies and materials left behind at the end of the 1578 voyage. George Best's account of the final Frobisher voyage states that, before leaving the island, "We buryed the timber of our pretended forte, with manye barrels of meale, pease, griste and sundrie other good things" [Stefansson 1938, 1:116]. Edward Sellman's account [Stefansson 1938, 2:70] states that these things were "hidden and covered in the place of the myne."

Hall [1865, 429] found chips of wood buried in the Ship's Trench, and this was confirmed by Fitzhugh's 1981 tests, which recovered ceramic fragments, charcoal, and wood, as well as two iron blooms similar to the one found by Hall in the same area. No obvious signs of excavation or other disturbance were apparent in 1990, although even the small amount of foot traffic from our visit resulted in gouging and slumping of the fine gravel and sand sediments that cover the sides and upper portion of the feature.

"Reservoir" or "Mine": (*Fig. 1 #18; Fig. 6*)

The other prominent feature of the island is a large trench which was labelled by Hall [1865] the "Reservoir or Mine". Although the trench does hold water during the early summer, it seems very unlikely that this amount of earth and rock was dug in order to create a reservoir. It should probably be referred to simply as the "Mine". The feature is located 100 m southeast of the Ship's Trench and runs for 25 m further to the southeast; the orientation is the same as that of the Ship's Trench, as if a single vein of ore was being followed across the island. A cluster of large boulders of black ore stand on the surface just beyond the southern end of the trench; these boulders may have attracted the miners to the location. The Mine is about 5 m wide and from 1 m deep at the northern end to over 2 m deep at the south end. As in the Ship's Trench, earth and rock spoil are piled on the surface to either side. Small pieces of black ore are scattered over the surface and there is a pile of discarded ore at the southwestern end.

A test pit made by Fitzhugh (1981) in the bottom of the Mine produced a few ceramic fragments but no sign of large-scale burial of material. In 1990, the only apparent disturbance was slumping of surface sediments caused by foot traffic.

Industrial Area: (*Fig. 7*)

Most evidence of industrial activity is concentrated in a flat and slightly sloping area of about one-quarter hectare in extent, lying between the Mine and the east coast of the island. It is the only part of the island that has a continuous vegetation cover, probably because the water-table is close to the surface. The vegetated area measures 21 m from north to south along the sloping bank that forms the eastern edge; charcoal and ceramics are slowly eroding from a few portions of this bank, where the edge has been disturbed by human trampling and archaeological testing. The area extends approximately 80 m inland to the northwest. There are surface indications of at least six structural features that appear to relate to Elizabethan activities, as well as two irregular patches that are barren of vegetation and which may have been stripped to provide caulking material for the walls of the structures. Surface collections and previous test excavations have yielded an assortment of coal and charcoal fragments, small pieces of slag, and fragments of industrial ceramics, suggesting that these structures were the main site of industrial activities associated with the Frobisher venture. The six structures visible in the Industrial Area (Features 1-6) are described individually:

Feature 1 ("Smithy"): (*Fig. 1* #10; *Fig. 8*) This is an unpatterned concentration of boulders and rock slabs, emerging from a low mound of turf approximately 6 m in diameter and backed against the hillock at the northeastern edge of the Industrial Area. The larger of the two barren patches of gravel lies immediately adjacent to the south of the structure. Test pits excavated by Fitzhugh in 1981 yielded slag and crucible fragments. Similar materials can be found in spoil from a small looter's pit and on the surface of the adjacent gravel area.

Feature 2 ("Assay Office"): (*Fig. 1* #8; *Fig. 9*) This is an amorphous jumble of boulders and turf slightly elevated above the surrounding surface, lying in the middle of the flat vegetated area approximately 50 m from the eroding bank. It probably represents a rectangular structure measuring approximately 6 m on a side The most apparent portion of straight wall appears along the western side, and there is a mound of boulders and turf 2 to 3 m across in the northern interior, perhaps marking the location of a furnace or other industrial structure. A small test pit excavated by Fitzhugh, and reopened in 1990, yielded fragments of charcoal and ceramics to a depth of 20 cm.

Feature 3 ("Charcoal Kiln"): (*Fig. 1* #7; *Fig. 10*) This small and poorly defined structure lies 15 m to the north of Feature 2. It is a pile of jumbled boulders and vegetation measuring 5 m east to west and 4 m north to south, against a little bedrock outcrop at the edge of the Industrial Area. A test pit excavated by Fitzhugh in 1981 produced quantities of charcoal. Small pieces of charcoal, coal, and slag can be found on the surface of the structure.

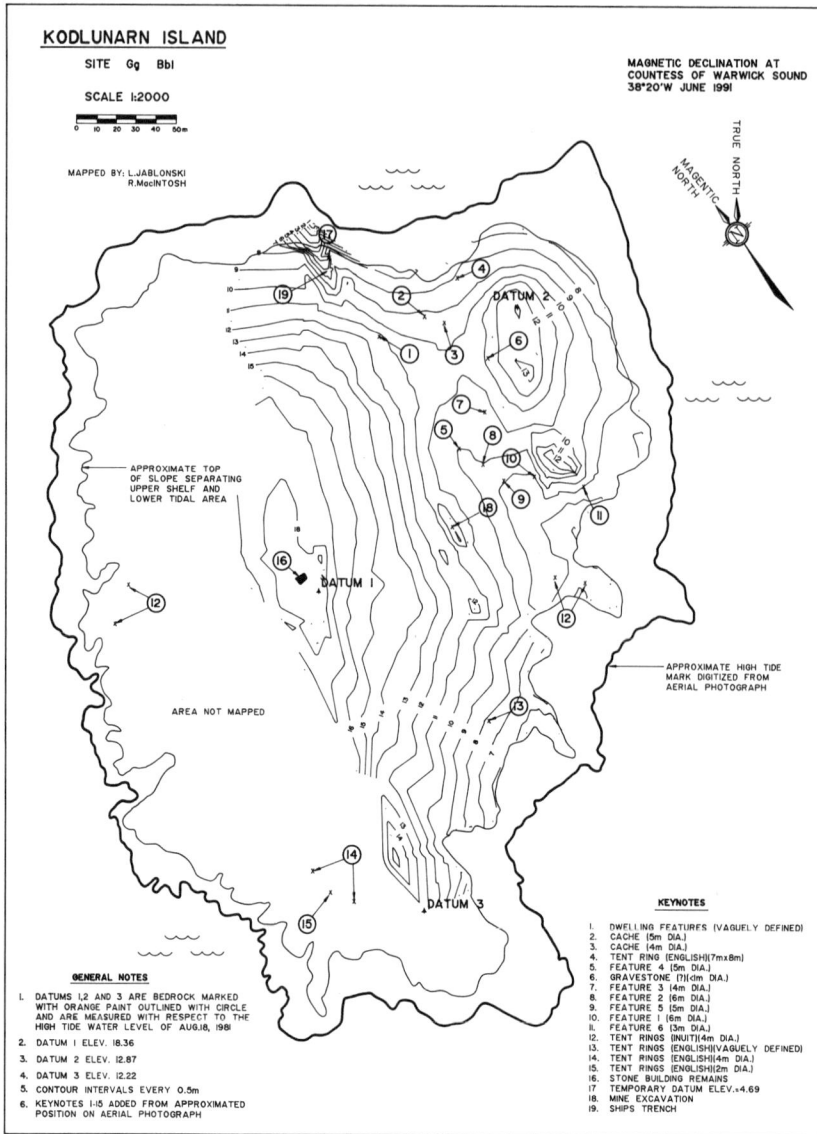

KODLUNARN ISLAND

SITE Gg   BbI

SCALE 1:2000

MAGNETIC DECLINATION AT
COUNTESS OF WARWICK SOUND
38°20'W JUNE 1991

MAPPED BY: L.JABLONSKI
R.MacINTOSH

APPROXIMATE TOP
OF SLOPE SEPARATING
UPPER SHELF AND
LOWER TIDAL AREA

APPROXIMATE HIGH TIDE
MARK DIGITIZED FROM
AERIAL PHOTOGRAPH

AREA NOT MAPPED

GENERAL NOTES

1. DATUMS 1,2 AND 3 ARE BEDROCK MARKED
   WITH ORANGE PAINT OUTLINED WITH CIRCLE
   AND ARE MEASURED WITH RESPECT TO THE
   HIGH TIDE WATER LEVEL OF AUG.18, 1981
2. DATUM 1 ELEV. 18.36
3. DATUM 2 ELEV. 12.87
4. DATUM 3 ELEV. 12.22
5. CONTOUR INTERVALS EVERY 0.5m
6. KEYNOTES 1-15 ADDED FROM APPROXIMATED
   POSITION ON AERIAL PHOTOGRAPH

KEYNOTES

1. DWELLING FEATURES (VAGUELY DEFINED)
2. CACHE (5m DIA.)
3. CACHE (4m DIA.)
4. TENT RING (ENGLISH)(7mx8m)
5. FEATURE 4 (5m DIA.)
6. GRAVESTONE (?)(<1m DIA.)
7. FEATURE 3 (4m DIA.)
8. FEATURE 2 (6m DIA.)
9. FEATURE 5 (5m DIA.)
10. FEATURE 1 (6m DIA.)
11. FEATURE 6 (3m DIA.)
12. TENT RINGS (INUIT)(4m DIA.)
13. TENT RINGS (ENGLISH)(VAGUELY DEFINED)
14. TENT RINGS (ENGLISH)(4m DIA.)
15. TENT RINGS (ENGLISH)(2m DIA.)
16. STONE BUILDING REMAINS
17. TEMPORARY DATUM ELEV.=4.69
18. MINE EXCAVATION
19. SHIPS TRENCH

Figure 1: Map of Qallunaaq Island.

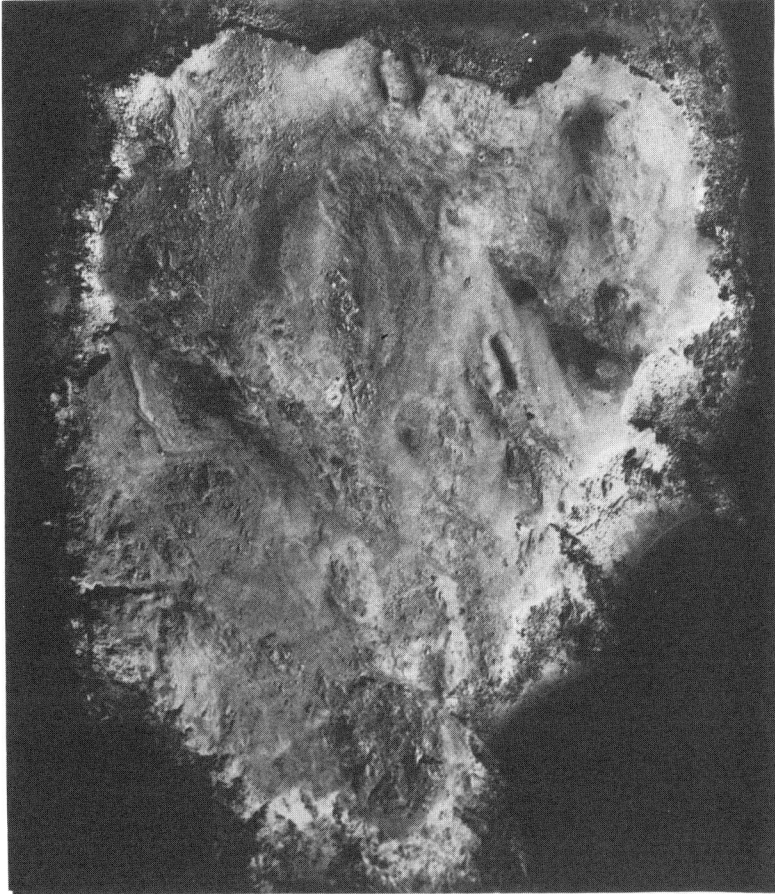

Figure 2: Aerial photograph of Qallunaaq Island.

Figure 3: The Ship's Trench mine from the southern end.

Figure 4: The vertical face (showing mining scars) that forms the lower eastern edge of the Ship's Trench.

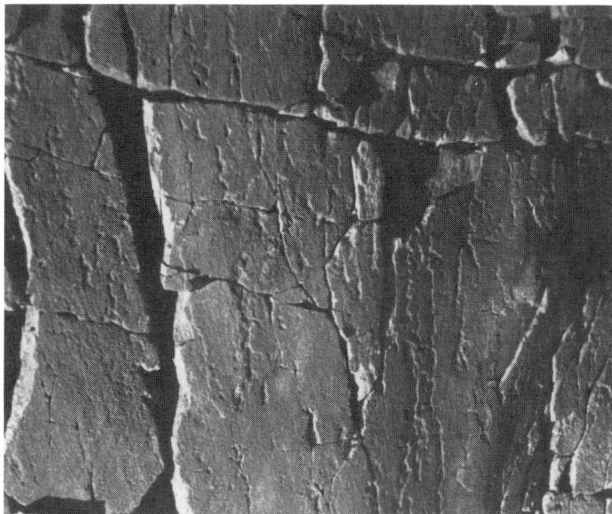

Figure 5: Close-up of hand-mining scars on rock face adjacent to Ship's Trench.

Figure 6: The Reservoir mine from the northwestern end.

Figure 7: The vegetated Industrial Area (where our tent camp was located), with the Reservoir mine in the foreground.

Figure 8: Feature 1 (Smithy) from east.

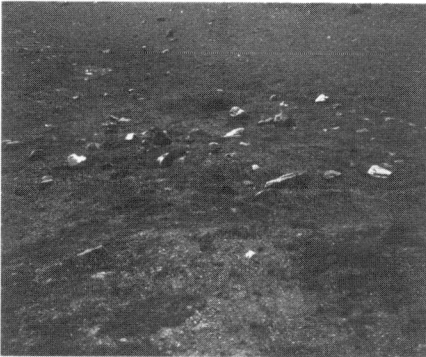

Figure 9: Feature 2 (Assay Office) from northeast.

Figure 10: Feature 3 (Charcoal kiln) from east.

Figure 11: Feature 4 (Workshop) from northeast.

Figure 12: Possible gravestones, from west.

Figure 13: Large cache features, from east.

Figure 14: Remains of Frobisher House from east.

Figure 15: Remains of House from south, showing nearby cairn built of looted boulders.

Figure 16: English (?) tentrings, with Ship's Trench mine in background.

Figure 17: Probable location of Best's Bulwark, from the west.

Feature 4 ("Workshop"): (*Fig. 1 #5; Fig. 11*) This is a vaguely defined structure located 5 m to the northwest of Feature 2. The scatter of boulders and turf is slightly raised above the surrounding area and measures approximately 5 m across. There is one small looter's pit in the interior.

Feature 5 ("Tent ring"): (*Fig. 1 #9*) A large boulder tent ring, circular in outline and approximately 5 m in diameter, lies 4 m to the south of Feature 2. The boulders barely emerge from the flat vegetated central tract of the Industrial Area, and the ring is difficult to detect from ground level.

Feature 6 ("Pit"): (*Fig. 1 #11*) This appears as a slight mound of earth, lying on the slope of a rocky hillock at the northeastern corner of the Industrial Area. It extends to the eroding bank, where a scatter of charcoal and ceramics fragments can be seen at a depth of approximately 30 cm below surface. No boulders or other structural features are apparent at the surface, perhaps because of burial by slopewash from the adjacent hillock.

A one-metre square test pit was opened in this structure at some time in the past, at a distance of 3 m from the eroding bank. Fitzhugh reopened the pit in 1981 and reports finding stone slabs and ceramics. It was reopened again in 1990, producing a few boulders, and coal and charcoal fragments to a depth of 1 m, where excavation was stopped. The nature and function of this feature is not determined.

In the northern section of the vegetated area, to the west of Feature 3, surface indications suggest either the remains of turf-cutting, or the concealed remnants of one or more structures.

Graves?: (*Fig. 1 #6; Fig. 12*)

A pair of isolated vertically-placed boulders were noted on a gravel plateau at the northern edge of the Industrial Area and approximately 20 m south of the tent rings along the northern coast of the island. These may mark one, or perhaps two, of the graves of Frobisher personnel.

Caches: (*Fig. 1 #2,3; Fig. 13*)

Two large boulder features lie on the gravel plateau above the northern shore of the island. These appear to be the remains of large boulder caches, with the boulders scattered and with a looting pit in the centre of each.

The more westerly of the caches, located approximately 30 m southeast of the upper end of the Ship's Trench, is marked by an irregular spill of boulders approximately 8 m in diameter. In the centre is a slight mound 5 m across and rising to 30 cm above the surrounding surface. A pit about 1 m across has been dug in the centre, but does not seem to have penetrated much beneath the original surface level.

The other cache lies a few metres to the east, with a sparser scatter of boulders over an area of approximately 8 m diameter, and a slight central mound 4 m across and 20 to 30 cm above the surrounding surface. A looter's pit, 80 cm across and 20 cm deep, lies slightly south of the centre of the feature; it does not appear to have penetrated below the original ground surface.

"Frobisher House": (*Fig. 1 #16; Figs. 14, 15*)

At the highest point of the island lie the remains of a small structure which was built at the end of the final Frobisher expedition. According to George Best's account [Stefansson 1938, 1:116]:

> This daye the Masons finished a house whiche Captaine Fenton caused to
> be made of lyme and stone upon the Countesse of Warwickes Ilande, to
> the ende we mighte prove againste the nexte yere, whether the snowe
> coulde overwhelme it, the frosts breake uppe, or the people dismember
> the same.

In order to attract the Inuit to better relations in coming years, the English provided the house with:

> dyvers of oure countrie toyes, as belles, and knives, wherein they
> specially delight, one for the necessarie use, and the other for the great
> pleasure thereof. Also pictures of men and women in lead, men a
> horsebacke, lookinglasses, whistles, and pipes. Also in the house was
> made an oven, and breade lefte baked therein, for them to see and taste.

The remains of this structure appear as a shallow irregular pit dug into the gravel surface. The pit and surrounding surface is littered with small fragments of yellowish lime plaster or mortar and occasional tiny fragments of ceramics. Approximately four hundred large boulders are scattered about the pit and the surrounding area, apparently having been tumbled from the walls of the house.

There appear to have been several attempts to excavate, and probably to reconstruct, the foundations of this small structure, through random digging and moving of rocks. A large nearby cairn was built of boulders from the Frobisher House, as well as incorporating an Inuit skull that had probably been removed from a grave elsewhere on the island. The cairn bears a brass plaque carrying the following inscription:

THIS CAIRN WAS ERECTED
IN MEMORY OF
SIR MARTIN FROBISHER
AS A CENTENNIAL PROJECT BY
LT. A. BROCKLEY
DR. R. WEST
MR. V.BROCKLEY
FROBISHER BAY 11.7.66

Tentrings [A] Probably English: (*Fig. 1 #1; Figs. 4, 13, 14, 15*)

The remains of dwellings relating to the Frobisher period seem to be more widespread on the island than had been previously reported. Several tentrings that have been ascribed to Inuit occupation seem more likely to be the remains of English tents. One cluster of features lies on the gravel plateau above the northern coast of the island, to the northeast of the two large cache-like structures (*Fig. 1 #4*). The most prominent lies 10 m northeast of the more easterly cache and 8 m south of the eroding bank (*Fig. 16*). The feature is rectangular in outline, measures approximately 7 m north-south by 8 m east-west, and has a central north-south wall; an alternative interpretation would see two adjacent seven-metre by four-metre structures with a shared wall. Other features in the area are smaller and comprise slight depressions and boulder scatters with less obvious outline patterns.

At the edge of a boulderfield, approximately 20 m south of the Ship's Trench, are the remains of three or four possible dwelling features, formed by removing boulders from a vaguely-defined linear area (*Fig. 1 #1*). Fitzhugh [1981] refers to this feature as a "longhouse" and reports that test excavations recovered ceramic fragments.

Other rectangular or sub-rectangular boulder features, likely representing the remains of English tent camps, occur in a cluster on a slightly sloping gravel plateau midway along the eastern shore of the island to the south of the main industrial area (*Fig. 1 #13*). In this area we also found a small slab hearth of likely European origin. Another cluster of three jumbled boulder structures lies at the southern end of the island, in a vegetated area which may conceal some occupation refuse (*Fig. 1 #14,15*). The

English origin of these features is suggested by the vaguely rectangular outline of the major feature, and by the ceramics that are eroding from the edge of the sea-cliff adjacent to one structure.

Tentrings [B] Probably Inuit: (*Fig. 1* #12)

A few tent rings and caches scattered along the western shore of the island may be of Inuit origin. Fitzhugh's party collected an iron arrowhead blade from the surface of one of these rings in 1990. The condition of the iron suggests an age of considerably less than four centuries, so the rings may have been the remains of Inuit occupation at about the time of Hall's visit to the area in 1861. Two Inuit tent rings, one with a characteristic sleeping-platform-edge of boulders, lie on the neck of a small promontory surrounded by sea-cliffs on three sides, above the eastern shore of the island adjacent to the Industrial Area.

"Best's Bulwark": (*Fig. 17*)

Shortly after arriving at Qallunaaq Island in 1577, the English fortified a position in expectation of an attack from the Inuit. This structure was known as "Best's Bulwark" and is described as "a small Forte" constructed in "a corner of a cliffe, which on thre parts like a wall of good heygth was compassed and well fenced with the Sea, & we finished the rest, with caskes of earth, to good purpose" [Stefansson 1938, 1:72-73]. Hall [1865] identified this feature with the small peninsula with a narrow neck, extending from the east coast just to the south of the Industrial Area. There are no remains suggesting that fortification of earth-filled casks, despite the fact that the fine gravel surface in this area should preserve indications of past construction activities. There are, however, remains of what appears to have been a linear boulder feature extending across the neck of the more amorphous headland 50 m to the south. This may be tentatively identified as the more probable site of the fortification.

Spring:

On the southwestern slope of the island is another probable English construction: a small irregular depression that appears to have been dug out, near the base of a drainage channel. At the time of our 1990 visit, this depression held the only surface water on the island. According to the rules laid down by Frobisher, no man was to "washe their handes or anye other things, in the Spring, uppon the Countesses Ilande, where the water is used, and preserved for the dressing of their victuals" [Stefansson 1938, 1:105]. The statement may refer to this apparent dugout.

Other Features:

During our examination of the island, we came across several signs of probable English activity: a Thule Inuit grave has had the cover removed and the skeleton taken; small boulders have been randomly piled on other boulders. And a strange cache-like structure has been formed by neatly plugging a crevasse in a rock outcrop with rectangular boulders.

Results of the 1990 Project

The results of the 1990 assessment project were presented to the Meta Incognita Project Committee in written form and in a videotape entitled *Kodlunarn Island, the 1990 Assessment*. The field party found the Frobisher-related sites to be in a better state of preservation than they had expected. Although there is little doubt that the late 16th century Inuit thoroughly dismantled the English structures and caches in search of usable materials, there is little evidence of major disturbance after that time.

The surface of the island is remarkably barren of potsherds, fragments of brick or tile, and the other occupational debris that must have been left by the Frobisher parties. Although occasional specimens can still be found, the surface appears to have been picked clean by generations of Inuit searchers, as well as by more recent souvenir-hunters. On the other hand, aside from the disturbance of the structure at the summit of the island, there is little evidence of excavation. Neither Kenyon nor Fitzhugh excavated more than a few small test pits. There are only two obvious looting-pits, and these may possibly be ascribed to the Rawson-MacMillan expedition; both are relatively small, old and neither appears to have penetrated the original ground surface of the two large cache structures in which they occur. The one portion of the site which has suffered considerable damage is the "house" built by Frobisher's men at the summit of the island, to test the durability of English construction techniques and for the edification of the Inuit.

Contrary to earlier report [Fitzhugh 1981], there was little evidence of active coastal erosion, and the sites did not appear to be immediately threatened by natural forces. Bank-edge erosion is occurring slowly along a sloping face that forms the eastern edge of the Industrial Area of the site. This erosion, however, appears to be caused primarily by archaeological testing along the eroding edge and by human use of this face as a route for scrambling up to the surface of the island.

The field party was surprised by the general state of preservation of the Frobisher-related archaeological sites on Qallunaaq Island. They were particularly impressed by the ambience of the island, by its palpable sense of history, and by its value as a historical landscape. They were not impressed by the island's potential as a source for archaeological research, and were persuaded that research-directed archaeology posed a significant threat to the value of the island as heritage landscape. These impressions led to three general recommendations which were made to the Canadian Museum of Civilization:

(1) In view of the probability that Qallunaaq Island will attract increased traffic from "adventure cruise" ships, or from individual tourists and history buffs, a management system should be put into place immediately in order to preserve the historical integrity of the island. In particular, measures should be taken to: (a) prevent camping on the island; (b) restrict access to a single landing-area, and restrict walking to a defined (signed, fenced or boardwalked) route that borders the main areas of interest.

(2) Archaeological investigations of the island should be carefully controlled, in order to preserve the limited archaeological resource as well as the quality of the historical environment. Proponents of research projects should be required to demonstrate that the proposed work can be expected to result in the recovery of information that significantly outweighs the detrimental effects on the sites investigated.

(3) In order to better assess both research and management possibilities, a moratorium of at least one year should be placed on any archaeological or site development projects relating to the sites. During this time, a major effort should be made to gather and analyse historical information relating to the Frobisher expeditions and their use of the area.

ACKNOWLEDGEMENTS: We wish to express our thanks to Chuck Arnold, who was a pleasant and perceptive companion and co-investigator during our stay on Qallunaaq Island. Thanks for help and hospitality to Bob Longworth and the Iqaluit Research Centre, as well as to Bill Fitzhugh and his companions on the *Pitsiulak*. The project could not have been accomplished without the fine flying and efficient organization of Aero Arctic helicopters, to which we wish to express our gratitude.

References

Fitzhugh, William W.
1981   Smithsonian Archaeological Surveys at Kodlunarn Island in 1981: Preliminary Field Report. Manuscript on file, Archaeological Survey of Canada, Canadian Museum of Civilization.

Hall, Charles Francis
1865   *Arctic Researches and Life Among the Esquimaux.* New York: Harper and Brothers.

Kenyon, Walter
1975   *Tokens of Possession: the Northern Voyages of Martin Frobisher.* Toronto: Royal Ontario Museum.

Stefansson, Vilhjalmur, and Eloise McCaskill, eds.
1938   *The Three Voyages of Martin Frobisher in Search of a Passage to Cathay and India by the North-west, A.D. 1576-8.* 2 vols. London: Argonaut Press.

The 1991 Investigations on Qallunaaq Island

James A. Tuck
Archaeology Unit
Memorial University of Newfoundland

J.A. Pilon
Geological Survey of Canada

Robert McGhee
Archaeological Survey of Canada
Canadian Museum of Civilization

RÉSUMÉ

L'évaluation faite en 1991 du site de l'île Qallunaaq comporte trois projets : des fouilles exploratoires dans la mine dite *Ship's Trench* pour connaître la nature et l'étendue des dépôts enfouis; des fouilles exploratoires en vue d'évaluer les restes de la maison de Frobisher; enfin, un sondage au géoradar d'autres éléments archéologiques. Un examen d'une surface de 1 x 4 m à l'extrémité nord du *Ship's Trench* a confirmé que les hommes de Frobisher ont enterré des provisions à cet endroit, mais que les lieux ont été fouillés de fond en comble par les Inuit. Les fondations de la maison de Frobisher étaient à ce point bien conservées qu'on a pu délimiter les dimensions et les formes de la construction, laissant espérer un examen plus détaillé dans l'avenir. Le sondage au géoradar (1) permet de croire qu'un dépôt est enfoui sous ce qui serait deux pierres tombales; (2) n'a indiqué que de légères perturbations sous deux caches importantes; (3) n'a fourni aucune preuve évidente que des structures ou des dépôts auraient été enfouis sous les éléments industriels variés sur le site. On recommande que soient entrepris d'autres travaux archéologiques sur l'île, mais à la condition que soit d'abord établi un plan global.

ABSTRACT

The 1991 assessment of Qallunaaq Island concentrated on three projects: test excavation in the Ship's Trench mine in order to assess the nature and extent of buried deposits; test excavations in order to assess the remains of the Frobisher House feature; and a ground probing radar survey of other features. A 4 m by 1 m test at the northern end of the Ship's Trench confirmed that the Frobisher party had buried supplies in this feature, but that the deposit had been thoroughly salvaged by Inuit. The foundations of the Frobisher House were found to be sufficiently preserved to delineate the size and shape of the structure and to encourage a more thorough investigation in future. The ground probing radar survey: supported the suggestion of a burial feature beneath a pair of possible headstones; indicated only shallow disturbance beneath two major cache features; and provided no evidence of significant buried structures or deposits beneath the various industrial features on the site. Further archaeological work on the island is recommended only within the context of a comprehensive management plan.

Introduction

In the summer of 1991, the Meta Incognita Project Committee requested the Canadian Museum of Civilization to undertake a more thorough assessment of Qallunaaq Island's archaeological resources. This commission arose, in part, in response to requests from archaeologists wishing to undertake extensive excavations on the island. The work was funded from a grant provided by the Friends of the Canadian Museum of Civilization. Logistic help was provided by the Iqaluit Research Centre (Science Institute of the Northwest Territories) and by the Polar Continental Project (Department of Energy, Mines and Resources).

The view presented to the Committee by the 1990 assessment team (cf. McGhee and Tuck, this volume) had stressed that heritage conservation should take precedence over archaeological research on this unique and vulnerable site. It was therefore an important aspect of the 1991 work that the assessment be carried out in such a way as to cause as little damage as possible to the island surface. The Canadian Museum of Civilization team even pioneered a new route from the shore to the surface of the island, discouraging use of the easiest route which led across the eroding face backing the main Industrial Area of the site. The erosion of this face seems to be caused, not by waves and tides, but primarily by human clambering and archaeological edge-excavation.

The project was carried out between August 13-24, under a permit issued to Robert McGhee (Canadian Museum of Civilization). Other members of the project team included: archaeologists James Tuck (Memorial University of Newfoundland) and Réginald Auger (Université Laval); Lee Jablonski (Novatech) who had offered to map the island; Jean Pilon (Geological Survey of Canada), who had been asked to undertake a ground-probing-radar survey of selected features; and Don Hogarth (University of

Ottawa) who was asked to estimate the rates of erosion apparent on the island. Field assistance was provided by Jeannette Smith (University of Calgary), Davin Ala (University of Ottawa) and Rob MacIntosh (Arctic College, Iqaluit). Malcolm Billings, a BBC radio journalist, joined the party in order to produce a documentary radio program, and also assisted in archaeological work.

The 1991 work comprised several distinct projects, each of which is briefly summarized below:

Site Mapping

Between August 16-19, Lee Jablonski (assisted by Rob MacIntosh) took several hundred readings with the "total station" instrument that he provided. The readings were successfully downloaded onto a portable computer. On returning from the field, these readings were combined with digitization of aerial photographic images to prepare the first accurate contour map of the portion of the island relevant to the remains of Frobisher activities [McGhee and Tuck, this volume: Fig. 1].

Estimation of Erosion Rate

Between August 16-19, Don Hogarth and his field assistant Davin Ala undertook a survey of erosion features on Qallunaaq Island. The primary technique involved comparison of contemporary topography with that shown on aerial photographs taken in 1953 and with a map drawn by Charles Francis Hall in 1861. No changes could be detected between current conditions and the 1953 photographs. No changes could be detected in the northern portion of the island (the area containing Frobisher sites) since the time of the Hall map, but Hogarth suggests that a very slight shoreline retreat can be detected on portions of the southern shore of the island, which is most subject to wave action. A more complete report on this portion of the project is provided by Hogarth elsewhere in this volume.

Archaeological Investigations

SHIP'S TRENCH

A description of the mine known as the "Ship's Trench" is given by McGhee and Tuck [this volume]. It had been suggested that a major burial deposit existed in this feature [Hall 1865; Fitzhugh 1981]. According to Inuit accounts recorded by Hall [1865], the feature had also been the site of ship-building activities carried out by some of the Frobisher party.

Excavation:

In order to detect evidence of these activities, a trench was laid out across the feature at a location just above the high water mark (*Fig. 1*). This area of the feature was selected because it lay at the lower and deeper end of the Ship's Trench but at the upper limit of wave action, thus providing the best chance for discovering undisturbed deposits with organic preservation. The location was also at the upper end of that portion of the mine subject to occasional storm activity. This activity has removed much of the earth and fine decomposed rock that comprises the surface of the upper reaches of the feature. The surface of this lower area is composed of large boulders, allowing the excavation to be backfilled and covered so as to leave little surface disturbance. In order to make backfilling easier and cleaner, all excavated backdirt was dumped and sifted on a large tarpaulin.

The excavation trench was 1 m wide and 4 m long, extending from the steep eastern face of the feature to a position part way up the sloping western face. The eastern end of the trench was formed by a vertical wall of rock, which follows the strike of the ore deposit and which bears the scars of hand-mining. The western end was composed of a jumble of angular cobbles and boulders which are clearly spoil from the mining operation. Since this concentration of rocks was difficult and dangerous to remove, excavations concentrated on the eastern and central portions of the trench. An estimated 4 m³ of deposit was removed by trowel and sifted through a 5 mm screen. A maximum depth of 160 cm was reached in the centre of the trench, over a horizontal area less than one metre square. No trace of intact deposits was found in the deepest part of the trench, nor in areas where bedrock was reached at lesser depths (*Fig. 2*).

At the completion of the excavation, the trench was backfilled and the surface covered with the boulders that had been removed from the surface before excavations were begun.

Figure 1: Excavation of test trench in Ship's Trench mine, from above (photo R. Auger).

Figure 2: The south face of the partially completed trench, showing undifferentiated fill (photo R. Auger).

Figure 3: Piece of cut wood from the lower levels of the test trench (photo R. Auger).

Stratigraphy:

No stratigraphy existed in the excavated portion of the deposit. The matrix consisted of homogeneous loose rock, gravel, and sand; the sand-sized fraction appears to be recently decomposed rock washed down from the spoil heaps on either side of the feature, and from the feature itself. The only distinction noted in different portions of the deposit related to depth below surface: the upper layers contained several fragments of charcoal and charred objects, while the lower levels contained proportionally less charcoal and more unaltered wood fragments. This is clearly a function of differential preservation, rather than an indication of stratigraphic distinctions in the deposit.

Artifacts:

Objects preserved in the deposit were few and generally badly fragmented. They included bits of wood and wood charcoal, which field identification suggests are largely oak (*Fig. 3*). Several pieces appear to be the fragments of barrel staves and at least one fragment has the shape of a barrel cant (one of the outermost pieces in the head of a wooden cask). Several fragments of what appear to be split osier or willow are visually identical to the thousands of sixteenth century barrel hoops recovered from the Basque whaling station at Red Bay, Labrador.

Other organic remains included several carbonized peas and numerous amorphous lumps of carbonized material which is suspected to be preserved hardbread (ship's biscuit). A sample of Newfoundland hardbread was experimentally carbonized on our camp stove; this produced a material that is visually indistinguishable from the excavated material.

Other artifacts included: a small unidentifiable fragment of flat iron and two stains of rust which apparently mark the decomposition of other small iron objects; and several fragments of red earthenware (probably mostly from flat tiles of the type represented by one relatively large edge-sherd), some of which bear traces of a green lead glaze and, in one instance, what appears to be a raised decoration. Sixty-one catalogue items were collected; further discussion of these finds is in Réginald Auger's paper in this volume.

Interpretations:

The archaeological findings are consistent with the evidence that the Ship's Trench was originally dug as a mine for "black ore". It was probably used secondarily as a landing point and ramp to the elevated surface of the island, but no archaeological evidence indicates such use. No evidence was recovered to suggest that any ship or boat repair took place in this feature. Wood chips, bits of plank, treenails, etc., were entirely absent from the deposits excavated. Rather, the material recovered suggests that the final European use of the feature was as a cache for materials abandoned during the late summer of 1578. Among the items cached in the feature at that time were peas and meal or hardbread, both of which were found in our excavations; the material was undoubtedly contained in wooden casks, fragments of which were also recovered.

If this was the case, it seems clear that the cached materials left by Frobisher's third expedition were thoroughly disturbed by local Inuit salvagers, very likely within a year or so after the English abandoned the island. The deposits in our excavation trench had been completely churned and all valuable materials salvaged by such efforts. Since our trench was located in the deepest and most inaccessible region of the feature, it seems likely that all other buried deposits in other portions of the mine had also been recovered at that time. It would not be inaccurate to say that the Ship's Trench was mined twice: once by Europeans searching for ore, and a short while later by Inuit in search of hardwood, nails, and possibly foodstuffs. As subsequent events indicate, the Inuit probably got a more valuable return for their efforts than did the English miners and investors.

FROBISHER HOUSE

The small stone building, which was constructed at the summit of the island in the late summer of 1578, has suffered considerable damage. The boulder walls have been tumbled and scattered over a wide area, and many of the boulders had been stolen in 1966 in order to construct a nearby cairn. The visible features of the structure are described by McGhee and Tuck [this volume].

Excavation:

The excavations at this feature were originally intended to remove and sift the disturbed deposit from the house interior (*Fig. 4*). A grid was laid over the structure, and three one-metre squares excavated within the house structure; the deposit was excavated by trowel and sifted through a 5 mm screen. This work revealed a totally disturbed matrix consisting of loose sandy soil containing rocks tumbled from the walls, fragments of lime mortar, small flint pebbles that had apparently derived from the mortar, and several small fragments of ceramic vessels and tiles. Twenty-seven catalogue items were collected; they are currently being analyzed by Réginald Auger.

Our excavations recovered no trace of the wealth of material left in the structure by the Frobisher party, as an enticement to local Inuit. The interior of the house appears to have been thoroughly excavated, probably on several occasions: by Inuit salvagers soon after the departure of the Frobisher expedition; by Charles Francis Hall; by the Rawson-MacMillan expedition in 1927; and by more recent curiosity seekers including the builders of the adjacent cairn.

The foundations of the house walls, however, were found to be surprisingly well preserved (*Figs. 5, 6*). In order to investigate the state of these foundations, two one-metre squares were excavated at the northwest and southeast corners of the building, and tumbled boulders were removed from portions of the south and east wall foundations. In places, the lower three courses of stone are preserved to a height of over 30 cm. Some of the rocks have been dressed, at least to the point where major projections were removed. This work was probably done with mining tools; no traces were found of the distinctive marks left by a walling hammer. The rocks were carefully fitted and mortared with lime mortar, and the interstices were packed with small stones and rubble detached from the shaped boulders.

Description of House:

Captain Edward Fenton, who supervised the building of this structure, described it as a "litle watche Tower I cawsed to be builded in the hight of the same Ilande with lyme and stone being xiiii foote in length and viii in bredthe with a litle rooffe covered with borde." [Kenyon 1981, 198]

The preserved wall foundations define a structure with external dimensions of 12 ft. by 14 ft. (3.6 m x 4.3 m; English units are used in this description, since the builders of the structure clearly used that system). The long axis is oriented roughly east-west (true). The north, east, and west walls are exactly 2 ft. (0.6 m) thick; the south wall, badly damaged on the portions of the interior edge that are exposed, may be a few centimetres thicker (*Fig. 7*). Another peculiarity of the south wall is a layer of mortar approximately 4 cm thick, plastered over the visible portions of the exterior surface of the wall (*Fig. 8*). This feature is not present on the other walls; whether the plastered surface covered the entire wall, or indeed whether it extended above the original grade surface, will probably not be determined by archaeology. What appears to be a door 30 in. (0.75 m) wide is located at the south end of the west wall. This area, which contains a jumbled pile of boulders, was not exposed; however, such a location for doorways was common in English cottages (at least in the Cotswolds and Somerset) from late medieval times until about A.D. 1700 [Barley 1967, 104]. Comparisons with existing Elizabethan houses and outbuildings might provide further information.

Figure 4: Remains of the Frobisher House, from west, prior to excavation.

Figure 5: Foundations of east wall of the House, from the south. The exterior of the wall is clearly visible; the bucket stands just inside the northeast interior corner of the foundation.

Figure 6: Northeast interior corner, from above.

Figure 7: Northwest exterior corner, from above.

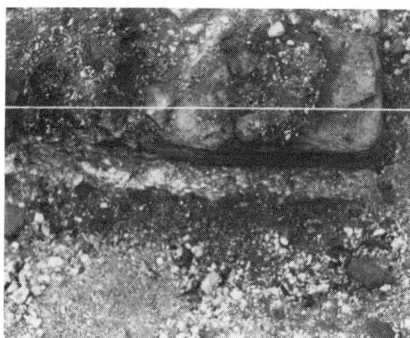

Figure 8: Southeast exterior corner, from above. Note line of light-colored plaster or mortar in the earth along the exterior edge of the corner stone.

In an attempt to determine the original height of the stone walls, the length, width, and thickness of each loose rock (including those from the 1966 cairn) were measured. It was assumed that the rocks scattered about the house site today are the original rocks from the structure (indeed, many bear traces of dressing or of adhering mortar) and that their number has not been significantly diminished by human or natural agents. An estimate of the volume of each rock was then calculated by multiplying the three dimensions. This method overestimates the volume, since it assumes that each rock is orthorhombic (with sides meeting at angles of 90°), but this compensates in a rough fashion for the volume of mortar and rubble that is not otherwise taken into consideration.

By these calculations, approximately 192 cu. ft. of rock are represented in the portions of the walls that are not currently *in situ*. This is sufficient to raise the walls about 26 in. (0.66 m) above their present level; the total original height of the masonry wall was probably 3 ft. to 3½ ft. (0.9-1.1 m). Despite the admittedly rough nature of these calculations, it is clear that the walls of the structure were built only partly of stone, while the upper portions of the walls must have been of wood construction. Again, comparisons with existing buildings might provide suggestions regarding the original appearance of the structure which, despite Frobisher's original plans for a much larger dwelling, was probably more in keeping with vernacular designs for one-room cottages of the late sixteenth century.

Finally, it should be noted that the original objective of clearing the interior of the structure was not accomplished. This was not done for several reasons. Clearing the interior would have resulted in the accumulation of a large amount of backdirt, which would have had to be dumped either at a considerable distance from the site, or on top of the deposits of disturbed soil (containing cultural material) that surround the feature. Clearing would also have exposed the already fragile wall foundations and made them more susceptible to damage. Finally, we thought it better to delay any major excavation until a management plan for the feature was in place.

As a part of the investigation of the House, we dismantled the boulder cairn that had been erected in 1966, using boulders that had been tumbled from the house walls. An Inuit skull was found inside the cairn and reburied in one of the prehistoric Inuit graves found on the island. The brass plaque that had been wired to the cairn [see McGhee and Tuck, this volume] was removed and delivered to the Prince of Wales Northern Heritage Centre.

At the completion of excavations, the exposed portions of the house foundations were covered with sifted backdirt. The entire foundation area was then covered with a large plastic tarpaulin and buried beneath a layer of boulders collected from the surrounding area.

Ground Probing Radar Survey

THE *GPR* TECHNIQUE

Ground Probing Radar (GPR) was developed as a means of rapidly and economically mapping near-subsurface features. In August 1991 the technique was used to conduct experimental surveys at several sites on Qallunaaq Island.

GPR operates on the same principles as conventional radar. The main difference is that the radar beam is directed into the ground. A short pulse of electromagnetic energy is emitted by the transmitter antenna, reflects off a distant electrical boundary, and the reflection is picked up by a receiver antenna. The travel time of the pulse from the transmitter to the receiver antenna via the reflector is measured [Davis and Annan 1989]. The depth to a reflector can be calculated, when the propagation speed of the pulse in the material is known. The propagation velocity can be measured *in situ* by conducting a Common Mid Point (CMP) or a Wide Angle Reflection and Refraction (WARR) survey [Arcone 1984]. In air the pulse travels at the speed of light (0.3 metres per nanosecond). In the subsurface the pulse travels at a velocity that is dependent upon the electrical properties of the material traversed; this velocity will be some appreciable fraction of the speed of light. Current operating frequencies vary from 10 MHz to 1 GHz and modern digital instruments incorporate signal stacking and digital data processing [LaFlèche, Judge, and Pilon 1987]. By moving the instrument along a survey line, one acquires a radar cross-section of the subsurface which can then be related to known earth material properties.

The overall depth to which a radar pulse will penetrate effectively depends on the electromagnetic absorption of the subsurface. Reflections detected by a GPR system are caused by dielectric contrasts in the subsurface materials. Common causes of subsurface reflections are material interfaces (e.g. overburden-rock, sand-clay, frozen-unfrozen, dry-wet, etc.). A large dielectric contrast exists between water and most geological materials. As a result, the presence or absence of water controls, to a large degree, the subsurface propagation characteristics of the radar pulse. Thus, the ability of a material to retain water within its pore space is an important factor in the determination of the bulk electrical properties. It is also important to remember that a GPR profile is a dielectric cross-section of the subsurface, which is strongly influenced by, but may not necessarily correspond only to, the stratigraphic cross-section.

RESULTS OF INVESTIGATION

Summaries of the operations and findings of the GPR study at various Qallunaaq Island sites are presented in the following section. The echoes recorded for each transect are printed as profiles in *Figure 9*. For those wishing to interpret these profiles, it should be noted that the uppermost echo line is the airwave, while the second line is a groundwave representing the ground surface traversed; this surface wave is interpreted as a straight line, so that undulations in the surface topography are transformed into apparent reciprocal undulations in subsurface echo lines. Descriptions of the visible surface characteristics of the various features investigated, as well as the locations of these features on a map of the island, may be found in McGhee and Tuck [this volume].

Graves?:

A 6x6 metre grid was laid out over the area where two isolated boulders had been noted as possible grave-markers. Six transects were run from south to north along the grid lines, each transect 1 m to the west of the last. The first transect (*Fig. 9*: FRO 0) shows a slight anomaly from a normal stratigraphic pattern. This anomaly is more apparent in the following three transects (FRO 1-3), at a point approximately 1 to 2 m from the beginning of the transects and at an estimated depth of approximately 1 m; a much weaker anomaly is visible at approximately the four-metre mark of these transects. No evidence of disturbance is seen in the final two transects (FRO 4-5). The findings are consistent with at least one elongated disturbance oriented east-west in the vicinity of the boulders found on the surface. Since the matrix in this area appears to be undifferentiated gravel, the anomaly may represent evidence of at least one burial.

Caches:

The next features to be investigated were the pair of large boulder caches located on the gravel plateau above the northern shore of the island.

The first transect (*Fig. 9*: CACH 1) was laid out from east to west across the centre of the caches, beginning about 1 m to the east of the easternmost cache. The findings show evidence of a disturbance between approximately 2 and 7.5 m from the beginning of the transect, and of a second anomaly between approximately 13.5 and 19 m. The maximum depth of these anomalies appear to be less than 1 m.

The second transect (CACH 2) was run from north to south, just to the east of centre of the western cache feature. This showed a similar anomaly to that of CACH 1, noted at 1 to 6 m along the transect but most strongly visible between 3 and 6 m. A strong point source is seen at approximately 3 m, and at an estimated depth of approximately 1 m; this may represent a small buried object, or a large boulder.

The third transect (CACH 3) was run as a control, from north to south across the barren area between the two caches. No significant anomalies are apparent.

The final transect (CACH 4) was measured from north to south across the centre of the smaller eastern cache. It shows slight evidence of disturbance from approximately 4 to 9 m along the transect, at a maximum depth of up to 1.5 m.

The findings are consistent with some amount of shallow excavation having been carried out in the central portions of the areas presently covered by scattered boulders. There is, however, no clear evidence of significant subterranean construction or the existence of large buried deposits.

Ship's Trench:

Three transects were run in this feature, as a check on whether our findings in the trench excavated near the lower end of the feature were representative of other areas of the deposit.

The first transect (*Fig. 9*: TRENCH 1) was laid out from east to west across the feature, approximately 2 m to the south and uphill from our excavated trench. The transect shows an apparently undifferentiated deposit extending to bedrock at an estimated maximum depth of 2 m. Near the centre of the transect, a small point source may suggest a piece of buried wood or metal lying close to bedrock.

The second transect (TRENCH 2) was run east to west, approximately 2 m downhill and to the north of our excavation trench. This transect is in the area of the Ship's Trench subject to occasional storm activity, and whose surface is comprised of heavy boulders. The transect shows no significant anomalies and suggests that the concentration of boulders extends to bedrock.

The third transect (TRENCH 3) was measured from north to south along the midline of the feature and runs for a distance of 22 m from bottom to top. The filled-in remains of our excavation trench shows clearly as a disturbance at approximately 5 to 6 m from the northern end. A second and weaker disturbance is visible between approximately 11 and 14 m, but the cause of this anomaly is not obvious. It should be noted that the sharply dipping echo visible between 19 and 22 m is an artifact of the steepening surface slope at the upper end of the feature.

The results of this survey suggest that the deposits filling the Ship's Trench are relatively amorphous, with no evidence of major anomalies or buried deposits. The deposits encountered during our excavations near the lower end of the feature are probably typical of those filling the remainder of the trench.

Industrial Area:

The remaining ground probing radar surveys were conducted on various features in the Industrial Area of the site. The aim of these surveys was to detect the existence of subterranean structural features or significant buried deposits, which would suggest the potential for recovery of useful information by excavation of these features.

Feature 1 ("Smithy"): This concentration of boulders and rock slabs emerges from a low mound of turf approximately 6 m in diameter and lies at the northeastern edge of the Industrial Area.

The first transect (*Fig. 9*: WORK 3) was laid out from southeast to northwest across the centre of the feature. It shows a shallow disturbance between approximately 1.8 and 8.5 m, obviously coinciding with the surface indications of the structure; the apparent dip in subsurface echoes in this area is an artifact of the rise in the surface topography from which the measurements were taken, above the feature. The second transect (WORK 4) is at right angles to the first, crossing the first at about the centre of the feature. A similar pattern of shallow disturbance can be detected at approximately 2 to 8 m from the northeastern end of the transect, again coinciding with the mounded surface of the feature. A point source can be noted at the 5.6-metre position on this transect, apparently emanating from just below the surface; this may represent a small buried piece of metal, wood or other organic material.

Feature 2 ("Assay Office"): This feature is a similar concentration of boulders in a slightly elevated turf mound. It lies in the centre of the flat vegetated zone of the Industrial Area. Surface indications suggest that it probably represents a rectangular structure measuring approximately 6 m on a side.

The first transect (*Fig. 9*: WORK 1) was laid out from south to north, crossing the mound inside the northern periphery of the feature. The results show a very uniform picture, with no anomalies that can be related to the structure. The second transect (WORK 2) runs from east to west at right angles to the first, with the centre of the feature at about the five-metre position. Again, the results are amorphous but show slight evidence of disturbance between approximately 2.9 and 5.5 m, with a possible point source at about the four-metre position.

Figure 9: Profiles of ground probing radar transects.

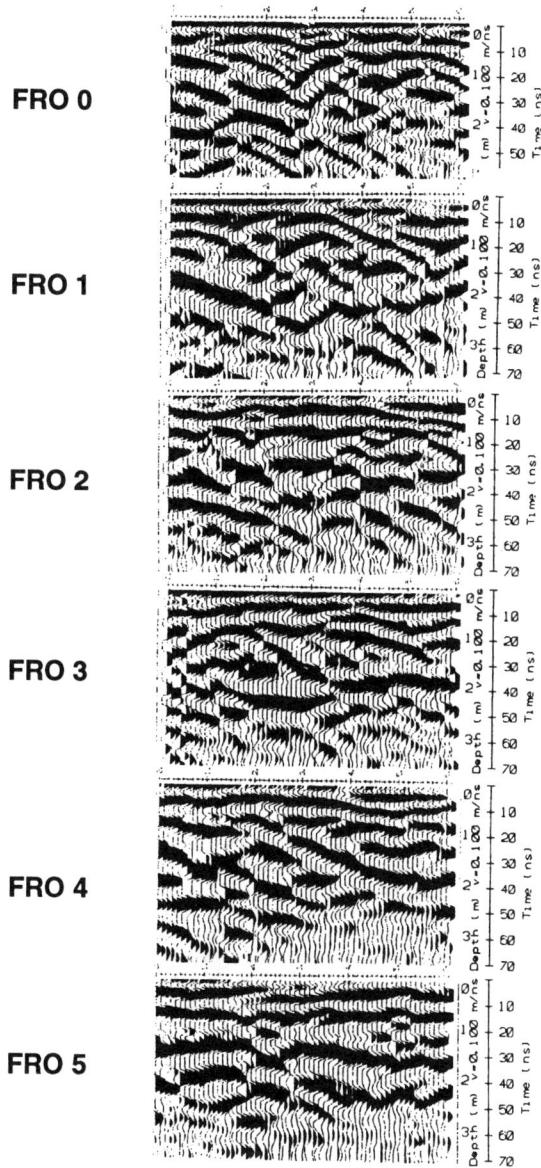

Figure 9 (cont.)

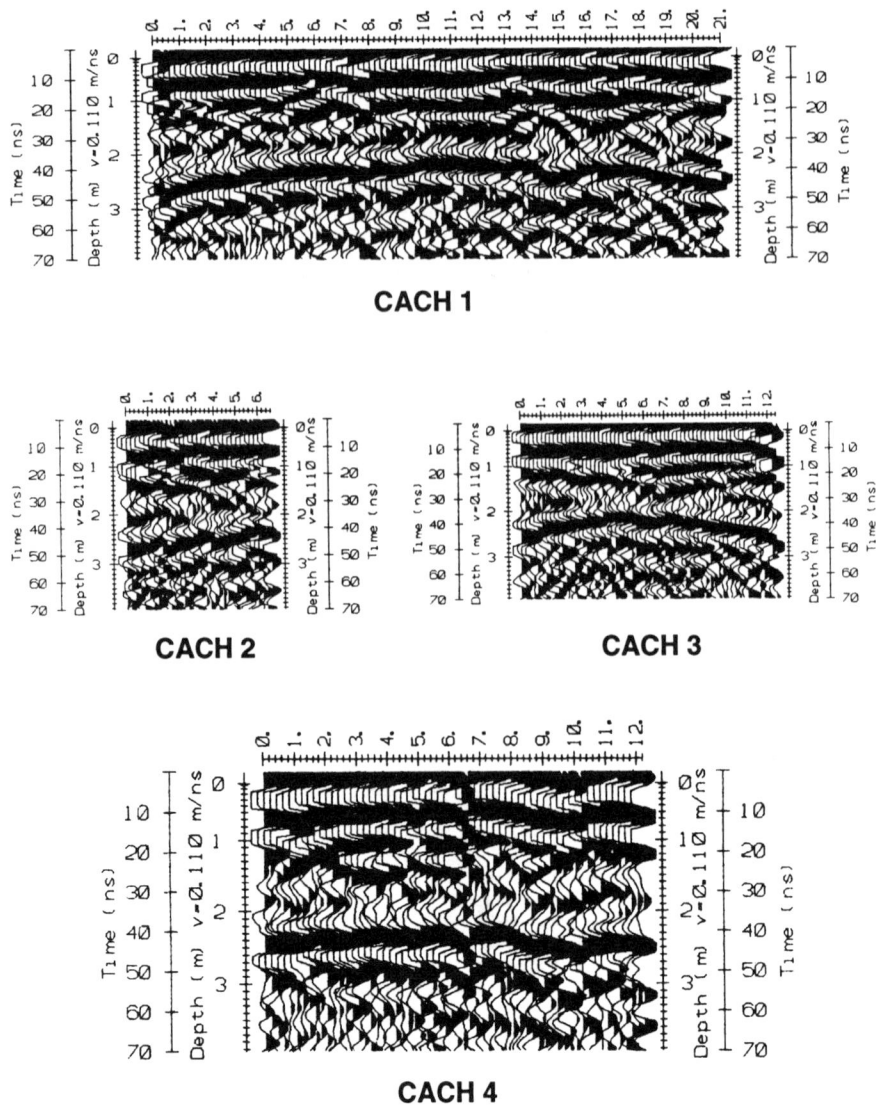

CACH 1

CACH 2

CACH 3

CACH 4

Figure 9 (cont.)

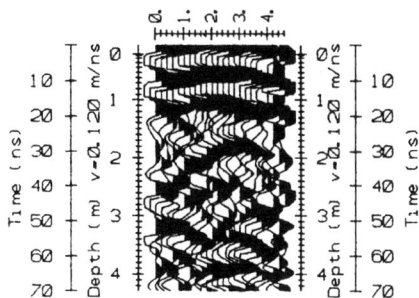

TRENCH 1

West to East trench

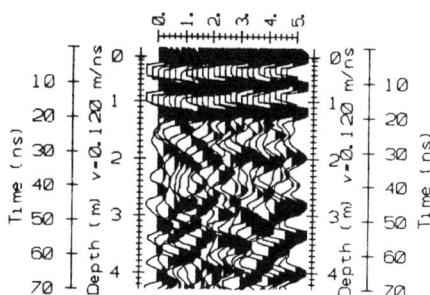

TRENCH 2

Ship's Trench

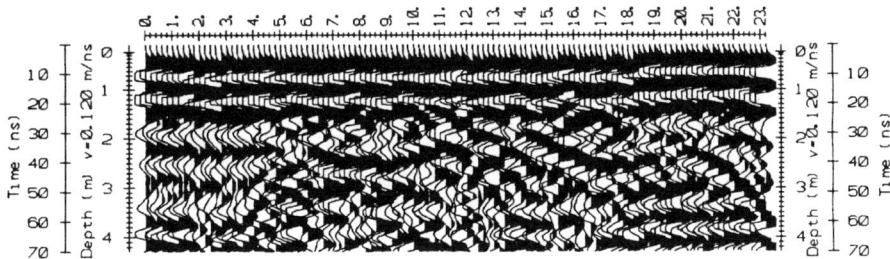

TRENCH 3

North to South trench

Figure 9 (cont.)

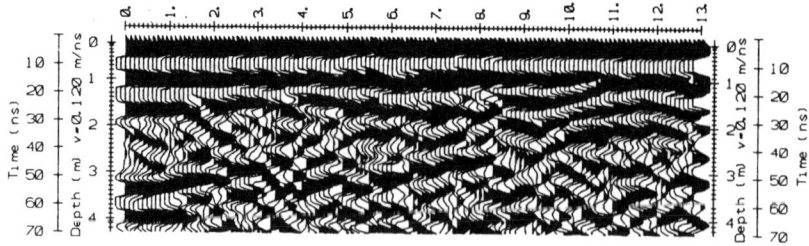

WORK 3

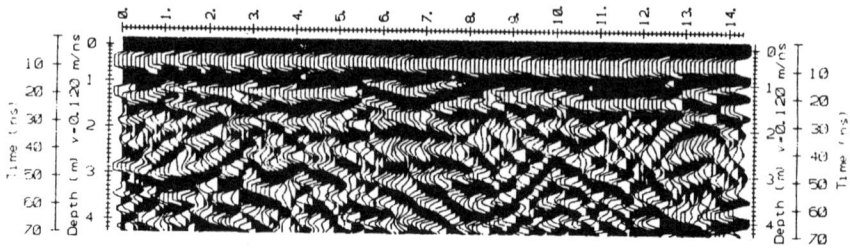

WORK 4

feature 1

Figure 9 (cont.)

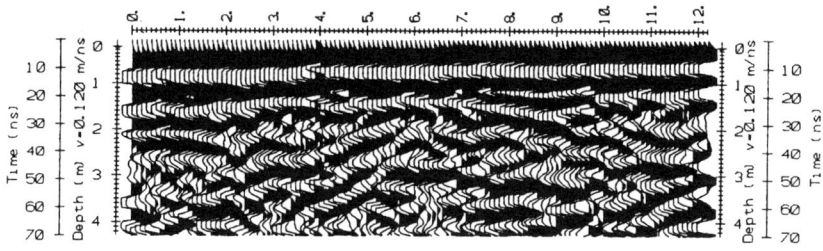

WORK 1

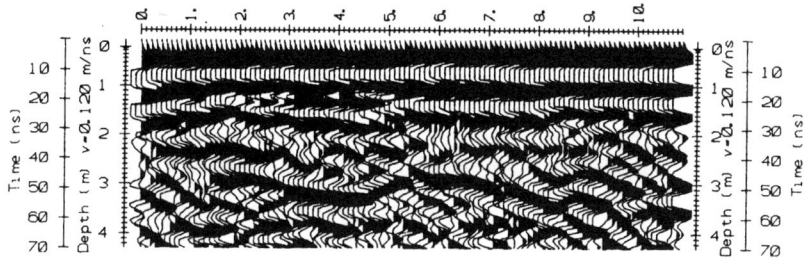

WORK 2

feature 2

Figure 9 (cont.)

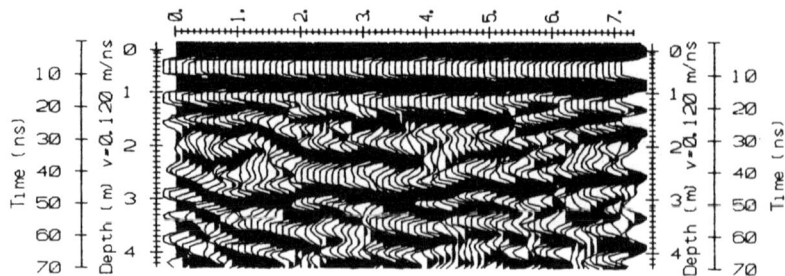

WORK 6

feature 3

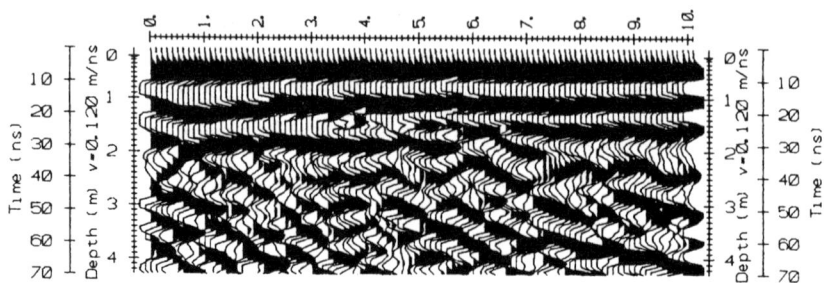

WORK 5

feature 4

Figure 9 (cont.)

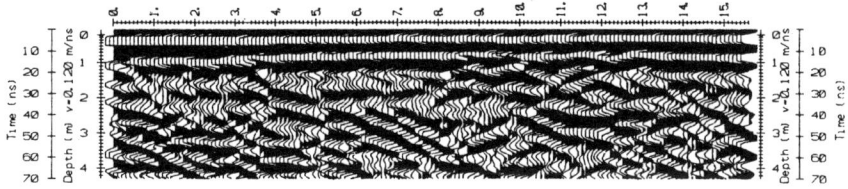

BAN 1

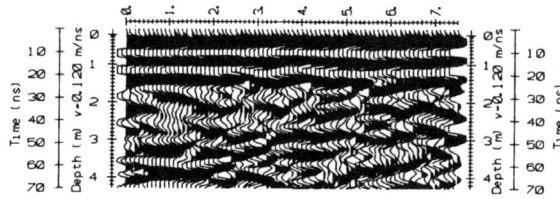

BAN 2

feature 6

Feature 3 ("Charcoal kiln"): This is a poorly defined feature, comprising a mound of boulders and turf measuring 5 m by 4 m, at the northern edge of the Industrial Area. A transect (*Fig. 9*: WORK 6) was laid out from northeast to southwest across the feature.

The profile shows a slight disturbance between approximately 1.4 and 5.9 m from the north end, coinciding with the dipping echoes which are an artifact of the raised surface topography over the feature. At the four-metre position, a point source (either a small buried object or a boulder) is visible at a depth estimated at less than 0.5 m. Bedrock appears to underlie the entire feature at a depth of about 0.5 m.

Feature 4 ("Workshop"): This feature is a vaguely defined scatter of boulders in a very slight mound of turf measuring approximately 5 m across. A transect (*Fig. 9*: WORK 5) 10 m in length was laid out from northeast to southwest across the centre of the structure. Evidence of a shallow disturbance can be seen between approximately 2 and 7 m from the northeastern end, coinciding with the surface manifestation of the structure, but no major anomalies are visible.

No ground probing radar transects were run on Feature 5, which is a simple tent ring with no indications of internal or subsurface features.

Feature 6 ("Pit"): Two transects were run at right angles across this puzzling feature, which appears as a slight mound with central pit adjacent to the eroding edge of the Industrial Area. The first transect (*Fig. 9*: BAN 1) was laid out roughly northeast to southwest and crosses the northern edge of the test pit in the mound. A shallow saucer-shaped echo can be noted between approximately 3.5 and 8.5 m; the shape is probably an artifact of the mounded surface from which the measurements were taken.

The second transect (BAN 2) is perpendicular to the first, beginning approximately 4 m to the northwest of the central test pit. There is evidence of shallow disturbance from approximately 2.6 to 5.5 m, and a discontinuity at 4 m which appears to represent the nearby test pit.

SUMMARY OF RESULTS

The results of the ground probing radar survey of selected Qallunaaq Island features can be summarized as follows:

1. The area beneath the suspected grave markers produced evidence consistent with at least one shallow burial.

2. The two large cache-like structures near the northern coast of the island produced evidence of shallow disturbance; aside from one point source suggesting a single buried object or boulder, there was no evidence of major buried deposits.

3. No evidence of significant buried deposits was found in the Ship's Trench.

4. Surveys of the five boulder features in the Industrial Area of the site produced no evidence of significant subterranean structural features such as stone floors, furnaces, etc., nor of significant buried deposits of artifacts or industrial refuse.

Plant Collection

An attempt was made to assess the vulnerability of the vegetation covering the main Industrial Area of the site to potential disturbance through excavation or human trampling. A systematic collection of plants in the area was made by Rob MacIntosh (Arctic College). Laurie L. Consaul (Canadian Museum of Nature) identified the following vascular plants in the collection:

Poa arctica R. Br.
Festuca brachyphylla Schultes
Trisetum spicatum (L.) Richt.
Carex membranacea L.
Salix arctica Pallas
Polygonum viviparum L.
Cerastium alpinum L.
Silene acaulis L.
Silene involucrata (Cham. & Schlecht) Bocquet, ssp. *involucrata*
Stellaria longipes Goldie
Dryas integrifolia M. Vahl
Potentilla pulchella R. Br.
Empetrum nigrum L.
Epilobium latifolium L.
Pyrola grandiflora Rad.
Arctostaphylos alpina (L.) Spreng.
Vaccinium uliginosum L.
Armeria maritima (Mill.) Willd.
Pedicularis flammea L.
Artemesia borealis Pall.
Taraxacum lacerum Greene

On the basis of these identifications, and of the notes and photographs taken by Rob MacIntosh, Susan Aiken (Canadian Museum of Nature) was able to make the following assessments:

(1) All plants represented are native to Baffin Island; there is nothing in the collection to indicate the use of the island by the Frobisher expeditions.

(2) The barren patches in the Industrial Area of the site appear to be the result of vegetation and turf removal at some time in the past. If this disturbance occurred during the sixteenth century, the rate of re-vegetation appears to be extremely slow and may be explained by the poor water-holding characteristics of the gravel substrate.

(3) The majority of dominant plants in the area (such as *Dryas*, *Salix*, *Empetrum*) are perennial shrubs that are quite resistant to trampling. Several of the more attractive flowering species would be more vulnerable to flower-picking by visitors, which might easily result in uprooting of entire plants from the gravel soil.

Conclusions and Recommendations

The 1991 assessment work furnished answers to several questions concerning the archaeological potential of Qallunaaq Island. It also provided a basis for recommendations regarding the archaeological resources of the island. These conclusions and recommendations can be summarized as follows:

[1] The major cache of material and supplies left by the 1578 Frobisher expedition appears to have been buried in the Ship's Trench. This material appears to have been thoroughly salvaged by Inuit, leaving behind a jumbled deposit containing only a few rejected remnants of unsalvageable materials. Our excavations did not produce evidence that the Ship's Trench had been the site of shipbuilding or other activities.

We recommend that, since excavation of the Ship's Trench is unlikely to produce significant information of research value, further excavation should not be undertaken.

[2] The ground-probing radar survey indicated the possibility of small burial deposits beneath the "headstones" and in the vicinity of the "cache" structures.

Subsurface investigation of these deposits should be carried out only within an overall management plan for the research and conservation of the island.

[3] The ground-probing radar survey showed that there were no major buried deposits, or buried structural features, associated with any of the structures in the main Industrial Area of the site.

It is recommended, in view of the surface damage that would be caused by excavation in this vegetated area of the island, that no excavation for research purposes is warranted in this portion of the site.

[4] The foundations of the Frobisher House at the summit of the island have survived in a surprising state of preservation.

We recommend that excavation and recording of these foundations should be carried out, with adequate equipment and expertise, within a management plan for the heritage resources of the island. Consideration should be given to preserving the foundations in the form of a mould.

[5] The site and its environs appear to be relatively safe from the forces of natural erosion. The surface of the site has already been picked relatively clean by tourists and archaeologists, so that the increasing tourist visitation to the site will probably not lead to a major degradation of the research value of the site.

However, the value of the site as a heritage landscape can be expected to undergo severe degradation at the hands and feet of visiting tourists. Despite our precautions in leaving as few marks as possible on the surface of the island, our activities resulted in the creation of several footpaths in the Industrial Area, across the gravel flats near the northern end of the island, and most notably down the central axis of the Ship's Trench. Heavier use can be expected to cause the development of more permanent footpaths, and slumping of the bank adjacent to the Industrial Area as well as of the edges of the Ship's Trench and Reservoir mines. Simple camping on the island, with the attendant shifting of boulders to hold down tents, would soon erase or confuse the sparse evidence of Elizabethan camping activities.

It is recommended that a management plan be put into place as soon as possible, to deal with the effects of human visitors on Qallunaaq Island.

ACKNOWLEDGEMENTS: We wish to thank those co-workers who joined us on Qallunaaq Island in August 1991: Davin Ala, Réginald Auger, Malcolm Billings, Don Hogarth, Lee Jablonski, Rob MacIntosh, and Jeannette Smith. For logistic help, we are grateful to Bob Longworth and his assistants at the Iqaluit Research Centre; Bill Fitzhugh and the crew of the *Pitsiulak*; Fred Alt and Bradley Aviation; and our pilots from Aero Arctic. We owe thanks to Laurie Consaul and Susan Aiken of the Canadian Museum of Nature, for their work in identifying and assessing the plant collection from Qallunaaq Island, as well as to Gregory Young, Elizabeth Moffatt, and Jeremy Powell of the Canadian Conservation Institute, for their analytical work on the organic materials recovered during excavation.

References

Arcone, S.A.
   1984   Field observations of electromagnetic pulse propagation in dielectric slabs. *Geophysics* 49:1763-73.

Barley, M.W.
   1967   *The English Farmhouse and Cottage.* London: Routledge and Kegan Paul.

Davis, J.L., and A.P. Annan
   1989   Ground penetrating radar for high-resolution mapping of soil and rock stratigraphy. *Geophysical Prospecting* 37:531-51.

Fitzhugh, William W.
   1981   Smithsonian Archaeological Surveys at Kodlunarn Island in 1981: Preliminary Field Report. Manuscript on file, Archaeological Survey of Canada, Canadian Museum of Civilization.

Hall, Charles Francis
   1865   *Arctic Researches and Life Among the Esquimaux.* New York: Harper and Brothers.

Kenyon, Walter
   1981   The Canadian Arctic Journal of Capt. Edward Fenton, 1578. *Archivaria* 11:171-203

LaFlèche. P.T., A.S. Judge and J.A. Pilon
   1987   Ground probing radar in the investigation of the competency of frozen tailings pond dams. In Current Research, Part A., *Geological Survey of Canada Paper* 87-1A, pp. 191-97.

Martin Frobisher's Base Camp on Kodlunarn Island: A Two-Year Time Capsule in the History of Technology

Réginald Auger
Célat, Université Laval

Michel Blackburn
Département des Sols, Université Laval

William W. Fitzhugh
Arctic Studies Center, Smithsonian Institution

RÉSUMÉ

Les exploits de Martin Frobisher (1576-1578) dans sa poursuite de la découverte du passage du nord-ouest n'ont d'égal, que son habileté à convaincre ses créanciers de lui fournir les fonds nécessaires à l'établissement d'une colonie de quatre cent mineurs sur l'île Kodlunarn. Au cours des trois années consécutives que Frobisher dirigea ses expéditions dans l'Arctique, la première visait à découvrir la route vers la Chine, alors que les deux autres avaient pour objectif l'exploitation de minerais dans le but d'en extraire l'or qu'ils devaient contenir. Cette entreprise pour le moins audacieuse résulta en l'implantation de l'établissement industriel anglais le plus ancien au Nouveau Monde. Cette contribution vise donc à démontrer le potentiel archéologique du poste de transformation des minerais construit sur l'île Kodlunarn. Nous présentons les résultats de la reconnaissance archéologique de l'île Kodlunarn et des sondages pratiqués sur le fourneau d'essai, la forge, la rampe de lancement des navires et de l'analyse de la collecte de surface dans une zone d'érosion. Bien que très préliminaires, les données architecturales, les témoins archéologiques et l'archéométrie apportent des éléments d'explication à des questions d'aspect technologique reliées à l'entreprise de Frobisher. Enfin, il est à noter que les problématiques de cette étude n'ont jamais été soulevées dans les études utilisant un cadre traditionel dans l'analyse des documents historiques.

ABSTRACT

The exploits of Martin Frobisher in search of the Northwest Passage (1576-78) were less successful than his ability to persuade financiers to provide the backing for the establishment of a colony of 400 miners on Kodlunarn Island. In three consecutive years Frobisher led expeditions to Arctic waters, the first being an attempt to discover a route through to China, but the latter two having as their goal the exploitation of mineral resources from which it was believed gold could be extracted. This was the earliest industrial enterprise in the New World undertaken by the English. This paper argues the archaeological potential of the mining/industrial complex set up on Kodlunarn. It indicates the results from archaeological survey of the island, from test excavations at the assay shop, smithy, and Ship's Trench, and from analysis of materials collected from the surface of areas threatened by erosion. Although very preliminary, data from architectural, archaeological, and archeometric evidence throw some light on questions related to technological aspects of the Frobisher expeditions. It is important to note that the problems addressed by this study are not capable of resolution through the traditional approach of study of historical documents alone.

Introduction

While the narratives of the Frobisher voyages and their related State Papers have been published on various occasions, none of these documents have ever been submitted to detailed analytical study. Some publications of these accounts present the texts verbatim with no commentary or analysis [e.g. Collinson 1867; Stefansson and McCaskill 1938] while others, such as Morison [1971] and Kenyon [1975], use the documents only as accessory illustrations to the historical story. For years, these accounts have attracted the attention of historians. It is only recently, however, that attention has shifted to the most neglected part of the Frobisher saga: the physical remains left by the expeditions and the impact these voyages had on Inuit populations in the Eastern Canadian Arctic.

Apart from Hall's publication [1865], everything we know of the Frobisher voyages is contained in the "official" documentary accounts rather than from study of the sites and their physical remains, which have been known since Hall's discoveries in 1861. The reasons for neglect by archaeologists and specialists in historical technology are clear. First, the Frobisher base camp is located on a remote Eastern Arctic island accessible to scientists for only a limited time during summer months. Second, the archaeological remains of the Frobisher voyages are less spectacular than southern sites such as the Louisbourg Fortress, Lower Fort Garry, or Place Royale. Ironically, the

Frobisher site has been, and may continue to be, ignored for reasons expressed in a 1981 proposal review which stated that archaeological work was unnecessary "because the events of the Frobisher voyages are so well documented historically." A more recent view continues this line of reasoning:

> The 1991 [field] work led to the conclusion that the Frobisher sites on Kodlunarn Island are not threatened immediately by either natural erosion nor by an expected influx of tourists. However, the value of the sites as a heritage resource would be threatened by insensitive excavation. The work confirmed that there is little justification for research-based archaeology on the site, and substantiated the need for establishment of a management plan to protect the heritage value of this unique location. [McGhee 1992, 27]

As a physical monument, the Frobisher site might be considered a "footnote to history." Kodlunarn Island cannot rival the larger and more impressive European sites found in southern regions, and its symbolic importance is diminished by the ultimate failure of Lok's and Frobisher's settlement, mining, and empire aspirations. Still, the site is important in the history of European exploration of the New World for three reasons principally. As the northernmost post-Norse European site, it documents an important stage in the discovery and exploration of the New World. Its mines, masonry building, smithy, and assay shop provide important information on building, economic pursuits, and the history of technology. Finally, it represents the first wave of a long tradition of European-Inuit contact and cultural exchange. The preliminary findings presented in this paper are intended primarily to highlight the research potential of the Kodlunarn Island sites - scene of one of the earliest pages of the story of European exploration in Canada.

The Three Voyages of Martin Frobisher

Martin Frobisher departed on his search for a route to Cathay the same year that Drake was sailing the Pacific [Payne and Beazley 1907; Aker and Von der Porten 1979]. Frobisher left Blackwall, England, on his first voyage on 15 June 1576[1] with a squadron consisting of the *Gabriel* (25 tons), the *Michael* (25 tons), and a 10-ton pinnace. As the flotilla approached Greenland the pinnace sank in a storm with everyone aboard. Fearing their own loss, the crew of the *Michael* turned back, while Frobisher, not without opposition from his own crew, pushed farther west in the Gabriel. On 26 July, he sighted a cape which he named Queen Elizabeth's Foreland and another promontory to the north which was named Cape Walsingham.[2] The Gabriel sailed between the capes to a distance of fifty leagues, Frobisher believing the land on his left was America and that on his right, Asia. Finding no end to that body of water,

Frobisher decided to explore the region around what is now the entrance to Hudson Strait. He returned to England on 2 October after naming present-day Frobisher Bay "Frobusher Straightes" [3] (*Fig. 1*).

Frobisher met native people immediately upon arriving in Frobisher Bay. During the first voyage Inuit came aboard the *Gabriel* and exchanged gifts with the crew, but mutual trust soon vanished when a group of five sailors, contrary to orders, strayed too far from the ship and were captured by a group of Inuit. The five sailors and their boat were never seen again, although remains of their clothing were found at an Inuit camp the following year. Frobisher having lost his only means of getting ashore and part of his crew, a rescue was out of the question. Nevertheless, he devised an ingenious scheme to take a captive, for possible ransom for his crew and to bring home to England to present to the royal court. Knowing Inuit fondness for European hardware, he lured an Inuk in his kayak close to his ship by offering him a small metal bell. When the Inuk was within reach, Frobisher grabbed him and plucked him and his kayak from the water. Abandoned by his friends, who refused to negotiate over the lost sailors, the Inuk was taken to England as one of Frobisher's "tokens of possession", but he died shortly thereafter.

Frobisher also returned with another "token" as proof of his discoveries. When asked by Lok and other investors about his finds, Frobisher produced a small chunk of black rock. History claims that one of the investors' wives thought this an insignificant trifle and angrily threw the rock into the fire. After the rock was withdrawn and quenched in vinegar "it glistered with a bright Marquesset of golde" [Collinson 1867, 75]. Believing the rock might be a gold-bearing mineral, Lok delivered a sample to an assayer. The "goldfiner" concluded that it contained gold and would yield a wealthy return; he backed his finding with a promise of personal investment. Thus began the first Arctic gold-rush.

Before further plans were made, Michael Lok, Treasurer of the Muscovy Company and an entrepreneur *par excellence* [McDermott 1984], arranged for other assays. Three new samples of the black rock were provided to different assayers, all of whom concluded that the black ore was a "marquesette" (pyrites) stone with no gold content. Dissatisfied with these results because he believed the ore contained gold, Lok submitted another sample to an Italian assayer named Giovanni Baptista Agnello. After some days, Agnello showed Lok a fine gold powder. Three more samples were submitted to Agnello, with similar results. Marvelling at the outcome, which was contrary to the earlier assays, Lok is reported to have received the perplexing response, "bisogna sapere adulare la natura" (one sometimes has to coax nature).

In spite of the equivocal results, the prospects of a major gold discovery prompted financiers and the Queen, with support from the Privy Council, to encourage a second voyage - this time a commercial venture organized as the Cathay Company, rather than one of exploration and discovery. The 1577 expedition was directed at mining the black ore deposits Frobisher had discovered and searching for new sources. On 18 July Frobisher reached the island where the ore had been collected the year before. The expedition then proceeded to explore the south shore of Frobisher Straits (west coast of Frobisher Bay). On the twenty-sixth *Michael* and *Gabriel* left the *Ayde* in Jackman Sound and proceeded north for further exploration. They anchored that night in Beare's Sound, where the crew began work at mining, but found their efforts cut short when the ships were suddenly endangered by drifting ice.

Sailing farther into the Straits on the twenty-ninth, Frobisher discovered a protected bay about five leagues from Beare's Sound. This place, which he named Countess of Warwick's Sound, was the farthest the expedition reached into Frobisher Straits in 1577. Here, on a small island also named in honour of the Countess, he spent the rest of the short season mining black ore in the feature we now know as the Ship's Trench (*Fig. 2*).

Back in London with three shiploads (*ca.* 200 tons) of black ore, it was estimated that 900 lb. of ore would pay for furnace construction in Dartford and the cost of refining the ore into gold. These funds were raised from people who had already ventured money in the enterprise. An alchemist named Jonas Schütz, who seemed particularly skilled at producing gold from the ore, was retained to oversee the work.

While the first and second voyages were relatively modest operations for such an ambitious endeavour, Frobisher's third voyage was, by sixteenth century standards, extremely lavish. He sailed from Portsmouth on 15 May 1578 with fifteen ships and four hundred men. The stated purposes of this voyage were to mine and return to England a large quantity of black ore, and to found a colony in the land Queen Elizabeth, a principal Cathay Company investor, had designated as *Meta Incognita*.

The proposed mining and exploration colony consisted of one hundred volunteers and three ships, to be left under the governorship of Edward Fenton. The skills of the proposed colonists were of prime importance. Since ships were to be used, forty were selected as mariners, gunners, shipwrights, and carpenters. Thirty soldiers were designated to protect the colony, and thirty others were assigned as "pioneers" (miners). Ammunition and provisions were to be left in sufficient quantity to last for eighteen months. Besides being asked to mine ore, the colonists were requested to make observations on climate, temperature, and ice conditions; weekly journal records were to be kept. They were also directed to befriend and gather information from native people, since the latter were expected to become guides and intermediaries in the projected Cathay voyages to follow.

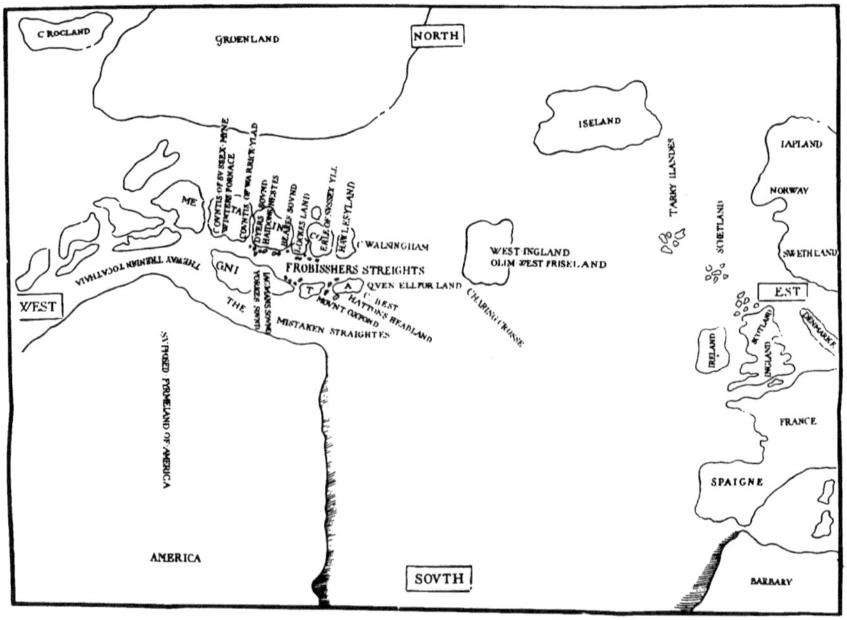

Figure 1: Sixteenth century representation of Frobisher Bay (reproduced by kind permission of the Hakluyt Society, London).

Figure 2: The Ship's Trench, site of the 1577 mining activities in Countess of Warwick Sound.

As a result of extremely severe sea-ice encountered off the east Baffin coast, the bark *Dennis*, which was transporting the expedition's prefabricated houses, sank together with her essential cargo. Storms and ice also took a toll on other expedition supplies, including lumber and another essential commodity, beer. As a result of these losses and the lateness of the season, the plan of founding a colony had to be abandoned, and Frobisher ultimately brought his entire expedition back to England in the fall of 1578.

On 1 August Frobisher ordered the expedition's miners and soldiers to begin work; victuals, tents, and tools for mining ore were landed on Countess of Warwick Island. Time was of the essence since autumn was fast approaching.[4] That summer the Frobisher expedition mined black ore at four locations [see Hogarth, this volume]. All ore was assayed on the island before being loaded aboard the ships.

Discovery of the Frobisher Sites' Remains

Apart from the published record, interest in the Frobisher expeditions began with discovery of Martin Frobisher's base camp on Kodlunarn Island by Charles Francis Hall in 1861 [see Hall 1865] and subsequent deposit of his collections and papers with the Smithsonian Institution and the Royal Geographical Society. Since the present research effort emerged from these early beginnings, a brief account of these events follows.

Like many adventure-seekers, Hall was enthralled with the mystery of the lost Franklin expedition of 1847 and decided to make his own search for survivors. Unlike official expeditions and naval parties, Hall decided to follow Inuit ways, learning to speak some Inuktitut and travelling with Inuit for extended periods. During his stay with the East Baffin Inuit he learned nothing of the Franklin sailors but, rather, heard much about Europeans who had visited the area in more ancient times. With his Inuit companions, he went to the site of these visitations, an island the Inuit called Kodlunarn, or "white man's" island - literally, the place where white men lived. There he found relics including pottery fragments, flint-tempered mortar, slag, bricks, and iron scattered among the ruins of a small settlement. The nature of his finds and Inuit oral accounts convinced him he had discovered Martin Frobisher's sixteenth century base camp [see Rowley 1993].

During his stay on Kodlunarn Island, Hall was much impressed by the detailed Inuit oral accounts and wondered about the five men Frobisher had lost on his 1576 expedition. Koojesse, one of Hall's informants, mentioned that the men who built the ship and embarked in it had all "died with the cold." When Hall asked how he knew this, Koojesse answered that "all the old Innuits said so" [Hall 1865, 390].

Frobisher's Base Camp at Countess of Warwick Sound

It is frequently asked why such a small desolate island was selected as the centre for Frobisher's 1578 operation? One reason is that Countess of Warwick Sound offers protection from drifting ice, which in summer can suddenly move in and crush vessels anchored in unsheltered harbors. In addition, Countess of Warwick Island, due to its small size (only 300 m in its longest dimension), is difficult to attack because approaching parties can be seen from all directions from a vantage point at the island's summit. The fact that the island had been the expedition's base and principal mining site in 1577 were no doubt added incentives. Most important, however, was that its mines had yielded a high-grade ore.

Not only was Countess of Warwick Island a mining centre; it also became the staging point for mining activities carried out elsewhere in Frobisher Bay in 1578. As a result it is here, on a small, low, and desolate Arctic island, that almost all of the physical remains of the earliest English settlement in the Americas are to be found.

Two activities carried out by the Frobisher party are of particular interest: blacksmithing and assaying of ores. Hogarth [1993] maintains that the mining methods were rather primitive. Miners did not have the advantage of explosives and had to extract the black ore by manpower alone. Exposed to the harsh task of breaking up local bedrock, the miner's iron crowbars, sledges, pickaxes, and wedges were frequently damaged and dulled; they required constant repair by blacksmiths. The assay office was also an essential component of the Kodlunarn Island base camp. Here the ores were assayed before being loaded, for the assayers had the responsibility of ensuring that only precious metal-bearing minerals were mined and returned to England.

Life at the Kodlunarn Island base camp was strictly regulated. Codes of behavior included regulations against polluting freshwater supplies, and dumping ballast and garbage into the bay. Strict secrecy governed the assaying of ores. A Frobisher order of 2 August 1578 stated that no person should assay any ores unless appointed by the general (Frobisher) or his lieutenant in his absence. Nor was any person allowed to keep as personal property any ore or precious metals. All such materials were to be delivered to the general or his lieutenant. Anyone failing to comply with the regulations was to forfeit, for each ounce, three times the value of his daily wages and to receive such punishment as Her Majesty would decide.

Hogarth [1993] has synthesized information from sixteenth century works on pyrotechnology [e.g. Agricola 1950; Ercker 1951], and explains the four basic steps involved in the process of rendering minerals. First, the minerals were melted in crucibles and, with the aid of metallic lead flux, precious metals were precipitated to the bottom of the crucible. The lead button thus produced was then subjected to a second operation called cupellation, in which the molten lead button was heated in a porous bone ash cupel into which the lead diffused; the remaining metal was collected from the bottom of the cupel in the form of a silver and gold bead. The third step involved the separation of silver from gold, achieved by dissolving silver with acid ($HNO3$). The final operation was the precipitation of silver as insoluble silver chloride ($AgCl_2$), by addition of sea water.

A fascinating aspect of the 1578 enterprise was the construction of a masonry house on Kodlunarn Island during the 1578 visit. The documents of the expedition reported that a cottage built of lime and stone was finished on 13 August, shortly before the expedition's departure for England. The purpose of building that house was twofold. First, it was erected as a test to see how it would withstand the cold climate of Frobisher Straits and whether the Inuit would dismantle it. Second, Frobisher thought that exposure to the cottage would convince the Inuit of the benevolence of English civilization and thus encourage them towards friendly relations. For the same reasons an oven was built and bread baked therein left in the house, together with engravings on metal of men and women on horseback, and gifts of bells, knives, mirrors, whistles, and pipes.

Finally, before departing in 1578 Frobisher cached unused supplies in anticipation of his return the next year. Best relates that:

> We buried the timber of our pretended forte, with manye barrels of meale, pease, griste, and sundrie other good things, which was of the provision of those whych should inhabite, if occasion served. And insteede therof we fraight oure ships full of ore, whiche we holde of farre greater price. [Collinson 1867, 272]

He goes on to report that, eternally hopeful, the English tested the island's fertility and ability to sustain civilized life by planting crops: "Also here we sowed pease, corne, and other graine, to prove the fruitfulnesse of the soyle against the next yeare."

Research on Kodlunarn Island: the 1981, 1990, and 1991 expeditions

The Kodlunarn remains of the 1577 and 1578 English expeditions constitute a unique two-year time capsule unsurpassed anywhere, in terms of its value as a sealed early exploration and mining enterprise. The fundamental importance of the site lies in its historical significance as the first English settlement in North America, and in the understanding it can give of the organization and activities of an early English mining and exploration enterprise. In addition to showing interest in the blacksmith and assay shops (as key components of a mining enterprise), research has concentrated on the Ship's Trench. This, according to Inuit oral tradition, was used by a group of English sailors who found themselves abandoned after the departure of the Frobisher expedition, and who built (or rebuilt) here a ship for their escape. Whether these were the original lost sailors of 1576 or another group is unclear. Frobisher records note that the 1578 expedition's excess supplies were cached in the Trench to preserve them for use the next year.

Given the Elizabethan dependence upon iron and the necessity for maintaining iron tools for mining, the blacksmith played an essential role in the expedition. The expedition certainly could not have been contemplated without the presence of a smithy. On the other hand, the assayer, through the secrets of his trade, provided necessary expertise to avoid filling the limited space in the ships with worthless rock. The smithy and the assay office on Kodlunarn are not only the earliest English structures of their type in North America, but were also focal points of the activities at the Frobisher base camp.

Archaeological investigation of the Kodlunarn Island smithy has potential value to the history of technology, since blacksmithing is the fundamental technology in the history of industry. Before the Industrial Revolution of the eighteenth century, the blacksmith was the primary manufacturer of the vast majority of all tools, as well as the maker of other hardware and equipment. As Moxon [1683] remarked:

> without the invention of smithing primarily, most other mechanik invention would be at a stand: the instruments, or tools, that are used in them, being either made of iron, or some other matter, form'd by the help of iron.... They all (other trades) have dependence upon the smith's trade, and not the smith upon them.

The smithy on Kodlunarn is therefore central to all other industrial activities at that site. Yet, despite its importance as an artisan's trade, little is known about technical aspects of smithing before the nineteenth century. Because early writers could not anticipate the sweeping technological changes to come in metallurgy, writings such as those by Biringuccio [1540], Agricola [1556], and later Moxon [1683] are either silent, terse, or obscure on many matters concerning the history of iron technology. With literature on smelting, forging, and other aspects of iron technology scanty, most of our evidence will have to come from archaeology and archaeometric analysis of iron products and remains [Light and Unglik 1987]. Archaeometallurgical examination of smithy slag is the best means of characterizing the technology and techniques used by sixteenth century ironsmiths.

Concerning the assaying activities, we know that, despite the precaution of field assaying, twelve shiploads of worthless ore were brought back to England in 1578. What went wrong with the assaying? Was it faked? Or more likely, as Donald Hogarth has hypothesized [pers. com.], was the lead used in separating gold and silver from the other minerals already contaminated with minute quantities of gold and silver? Recovery and analysis of soil samples from the assay office, as well as microprobe and thin-section analysis of ceramics used in the assaying, should allow us to determine the answer to this question.

The Blacksmith Shop:

Hall's map does not identify an assay shop, but appears to identify a blacksmith shop in this location. We believe Frobisher's blacksmith shop was a few metres to the southeast, based on the existence of a large turf-walled structure containing remains of slag, firebrick, coal, charcoal, and other materials. Both the assay and blacksmith structures are located near a drainage channel alongside small ponds that in former times (and seasonally today) hold water draining off the island.

The smithy feature (*Fig. 3*) consists of a poorly delimited, low rectangular foundation roughly 8 m by 7 m in area and approximately 30 cm higher than the surrounding ground. It is well covered by grass and moss and is bounded by an intermittent pond on its southeastern corner and by a small rocky hill to the north.

The test pit dug in that feature in 1981 exposed a dark charcoal-stained deposit with cultural remains [Fitzhugh 1993c]. A few of the finds recovered from this test include fragments of roof tiles, brick, crucibles, and iron blooms, as well as quantities of coal, clay, slag, flint, and charcoal [see Unglik 1993]. The charcoal recovered was identified by Laeyendecker [1993] as being of two categories: coniferous woods and hardwoods. While the coniferous wood might have originated from local driftwood collected on the beaches, Laeyendecker maintains that most of the hardwood species identified - notably oak, beech, ash, hazel, and maple - must have been brought to Kodlunarn Island from England for use in the smithy and assay shops.

Detailed analysis of these materials cannot be provided here. However they are of fairly common generic types. Roof tile fragments indicate that the parent materials were 1.5-2.0 cm thick, made from a fine pink-red paste pocked with lenticular air bubbles, and tempered with sand or grit. None of these tile fragments was of sufficient size to allow measurement or definition of overall shape. Most were highly frost-fractured. Larger fragments of both yellow and red bricks were found, also sand-tempered but without gaseous matrix, but none were in a whole or measurable condition. Samples from the blacksmith shop also included large amounts of smithing slag, bits of flint-tempered mortar, charcoal, coal, and a few ceramic crucible fragments.

Figure 3: The blacksmith shop.

Figure 4: The assay office.

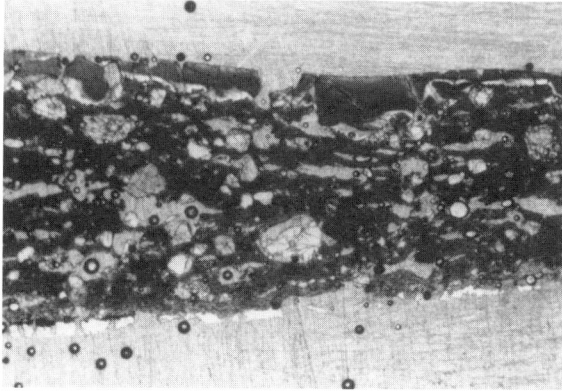

Figure 5: Thin section in plain-polarized light of the crucible showing a vitreous layer at the top. 15x

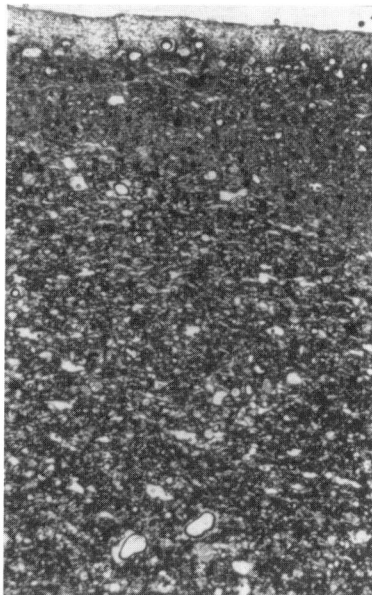

Figure 6: Thin section in plain-polarized light of the first cupel type showing a vitreous layer at the top. 15x

The Assay Shop:

The second site feature that has received special attention is the assay office (*Fig. 4*). The wall remains of this structure rise a few centimetres above the level of the ground surface and are evidence of sixteenth century human activity at that location. The three most visible walls meet at right angles and form a square enclosure 18 ft. by 18 ft. Geo-radar exploration by Pilon [pers. com. August 1991] in 1991 suggested the presence of a buried layer in the northwest corner of this structure. This may be the floor of an assaying oven.

Analysis of the ceramics recovered from a test excavation in 1990, in conjunction with historical research, [see Auger 1993] suggest that the assaying activities represented here include use of crucibles, cupels, and refractory ceramics. Further analyses have allowed us to quantify our initial interpretation with regard to the ceramics used in the assays. These analyses include a microscopic study of ceramic and rock specimens used in the assays. First, thin sections of both ceramic sherds and a rock were examined under a Leitz Orthoplan-pol microscope equipped with an Orthomat photographic system, and were described according to the terminology of Brewer [1976] and Bullock et. al. [1985]. Second, samples were analysed with a Geol 840 scanning electron microscope (SEM) operated at 15 kV accelerating voltage. That instrument was equipped with a Noran 5500 analyser, a germanium crystal detector, and an energy-dispersive analysis system. Total elemental analysis was performed using $LiBO_2$ extraction method and atomic absorption spectrophotometry. Major and minor elements were also analysed by X-ray diffraction with a copper tube.

Microscopic study of the thin sections reveals significant differences between crucibles, cupels, refractory ceramics, and rock minerals. Crucibles are made of coarse quartz grains embedded in an abundant brown clay matrix with few ferruginous nodules (*Fig. 5*). The basic structure (fabric of plasma, skeleton grains, and voids) is porphyroskelic (coarse skeleton grains in a dense groundmass), while the plasmic structure (fabric of plasma and simple packing voids) is anisotic parallel (total extinction parallel to the surface). Cupels are of two types. One is composed of small quartz grains and a small amount of light brown clay matrix (*Fig. 6*); the other is composed of greyish brown grains that polarize in an iridescent yellow-green-pink colour, rare quartz, and feldspar grains joined together by a brown matrix (*Figs. 7a, 7b*). The basic structure varies from fine porphyroskelic to intertextic (skeleton grains linked by intergranular braces) and no plasmic structure is present. The refractory ceramic shows quartz grains, small stick-like muscovite, and rare plagioclasic feldspar with few ferruginous nodules (*Figs. 8a, 8b*). Clay is almost absent from the matrix, which is rich in small grains similar to those of the skeleton. The basic structure is mostly intertextic. The rock specimen is almost entirely composed of amphibole crystals with typical cleavage and a few iron oxide grains. The chemical composition of our rock sample is comparable to the results of Hogarth and Roddick [1988], excepted for the TiO2 content which is higher in our sample (4.27%).

The X-ray diffraction analysis showed that the greyish brown mineral present in one of the two types of cupel could be cerrusite, a lead carbonate mineral ($PbCO3$). The presence of lead was confirmed by X-ray fluorescence and total elemental analysis. It represents 30% of the cupel, while calcium and phosphorus account for, respectively, 32.5% and 25.4%. These latter elements form the hydroxyl-apatite identified on the X-ray diffraction spectrum. The macroscopic examination of the crucibles and one of the two types of cupels shows a black vitreous coating on one side. The coating was initially thought to be the residue of the minerals in fusion. It proved to be a vitrification of the crucible or cupel surface resulting from the heat of the minerals in fusion. From the microscopic examination of the thin sections, we conclude that, even if the vitreous layers of the crucible and the cupel differ slightly by their texture and colour (cf. *Figs. 5, 6*), both sections show heat-fractured quartz grains near their surface and quartz grains that are less altered when farther inside the matrix (*Fig. 9*).

The presence of heat-altered quartz remains detected in those vitreous layers supports the hypothesis of heat transformation of the surface material of both the crucibles and the cupels. Moreover, the energy-dispersive spectrum of the crucible vitreous layer is quite similar to the crucible core diagram (*Fig. 10*). Both are rich in Si-Al, have a lesser amount of O-K and traces of Fe. The presence of Na and Ca on the vitreous layer essentially suggests that they have an environmental origin, namely, the salt-water surrounding Kodlunarn Island. Pedological processes such as leaching and illuviation can account for the Na and Ca accumulation on the exposed vitreous surface, while the reading on the core comes from a freshly sawn surface. However, the energy-dispersive spectrum of the rock specimen differs from those of the crucible and its vitreous layer. Besides the absence of K, we found in that rock sample Mg, Ti, and a greater amount of Fe (*Fig. 10*). The chemical analysis showed that MgO represented 13.38%, TiO2 4.27%, and Fe_2O_3 17.83% of the whole rock.

From the microscopic observations, the chemical composition, and the energy-dispersive analysis we can conclude that the rock specimen is a Fe-Mg silicate of hornblende type which differs markedly from the vitreous coating of the crucibles and the refractory ceramics. We can also infer that crucibles, cupels, and refractory ceramics differ in composition and fabric. Finally, one of the two cupel types is further distinguished by its high lead content.

This evidence points to the probability that ongoing research will allow us to answer one of the basic questions unexplained to this day: why did the master assayer in charge of Kodlunarn Island assaying obtain positive readings to the point of allowing 1136 tons of worthless mineral to be loaded and shipped to England?

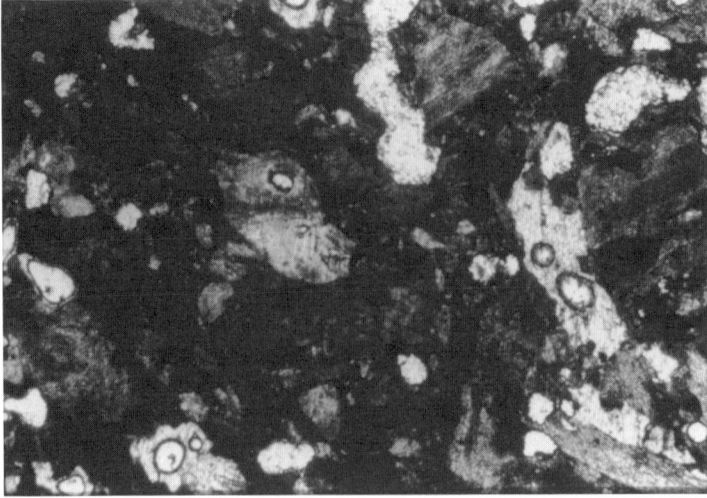

Figure 7a: Thin section in plain-polarized light of the second cupel type. 60x

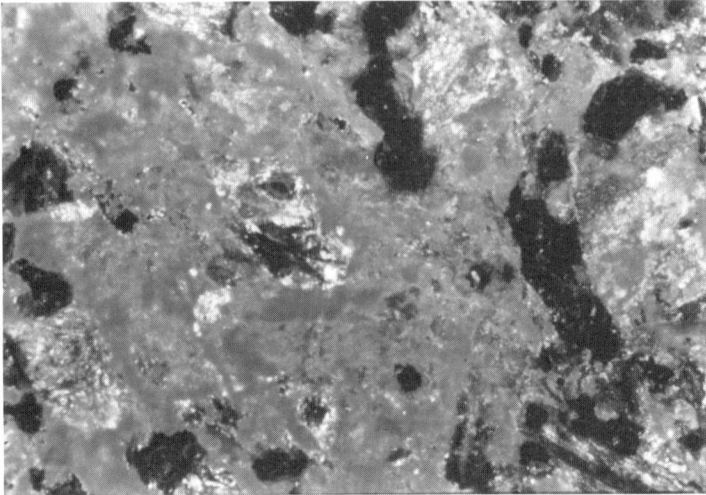

Figure 7b: Thin section under crossed polars of the second cupel type. 60x

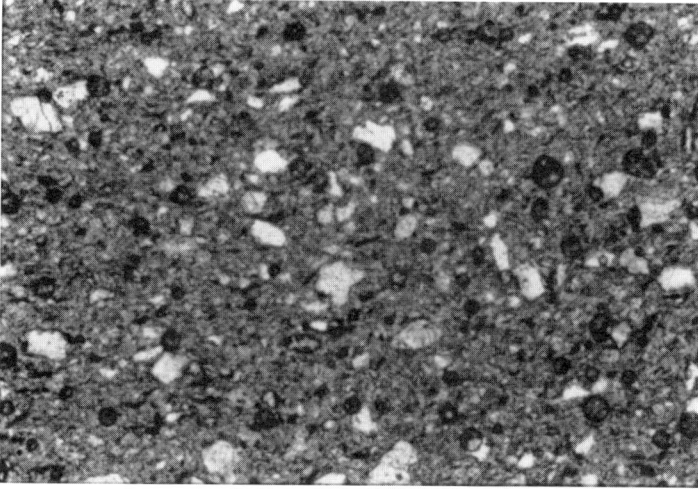

Figure 8a: Thin section in plain-polarized light of refractory ceramic. 60x

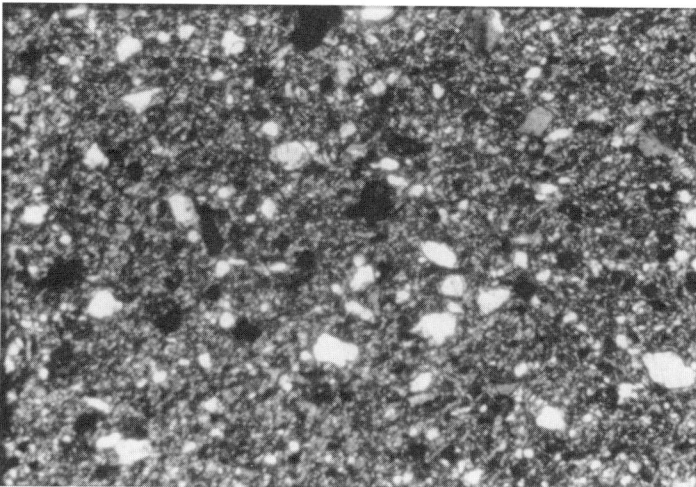

Figure 8b: Thin section under crossed polars of refractory ceramic. 60x

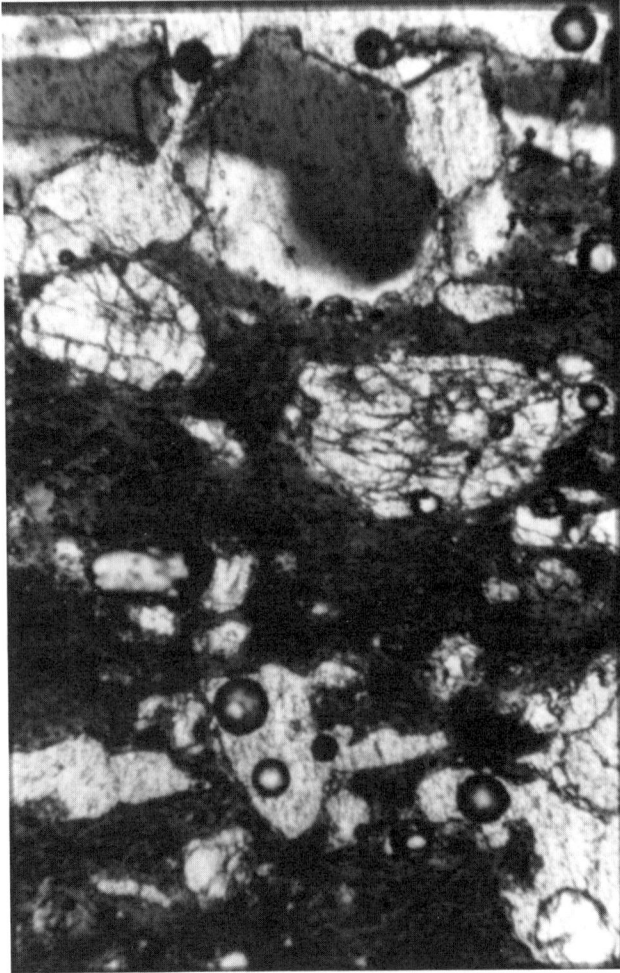

Figure 9: Thin section in plain-polarized light of heat-fractured quartz grains near the vitreous surface of the crucible. 55x (Note: close-up of figure 5.)

Laval University
Cursor: 0.000KeV = 0

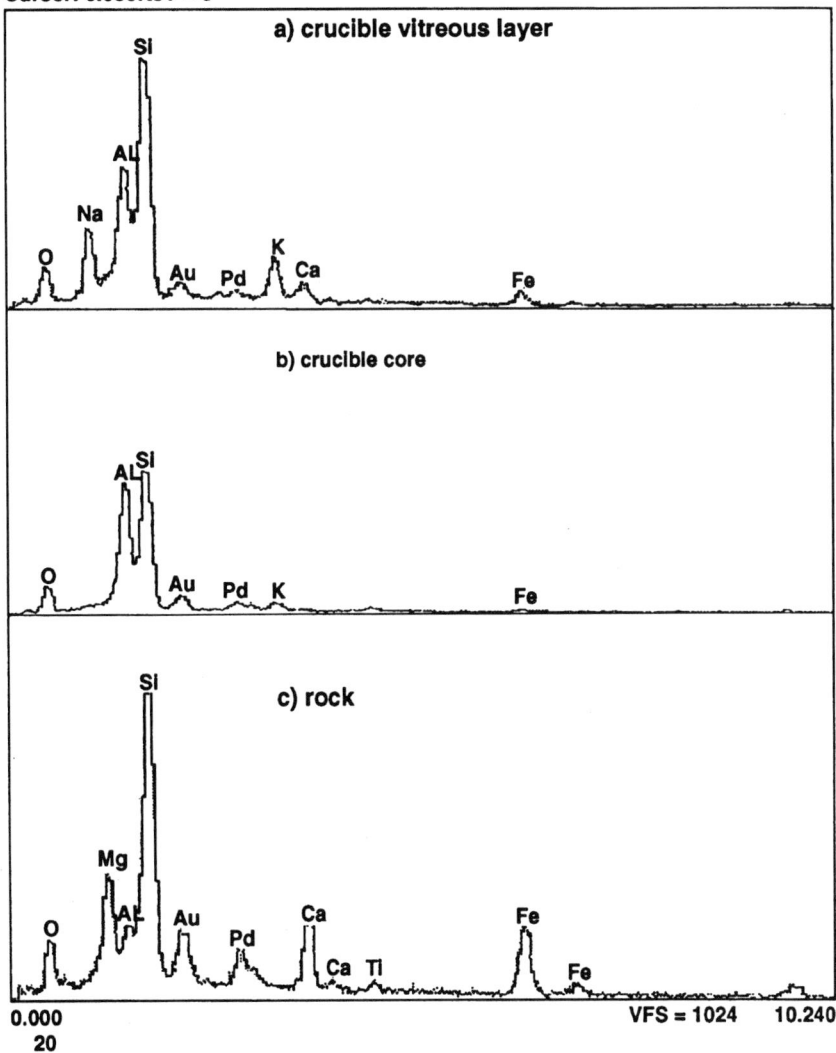

Figure 10: Energy-dispersive spectrum: a) crucible vitreous layer, b) crucible core and, c) rock. (Note: Au and Pd were used as coatings for the SEM.)

The Ship's Trench:

Produced initially by mining activities on Kodlunarn Island in 1577, the Ship's Trench is a large gully on the north shore of the island which has the same directional orientation as the 1578 mine in the centre of the island and appears to follow a vein of black ore. The profile of the Ship's Trench is accentuated by the deposition of mining spoil on its sides and artifacts eroding into the sea at the bottom of the Trench [see McGhee and Tuck, this volume].

Although it has not been submitted to systematic archaeological excavation, the Ship's Trench area has yielded four iron blooms to date. In addition to these artifacts, a small test pit excavated in 1981 revealed the presence of wood chips, dowels, ceramics, coal, flint, and other materials which have been attributed to caching and shipbuilding activities [see Fitzhugh 1993c and Laeyendecker 1993].

The most revealing data, however, come from the 1991 excavation of a one metre wide trench across the lower portion of the feature. This revealed that the sixteenth century deposit is much richer than anticipated. Because of lack of time, we had to terminate excavation at 1.53 m and failed to reach the bottom of the deposit. The order of deposition of the artifacts, as well as the fragmentary nature of the remains, suggest that the Ship's Trench was probably scavenged by Inuit shortly after the Englishmen departed in 1578.

The material recovered from the Ship's Trench included seeds (probably those seeds left by the 1578 expedition), culinary ceramics, roof tiles, carbonised matter, and a metal fragment. Among the wood artifacts collected (and examined by wood technology specialist Brad Loewen, Canadian Parks Services) there appear to be some pieces that are carbonised while others are blackened due to their depositional environment. Some are broken along the weakness points in the wood, and a few fragments still bear traces of sixteenth century cultural transformation. One fragment is a barrel hoop and one may be a barrel head-piece (cant), which had been re-used before its deposition. At least one fragment appears to be structural. It has been sawn or squared and could be from an oak plank. That latter evidence, when put in context with the wood chips recovered by the 1981 Smithsonian expedition, suggests that the Ship's Trench may bear the evidence of where elementary shipbuilding took place.

The Frobisher House:

The last structure investigated in 1991 was the house built by the Frobisher party in 1578 on the highest point of the island. That small house has attracted the attention of many well-intentioned people since the time it was built. Hall [1865, 390] described it as a house built of stones cemented together with lime and sand. He further mentioned that it was about 12 ft. in diameter and covered with aged moss. Hall and his Inuit friends excavated "down two feet [but] could not find bottom of the foundation." Hall was not, however, the first person to go through those remains, for he mentions that the wall stones had been turned over by Inuit searching for treasures. Finally, he added that, a few feet to the east, a pile of stones had been built as if by the Frobisher men to cover a memorial.

Later the Rawson-MacMillan Expedition (1927) churned the ground of the Frobisher house trying to uncover materials left by Frobisher. However, the first mission with an archaeological strategy was led to this location in 1974 by the late Dr. Walter Kenyon of the Royal Ontario Museum. Kenyon [1975] exposed part of the Frobisher house, in addition to investigating the mines and reporting on attrition of the Kodlunarn site by marine erosion.

All told, this little cottage has seen a lot of scrutiny during its four centuries of existence. When we undertook research here in 1991 [see McGhee and Tuck, this volume] the hope of finding any intact remains was rather slim. After surface cleaning we discovered that the original stone foundations were still preserved. We found the southeast and the northwest corners of the foundation still intact after four centuries - the foundations of the earliest English cottage built in North America. These foundations have withstood the elements to the point that they provide evidence of their original dimensions. They measure 14 ft. by 12 ft. on the outside and, with two-foot thick walls, the interior dimensions are 8 ft. by 10 ft. Still visible was the sixteenth century workmanship of the mason, who had laid a course of stone in mortar tempered with bits of crushed European flint. The ground had been levelled at the southeast corner prior to laying the foundation. Also recovered from the screening of the earth were fragments of roof tile and culinary vessels, all evidence of Frobisher's attempt to convince the Inuit of the benevolence of English civilization.

Conclusion

The central contention of this paper is that full understanding of the Frobisher voyages cannot be achieved without archaeological study of the physical remains of the voyages themselves. Among the things these remains evidence are pyrotechnological techniques used in rendering the minerals, mining technology for mineral extraction, and blacksmithing technology. Moreover, the results to date of research at the Frobisher base camp allow us to suggest that systematic excavation at the Ship's Trench, the blacksmith shop, and the assay office will produce data with the potential to throw light on processes of cultural change among the Baffin Inuit. Consequently, in conjunction with existing information from historical and archaeological research, future investigation of the assay office, the blacksmith shop, and the Ship's Trench is expected to enable us to answer specific questions regarding: a) the application of sixteenth century pyrotechnology, mining, and smithing within the framework of a remote outpost colony; b) the impact that the colony had on local Inuit society. Data from Greenland and Labrador have shown that increased interactions between Inuit and Europeans fostered the development, in Inuit society of those parts, of a class of leaders whose regional prestige and influence were based on the acquisition and redistribution of exotic goods. Did the goods acquired from the Frobisher expeditions stimulate a similar development among the Baffin Inuit?

The discoveries made by the Smithsonian Institution since 1981 and, more recently, by the Canadian Museum of Civilization have demonstrated that further in-depth studies at the unique archaeological site of Kodlunarn Island will be extremely rewarding and will augment our historical understanding of the early voyages of exploration and mining. Investigation of the Ship's Trench, reportedly used to cache goods in expectation of another voyage in 1579, should also contribute to better understanding of what supplies were used by sixteenth century expeditions. New knowledge of sixteenth century boat-building would be another potential benefit from Ship's Trench excavations.

The significance of the Frobisher base camp as a site of national and international historical merit adds further weight to the need for research at this early and unique European site in North America. Suffice to say that the Baffin Inuit still hold respect for that island, which was once at the crossroads of their cultural history. Ongoing research at Inuit sites near Kodlunarn is providing evidence of cultural transfer that occurred between English and Inuit cultures during the time of the Frobisher voyages and later, when Inuit returned regularly to "mine" Kodlunarn themselves. This time the "mining" was for materials precious to the Inuit - among them wood, iron, ceramics, flint, and coal - and ultimately of much greater use to *them* than the black ore was to be to the Elizabethans [see Gullason, Fitzhugh and Henshaw, this volume].

The Frobisher saga is an historical event that has been ignored from an archaeological standpoint. Nonetheless, the 1991 partial assessment of the Frobisher base camp by the Canadian Museum of Civilization shows that the site holds unique information on the history of technology and on English colonial history.

Notes

1	Because Frobisher records are in the Julian calendar the actual dates, using our modern Gregorian calendar, would be ten days later than given in the accounts.
2	These are presumed to be the headlands at the entrance of Frobisher Bay: respectively, Queen Elizabeth's Foreland and North Foreland.
3	After sailing these waters for two summers, with 35 foot tides rushing through the bay twice daily, we are not surprised that Frobisher thought he had discovered the Northwest Passage. There are no such tides known elsewhere in Europe or the North Atlantic. Another clue that may have lead Frobisher to think he had discovered the passage was the large amount of driftwood which accumulates on these beaches, in a landscape devoid of trees.
4	It was already 10 August by our modern calendar.

ACKNOWLEDGEMENTS: Financial support for field research was provided by the Smithsonian Institution for the 1981, 1990, and 1991 field seasons, and logistics support came from the Science Institute of the Northwest Territories. The Canadian Museum of Civilization provided partial financial support for 1991 field research, through a grant to Dr. Robert McGhee. Finally, we wish to acknowledge the Social Sciences and Humanities Research Council of Canada for a post-doctoral fellowship to Dr. Auger, and CELAT at Université Laval for secretarial support.

References

Agricola, Georgius
 1556   *De Re Metallica*. Translated from the first Latin ed. of 1556 by H.C. Hoover and L.H. Hoover. New York: Dover Publications, 1950.

Aker, Raymond, and Edward Von der Porten
 1979   *Discovering Portus Novae Albionis, Francis Drake's California Harbor*. Palo Alto: Drake Navigators Guild.

Auger, Réginald
1993   Sixteenth century ceramics from Kodlunarn Island. In *Archeology of the Frobisher Voyages*, ed. W. Fitzhugh and J. Olin, 147-54. Washington: Smithsonian Institution Press.

Biringuccio, Vannoccio
1540   *Pirotechnia*. Cambridge: MIT Press, 1966 (original ed. 1540).

Brewer, R.
1976   *Fabric and Mineral Analysis of Soils*. Huntingdon: Kreiger Publishing.

Bullock, P., N. Federoff, A. Jongerius, G. Stoops, T. Turisma, and U. Babel
1985   *Handbook for Soil Thin Section Description*. Wolverhampton: Waine Research Publication.

Collinson, Richard, ed.
1867   *The Three Voyages of Martin Frobisher in Search of a Passage to Cathaia and India by the North-west, A.D. 1576-8. Reprinted from the First Edition of Hakluyt's Voyages*. New York: Burt Franklin.

Ehrenreich, Robert M.
1993   An evaluation of the Frobisher iron blooms. In *Archeology of the Frobisher Voyages*, ed. W. Fitzhugh and J. Olin, 221-30. Washington: Smithsonian Institution Press.

Fitzhugh, William W.
1993a   Introduction. In *Archaeology of the Frobisher Voyages*, ed. W. Fitzhugh and J. Olin, 1-10. Washington: Smithsonian Institution Press.

1993b   Field surveys in Outer Frobisher Bay. In *Archaeology of the Frobisher Voyages*, ed. W. Fitzhugh and J. Olin, 98-136. Washington: Smithsonian Institution Press.

1993c   Archeology of Kodlunarn Island. In *Archeology of the Frobisher Voyages*, ed. W. Fitzhugh and J. Olin, 58-97. Washington: Smithsonian Institution Press.

Hall, Charles Francis
1865   *Arctic Researches and Life Among the Esquimaux*. New York: Harper and Brothers.

Harbottle, Garman, Richard Cresswell, and Raymond W. Stoenner
1993   Carbon-14 dating of the Kodlunarn Island iron blooms. In *Archeology of the Frobisher Voyages*, ed. W. Fitzhugh and J. Olin, 181-212. Washington: Smithsonian Institution Press.

Hogarth, Donald D.
1993   Mining and metallurgy of the Frobisher ores. In *Archeology of the Frobisher Voyages*, ed. W. Fitzhugh and J. Olin, 137-46. Washington: Smithsonian Institution Press.

Hogarth, Donald D. and, J.C. Roddick
1988   *Discovery of M. Frobisher's Baffin Island "Ore" in Ireland.* Geological Survey of Canada Contribution No. 35188. Ottawa.

Johnson, Adrian
1974   *America Explored: a Cartographical History of North America.* New York: Viking Press.

Kenyon, Walter A.
1975   *Tokens of Possession: the Northern Voyages of Martin Frobisher.* Toronto: Royal Ontario Museum.

Laeyendecker, Dosia
1993   Wood and charcoal remains from Kodlunarn Island. In *Archeology of the Frobisher Voyages*, ed. W. Fitzhugh and J. Olin, 155-72. Washington: Smithsonian Institution Press.

Light, John, and Henry Unglik
1987   *A Frontier Fur Trade Blacksmith Shop 1796-1812.* Rev. ed. Ottawa: Parks Canada.

McDermott, James
1984   The account books of Michael Lok relating to the northwest voyages of Martin Frobisher, 1576-1578: text and analysis. Master's Thesis, University of Hull.

McGhee, Robert
1992   Kudlunarn Island archaeological project. *Canadian Archaeological Association Newsletter* 12(1): 26-27.

Morison, Samuel Eliot
1971   *The European Discovery of America: the Northern Voyages A.D. 500-1600.* Toronto: Oxford University Press.

Moxon, Joseph
1683   *Mechanick Exercises: or the Doctrine of Handy-Works.* 1703 ed. London: Dans Midwinter.

Olin, Jacqueline S.
1993   History of research on the Smithsonian bloom. In *Archeology of the Frobisher Voyages*, ed. W. Fitzhugh and J. Olin, 49-57. Washington: Smithsonian Institution Press.

Payne, Edward John, and C. Raymond Beazley
  1907   *Voyages of the Elizabethan Seamen.* Oxford: Clarendon Press.

Rowley, Susan
  1993   Frobisher *miksanut*: Inuit accounts of the Frobisher voyages. In *Archeology of
            the Frobisher Voyages*, ed. W. Fitzhugh and J. Olin, 27-40. Washington:
            Smithsonian Institution Press.

Sayre, Edward V., Garman Harbottle, Raymond W. Stoenner, Wilcomb Washburn, Jacqueline
    S. Olin, and William Fitzhugh
  1982   The carbon-14 dating of an iron bloom associated with the voyages of Martin
            Frobisher. In *Nuclear Dating Techniques*, ed. L. Currie, 441-51. ACS
            Symposium Series, 1976. Washington: American Chemical Society.

Stefansson, Vilhjalmur, and Eloise McCaskill, eds.
  1938   *The Three Voyages of Martin Frobisher in Search of a Passage to Cathay and
            India by the North-west, A.D. 1576-8.* 2 vols. London: Argonaut Press.

Unglik, Henry
  1993   Metallurgical study of an iron bloom and associated finds from Kodlunarn Island.
            In *Archeology of the Frobisher Voyages*, ed. W. Fitzhugh and J. Olin, 181-212.
            Washington: Smithsonian Institution Press.

The Impermanence of Kodlunarn Island

Donald D. Hogarth
Department of Geology, University of Ottawa

RÉSUMÉ

Ce bref article traite de l'érosion sur l'île Kodlunarn, également appelée Qallunaaq et, à l'époque des expéditions de Frobisher, l'île Countess of Warwick. L'auteur s'intéresse tout spécialement aux risques encourus par les artefacts qu'ont laissés sur l'île les membres des expéditions de Frobisher. Il tire ses renseignements de trois sources : les cartes et les photographies, les perturbations d'origine humaine et les habitations, et les observations géologiques. En résumé, bien que des forces destructrices soient à l'œuvre, nul ne peut mesurer en toute certitude l'ampleur ou le degré d'érosion sur l'île.

ABSTRACT

This short paper deals with the erosion of Kodlunarn Island, also known as Qallunaaq Island and (in Frobisher's time) Countess of Warwick Island. It is specifically concerned with the resulting danger to Frobisher artifacts. Information has been derived from three sources: maps and photographs; human disturbance and dwellings; and geological evidence. In summary, although destructive forces are undeniably active, we cannot calculate magnitudes or rates of erosion with any certainty.

Location, Geography, and Geology

Kodlunarn Island, a barren rock of fifteen acres in Frobisher Bay, is about 190 km east-southeast of Iqaluit and 150 km west-northwest of Resolution Island. It is a low, inhospitable piece of land, on whose windswept surface crouch forty sickly species of plants, including a lonely dandelion. There is little protection from the wind and, after spring runoff, no water at all. Sharat Roy, who visited the island in 1927, said "it is incredibly desolate and a more forbidding place would be hard to imagine" [Roy 1937]. Were it not for its fascinating history, few visitors would be drawn to its hostile shores.

The island is rolling, with occasional outcrop projecting through the frost-heaved shingle, the highest point peering down 17 m to tidewater. It is fringed by a 5- to 7-metre scarp which abruptly fronts a pavement of tidal flat. The scarp is composed of solid rock in some places, unconsolidated material in others. It is this scarp or sea cliff that is of main concern here.

In situ rock is mainly yellow to pink biotite gneiss, less commonly grey hornblende gneiss - both Precambrian. Other rock types are comparatively rare. The predominant layering strikes north-northwest and dips southwest at 45° to 70°. Jointing is east-west and dips south at about 80°. The foliation and jointing influence the direction and magnitude of erosion. The dark hornblende gneiss is more easily eroded than its pale-coloured counterpart and tends to form undercuts and back indentations in bays [further information on bedrock geology is given by Blackadar 1967 and Hogarth, Loop, and Gibbins 1985].

Unconsolidated rocks seem to have been derived locally by weathering and frost heaving, but some were obviously transported. Thus, a few pieces of (Ordovician?) limestone were probably brought in from the south during Pleistocene glaciation. The large blocks of "black ore" south of the Reservoir Trench may also have been glacially transported. They are rather different from the Kodlunarn ores. Other loose rocks were imported by humans, e.g. a specimen of fused sillimanite-garnet gneiss, which probably represents an attempt at gold-production by one of Frobisher's alchemists. This rock is not indigenous, but *is* present at Tikkoon Point, 0.6 km east of Kodlunarn, and is abundant at Countess of Sussex Mine, 9 km west-northwest. Another loose piece from the island, a special type of "black ore", appears to have been derived from Victoria Bay, 10 km east-southeast.

Tides and Weather

Kodlunarn Island receives violent punishment from tide, tempest, and temperature. Mean high tide at Iqaluit is 7.8 m (maximum 12.3 m; 30-year record). At Resolution Island, the tide has decreased to 4.5 m ("large tides" attain 8 m). A measurement by the author gave 7.5 m at Kodlunarn. Therefore maximum tides may possibly attain 10 m. With the high tide comes a swift and unpredictable tidal current.

Precipitation is slight. At Iqaluit it averages 43 cm annually, producing a virtual desert climate; but this precipitation falls mainly in the summer, when daily rainfalls of 4 cm are not unknown. In August 1991 there was an unprecedented thunderstorm.

Winds can be strong and, in no time at all, increase from calm to gale force. Iqaluit has record of winds up to 84 knots per hour, Resolution Island winds to 107 knots. Winds are most violent in March and April, blowing from the west and northwest. Kodlunarn Island itself is protected in the north and takes its greatest lashing in the south and west. A permanent low, off the east coast of Baffin and Resolution Islands, ensures ample foul weather.

Grating of sea ice, cakes of which were lodged on the island's coast during all five of the author's visits, must play an additional role in erosion.

The temperature can be described as typically arctic. The annual average at Iqaluit is -9.3°C. In February it commonly dips to -30°C at night and goes as low as -45°C. There are 92 frost-free days per year, but diurnal spans from melt to frost can occur from May through September.

Under these severe and variable conditions it is not surprising that erosion takes its toll of the island. Most of the factual information in this section has been taken from *Sailing Instructions, Arctic Canada*, 3rd edition (Ottawa, Department of Fisheries and Oceans, 1982).

Maps and Photographs of Kodlunarn, Past and Present (*Fig. 1*)

Comparison was made of an aerial photograph of 1987 with the map of Charles Francis Hall [Hall 1865]. Hall visited the island on three occasions: 2 September 1861, 25 September 1861, and 14-17 July 1862. The map, on a scale of 1 : 4800, was made during his last visit, surveyed with tape, compass, and theodolite. Using "D" (the largest excavation of the "ruins of shop") as reference, and orienting Hall's north shore of the island parallel with the true (photographic) outline, the "ruins of house", "Reservoir Trench", and south end of the island have been rotated about three degrees clockwise from their true position. Hall's north line is about three degrees out, also rotated clockwise, with respect to true north.

It is apparent that Hall's outline of the island corresponds to the top of the sea cliff and that the greatest horizontal erosion (about eight metres on promontories) has taken place along the southern half of the island. Considering the prevailing winds and the unprotected south shore, this is not surprising. However, quite unexpected was erosion near the northeast corner of the island. This corner coincides with strata of the erodable hornblende gneiss. Fortuitously, the foliation, well marked here, transects the minor promontory shown in Hall's map. In fact, remnants of this cleaved and tumbled

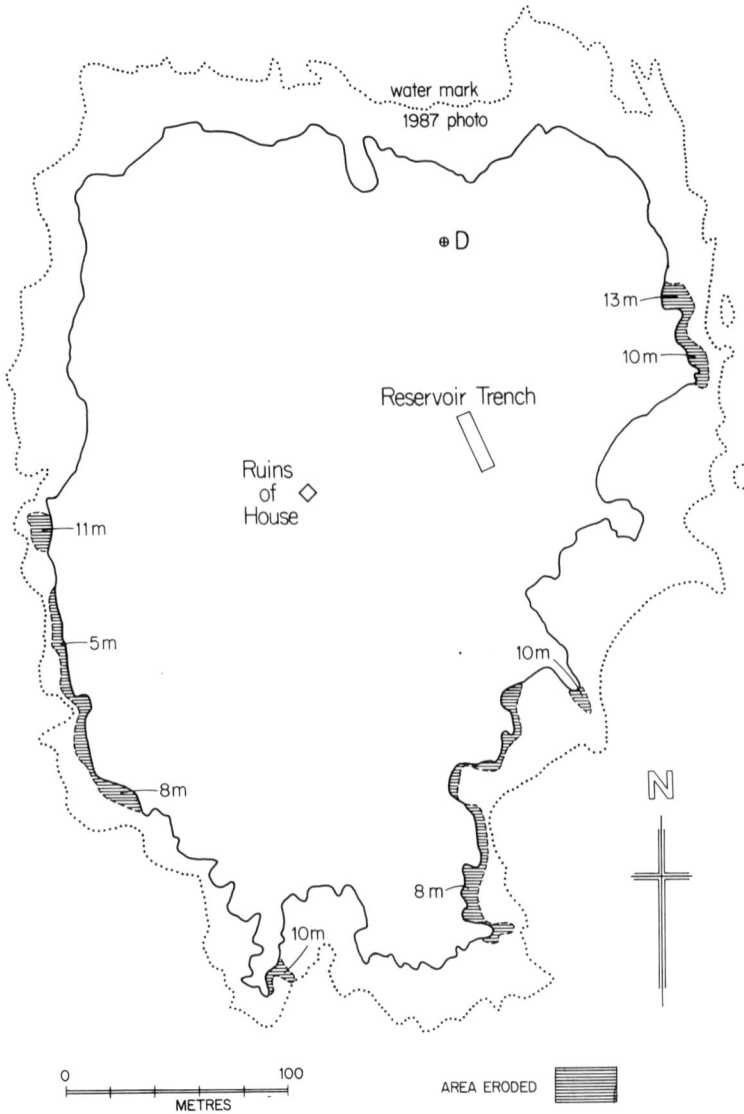

Figure 1: Kodlunarn Island outline. Heavy solid and dotted lines represent top of scarp and sea level, respectively, as shown on National Air Photograph A17261-170, taken in August 1987. The area eroded since Hall's survey of July 1862 is hachured, with typical land widths eroded since 1862 shown in metres.

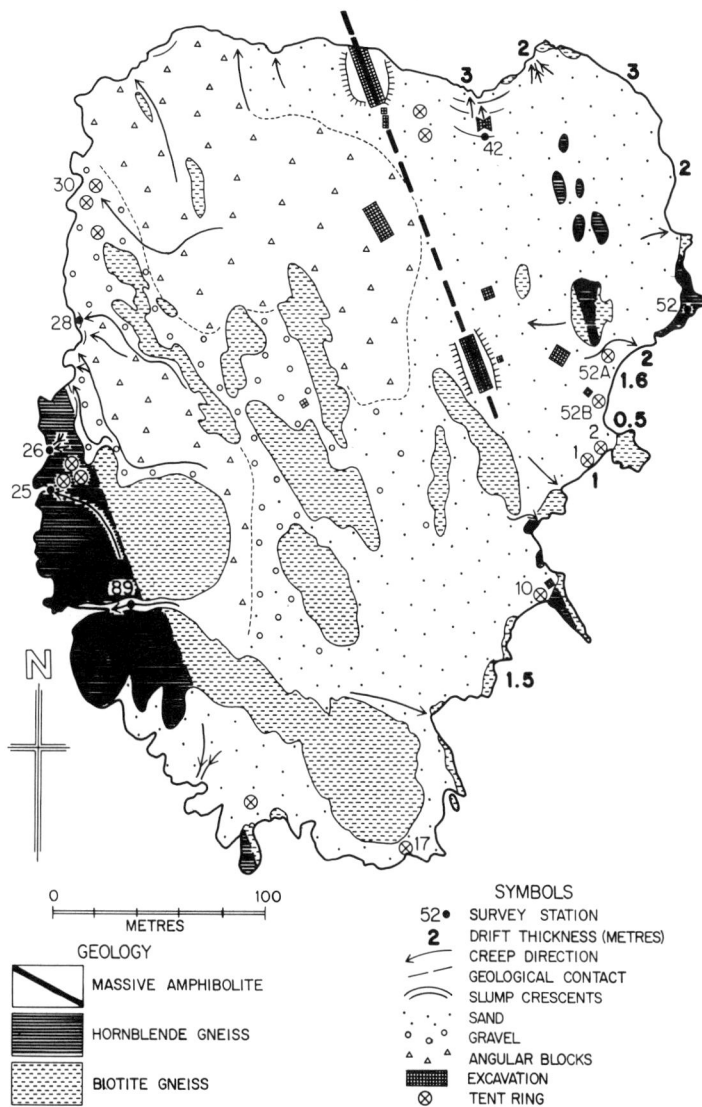

Figure 2: Surficial geology and outcrops of Precambrian rock on Kodlunarn Island. Frobisher's "pay zone" (massive amphibolite) is projected from the Ship's Trench in the north to the Reservoir Trench in the south.

rock can still be found on the beach below. It is interesting to note that an entry in this author's field book for station 52 records "saline deposit near top of scarp" (and perhaps three metres above high tide). Even here, solid rock is far from immune from the ravages of storm!

The coastline on the 1953 air photograph is virtually identical with that of 1987, although the less detailed scale and lack of clarity on the earlier photograph leave much to be desired. Air photographs taken in the 1940s, during reconnaissance connected with DEW line installations, were not available for comparison.

Inuit Habitation / Frobisher Relics (*Fig. 2*)

Tent rings have been decapitated by the advancing coastline in at least 3 places, marked as stations 2, 10, and 17 in *Figure 2*. Each of these appears to be missing at least one metre on the seaward side to complete the ring, let alone be spaced a safe distance from the edge of the scarp. Other tent rings, near stations 1, 30, 52A, and 52B, appear to be uncomfortably close to the brink (< 1.5 m). While erosion has undoubtedly taken place at these sites, the author is unqualified even to guess at their ages. Attempt to locate the datable lichen *rhizocarpon sp.* in suitable locations proved unsuccessful.

Réginald Auger [pers. com. 1991] pointed out certain exposures of coal and tile, on the scarp just north of station 1 (near the traditional siting of "Best's Bulwark"), that were no longer visible in 1991. This shows that scarp retreat is still in progress in sensitive areas.

Geological Evidence of Scarp Retreat (*Fig. 2*)

Two major rock types, plus the projected "pay zone" or massive amphibolite, are shown in outcrop on the map. These can be regarded as solid anchor rock. Between and surrounding the outcrops are unconsolidated materials, or active rock, that apparently move through downslope creep, aided by freeze and thaw activity. These migrations, shown as arrowed lines on *Figure 2*, are marked by fractured ground, crescents, slump stratification, and gullies near the sea cliff, especially at stations 25, 28, and 42. In other words, erosion proceeds along two paths: encroachment of the sea on the land and movement of the land towards the sea. It should be kept in mind that this mobile piece of land, the unconsolidated cover, is that which houses the bulk of artifacts. How much creep has occurred in recent years is not known, but at station 89 small fragments of pale biotite gneiss were identified in the soil and must have moved at least eight metres from their source. At station 26, fragments of the rock have moved at least fifteen metres. The fact that these fragments were truly angular suggests they were *not* glacially transported; but just when these fragments were dislodged from their source is, of course, not known.

Conclusions

Evidence has been presented to show that both shoreline retreat and downslope creep have been active at Kodlunarn and were probably appreciable over the years. However, the rate of the latter cannot be determined from the data at hand. Shoreline retreat of active areas may be 8 m in 126 years (or 6 cm per year). This figure assumes an accuracy of survey quite within range of the methodology, even in Hall's time, although the magnitude of retreat seems somewhat large. The danger of loss of artifacts from natural causes may, however, be greatly surpassed by insatiable appetites of enthusiastic collectors who visit the island.

Kodlunarn Island is a treasure in jeopardy. Natural erosion has changed, and will continue to change, its face. Furthermore, with increased accessibility, unauthorized treasure-hunters have already begun to arrive. The island cannot be protected from these two destructive forces. At this point, a rhetorical question may be posed: do not archaeologists have a mandate, if not a duty, to collect on-site, and then reassemble artifacts in their correct historical context in large centres, for the general education of the public? Surely it is now time for controlled archaeological studies of this unique site?

References

Blackadar, R.G.
   1967   Geological reconnaissance, southern Baffin Island, District of Franklin. *Geological Survey of Canada Paper* 66-47.

Hall, C.F.
   1865   *Arctic Researches and Life Among the Esquimaux.* New York: Harper and Brothers.

Hogarth, D.D., J. Loop, and W.A. Gibbins.
   1985   Frobisher's gold on Kodlunarn Island - fact or fable? *CIM Bulletin* 78:75-9.

Roy, S.K.
   1937   The history and geography of Frobisher's "gold ore". *Field Museum of Natural History. Geological Series* 7:21-38.

Archaeology of the Frobisher Voyages and European-Inuit Contact: Overview and 1991 Field Report

William W. Fitzhugh
Arctic Studies Center, Smithsonian Institution

RÉSUMÉ

L'exposé qui suit présente les objectifs et les résultats préliminaires des recherches menées sur le terrain en 1990 et 1991 dans le cadre du projet *Meta incognita* dans la baie de Frobisher, dans la région sud-est de l'île de Baffin. Des recherches récentes ont agrandi nos connaissances sur l'histoire culturelle de cette région, de façon générale, et sur l'histoire de la culture inuit de 1500 à 1900, en particulier. Des fouilles dans cinq habitations inuit de la période historique, à Kuyait et Kamaiyuk, ont livré les premiers témoignages archéologiques sur la culture des Inuit et leurs contacts avec les Européens dans cette région. De plus, malgré les difficultés, aussi immenses qu'inhabituelles, créées par les glaces, les recherches se sont poursuivies jusqu'à Beare Sound et Chapell Inlet, et sur les côtes méridionales de la baie de Frobisher, de York Sound à East Bluff. On y a trouvé entre autres des sites dorsétiens et paléo-esquimaux anciens, d'autres mines et décharges de charbon dans la baie de Frobisher, le site probable du massacre de Bloody Point en 1577, et des postes de baleiniers qui exercèrent une grande influence sur la culture inuit au sud-est de l'île de Baffin aux XIXe et XXe siècles. Les chercheurs ont pu faire rapport sur l'état de conservation de tous les sites, notant au passage la présence d'une importante érosion qui menace les sites archéologiques côtiers. C'est à Kamaiyuk, plus particulièrement, que la destruction de sites inuit, où l'on retrouve des objets datant des premiers contacts avec Frobisher, est particulièrement importante. Il faut sauvegarder les lieux et renseigner le public sur l'importance de ces ressources historiques.

ABSTRACT

This paper outlines the objectives and preliminary results of field studies conducted during 1990-91 as part of the Meta Incognita Project in the Frobisher Bay region of southeast Baffin. Recent research has greatly expanded knowledge of regional culture history in general and of Inuit culture history from *ca.* A.D. 1500-

1900 in particular. Excavation of five historic period Inuit houses at Kuyait and Kamaiyuk has provided our first archaeological evidence on historic Inuit culture development and European contact in that region. In addition, despite unusually severe ice conditions, surveys were extended into Beare Sound and Chapell Inlet, and on the south side of Frobisher Bay from York Sound to East Bluff. Among the finds are important Dorset and early Neoeskimo sites, new Frobisher mines and coal dumps, the probable site of the Bloody Point massacre in 1577, and whaling stations that had a major impact on nineteenth/twentieth century southeast Baffin Inuit culture. Conservation status was determined for all sites. Evidence of serious erosional destruction of coastal archaeological sites was noted. Destruction of Inuit sites containing Frobisher contact materials at Kamaiyuk is particularly serious. There is need for archaeological salvage and public education concerning the importance of these historical resources.

Introduction

The three voyages of Martin Frobisher seeking a route from England to Cathay via the Northwest Passage (1576-78) are among the most celebrated and best documented of the early discovery period. Ironically, Frobisher is best known for what he failed to do. His attempt to pioneer an Arctic route to Asia was doomed from the beginning, as was his gold-mining enterprise in the mineralogically poor rocks of Frobisher Bay. Less well-known is the fact that the Frobisher voyages resulted in the implementation, transient though it was, of the first English establishment on the soil of the New World - the first English buildings constructed in North America (on Kodlunarn Island in outer Frobisher Bay) - and also in the first scientific observations on Arctic regions and Inuit ethnography.

The significance of the Frobisher sites in British and North American history is indisputable. Few European enterprises in the history of New World discovery rival Martin Frobisher's exploits in search of the Northwest Passage. For three summers he led expeditions into the Canadian Arctic. When a route to Cathay eluded him, he turned to mining tons of "black ore" for gold. His third voyage of 1578 was the largest English naval venture ever mounted, but it returned in disarray. Its ore worthless, the Cathay Company (which included Queen Elizabeth) declared bankruptcy, and a disgraced Frobisher slipped forever from the pages of history to die in relative obscurity in the Battle of Brest (1594).

During the four centuries following the departure of Frobisher's mining expedition, the sites associated with that enterprise have been "mined" by Inuit scavengers, and the exceptional records and narratives [Settle 1577; Best 1578; Ellis

1578; Collinson 1867; Stefansson and McCaskill 1938; Kenyon 1980/81] have been "mined" by historians. Yet the archaeological significance of these sites has not been similarly appreciated, until recently. Walter Kenyon's visit in 1974 was the first to confirm Charles Francis Hall's discovery, in 1861, of the association between Kodlunarn Island and Frobisher [Hall 1865; Kenyon 1975a, 1976, 1980/81], but resulted in little new documentation. A Smithsonian survey in 1981 provided the first detailed archaeological documentation of the principal Frobisher sites on the island, and recovered iron artifacts suspected by some as having a Norse connection. To follow up that pilot project, a joint American-Canadian programme was organized [Fitzhugh 1989]. The goals of this work have been two-fold: to provide archaeological documentation of the Frobisher sites and mines; and to study Inuit culture history and environmental relationships in southeast Baffin Island from pre-contact times (*ca.* A.D. 1500) to the present. In particular, we have explored Inuit culture response to Frobisher and to later contacts with European whalers, missionaries, and traders.

In 1990 the work was reorganized as an official Canadian project under the auspices of the Meta Incognita Project Steering Committee. Like the earlier Smithsonian effort, the current Meta Incognita Project has two major field components: 1) historical and archaeological study of the physical remains of the Frobisher settlements, workshops, mines, and shipways; 2) archaeological and ethnohistorical studies of Inuit sites associated with the Frobisher voyages and later contact periods. Under Meta Incognita guidelines, part of the first thrust - that relating to Frobisher sites on Kodlunarn Island - is being conducted by a Canadian team, while "off-island" surveys and documentation are being conducted by an international team coordinated by the Smithsonian Institution. Both programmes are being pursued by research teams sharing information on Frobisher sites, collections, and European-Inuit interactions.

The Frobisher voyages provide a remarkable opportunity for interdisciplinary studies of a pioneering European exploration venture and its impact on native Arctic peoples. Among the disciplines participating in this project are historical and Inuit archaeology, archival studies, history and native oral history, archaeometry, geology, metallurgy, and a variety of environmental sciences. In addition to these interdisciplinary studies, the Frobisher project involves broader themes of global change, human-environmental interactions, native studies, and "Europe and America" interactions that reverberate to wider audiences in this Quincentennial era of historical reflection and internationalism. As the principal northern branch of the "Columbian exchange" - the first well-documented contact between Europeans and Arctic peoples - the Frobisher voyages offer an important source of new, untapped knowledge, through archaeology.

The Author and his Innuit Company on Kodlunarn, or White Man's Island, gathering Frobisher Relics, July 14th–17th, 1862.

Figure 1: Hall engaged in field work on Kodlunarn Island [Hall 1865].

Figure 2: The Kodlunarn Island iron bloom given to the Smithsonian Institution by Hall in the mid-1860s. Medieval period radiocarbon dates from this bloom in the 1970s initiated the Smithsonian's Kodlunarn Island investigations of 1981. Hall's inscription reads: "Iron smelted by the Frobisher Expedition A.D. 1578".

A. Frobisher Bay.
B. Countess of Warwick's Sound.
C. Lupton Channel, which leads down to Bear Sound.   On the
    right is Lok's Land; on the left, Bache's Peninsula.
D. Cyrus W. Field Bay.
E. Cornelius Grinnell Bay.
F. Robinson Sound.
G. Resolution Isles.
H. Hudson's Strait.
X. Cape True, on Blunt's Peninsula.

Figure 3: "Esquimaux Chart, no. 2, drawn by Kooperneung (Charley) while we were at Cape True, August, 1862" [Hall 1865].

Research Themes

European-Inuit Contact Studies

Most archaeological studies of culture contact have been pursued with either a European or an indigenous point of view. Research on Inuit and European contact in the Arctic is no different. In Greenland, investigations of Norse and Inuit sites have been conducted independently, and often in isolation, by historians, ethnologists, and archaeologists. More recently, studies of sixteenth century Basque whaling sites in southern Labrador have been pursued, again largely separately, by archaeologists and historians. In both cases there is no settlement proximity or local context for cultural interaction. In southern and central Labrador archaeological studies of contact-period Inuit sites have revealed much about Inuit adaptation to European materials and economies [Jordan 1978; Jordan and Kaplan 1980; Kaplan 1983, 1985; Auger 1989]; but, here also, the specific sources and sites of European outposts, many of which were shipborne, are not known.

By contrast, in Frobisher Bay evidence of European-Inuit contact and interaction is abundant both in the historical record and in archaeological sites. The Frobisher episode stands out clearly in the historical record as a brief, intense incident followed by nearly two hundred and fifty years of isolation in the east Baffin region before European contact begins again after the arrival of nineteenth century whalers. The Frobisher voyages are therefore an ideal case for studying culture contact and accommodation from both European and Native perspectives.

Frobisher History and Archaeology

Previously, the Frobisher voyages have been exclusively the domain of the historian. Only recently have we realized the importance of the sites for elucidating, clarifying, and expanding upon the extensive documentary evidence for this pioneering English entry into the New World. Still, it is universally recognized that documents tell only a small and often biased part of "real" history. Archaeological data offers another line of evidence for historical reconstruction.

Archaeological work at the Frobisher sites began with the discovery of Martin Frobisher's base camp and mines at Kodlunarn Island by Hall in 1861 (*Figs. 1-3*). After more than a century of neglect, interest in the site was rekindled when an iron bloom (a partially processed smelter mass) Hall had given to the Smithsonian in 1864 was radiocarbon-dated to the twelfth/thirteenth centuries [Sayre et al. 1982], raising questions of possible Norse affiliation. Subsequently, a Smithsonian field expedition was organized in 1981 to conduct a preliminary survey, search for more dating samples, and examine the question of possible Norse involvement. The survey produced many new finds including three further iron blooms and confirmed the Frobisher attribution of the site [Fitzhugh and Olin 1993]. But the mystery of the bloom dates was not resolved and, in fact, became more mysterious when dates from the new blooms matched the early medieval dates obtained from the Hall bloom.

While many explanations have been offered, including theories of Norse origin [Sayre et al. 1982; Harbottle et al. 1993; Unglik, 1993], the discovery of the blooms in securely-dated sixteenth century site of known historical origin has called for other theories to explain the early dates. Among the possibilities are production from local iron ore with charcoal made from centuries-old Arctic driftwood, or contamination of the bloom matrix by smelting with coal. The dating problem is compounded by the question of why the blooms were present on the expedition in the first place. Were they intended as raw materials for iron production; for shipwright's hammers or anvils ("dollies"); ship's ballast; or some other function [see discussions in Fitzhugh and Olin 1993]? Recently, Ivor Noel Hume [pers. com. 1992] pointed to a lading entry for the 1576 voyage recording purchase of "V^c of yron stones of Russia ... for balliste for the Gabriell." If this describes the blooms it may provide a solution to their function and presence in the Kodlunarn Island region - in particular, in the Ship's Trench. Perhaps these "yron stones" were abandoned by Frobisher's men when they loaded ore at Kodlunarn; alternatively, perhaps they were used as tools, ballast, or for forging new iron fittings for the vessel that, according to Inuit oral history, was built by a group of sailors the Inuit say were lost or abandoned by the "kablunat" - events that could only have occurred at the end of the 1578 season. Although only one example, this story aptly points out the need for interdisciplinary study of historical and archaeological data. Whether or not the above hypothesis is correct, we can be sure that excavations on Kodlunarn and elsewhere will reveal much about European outpost life, early mining and assay technology, and details of Frobisher expedition history that can only be retrieved by excavation and archaeometric analysis.

Inuit Culture History and European-Inuit Accommodation

The second and dominant strand of our programme involves Inuit archaeology and exploration of the last large unexplored area of the Eastern Arctic. Of particular interest is the appearance during the past thousand years to a series of European visitors - Norse, Dutch, and British-American - and the effects of these ethnically and motivationally diverse groups on Inuit material culture, economy, settlement patterns, socio-political organization, and worldview. In addition to documenting the past four thousand years of Inuit culture history, regional and environmental relationships, and interactions with other European groups, research is directed primarily at excavation of Frobisher-Inuit contact sites. The goal of this work is to reconstruct an archaeological history of Elizabethan-Inuit contact and to assess the manner and degree of Inuit adaptation and accommodation to this early episode of European presence. Our work also extends to the post-Frobisher period of southeast Baffin Inuit history through periods of relative isolation from European contact (A.D. 1600-1830), the whaling and fur trade era (1830-1940), and until the modern day. These studies represent the extension into southeast Baffin Island of a long-term research programme investigating patterns of Native culture history, European contact, and environmental relationships facilitated by ship-supported logistics.

In addition to descriptive historical archaeology and early European-Inuit contact studies, the Frobisher project addresses other questions including: the history of the Frobisher expeditions; technology of early European iron smelting, gold assaying, and mining procedures; baseline studies of historical climatology and effects of the Little Ice Age; regional Inuit culture history; and problems of Eastern Arctic communal house development.

Project Goals

This paper primarily addresses the Smithsonian's Inuit studies portion of the Meta Incognita Project. The goals of the Smithsonian programme include documenting: 1) four millennia of regional culture history; 2) Inuit cultural development *ca.* A.D. 1500 to the present; 3) the impact of the Frobisher voyages on sixteenth century Inuit culture; 4) changing patterns of European-Inuit interaction; 5) the history of human-environment relationships; and 6) integration of archaeological, historical, ethnographic, oral historical, and environmental data [previous reports on the project include: Sayre et al. 1982; Fitzhugh 1985, 1989, 1990a, 1990b, 1990c; and a monograph, Fitzhugh and Olin 1993].

The Frobisher voyages present an unusual and timely source of information about the history of Arctic exploration, settlement of the New World, and European-Inuit contacts and interactions. From the public standpoint it is remarkable how little is known about the pioneering nature of these voyages. Most people are only vaguely aware of Frobisher's search for a route to Cathay and the resulting mining fiasco. The Arctic destination of the voyages; their extremely early date; the fact that they resulted in the first English commercial venture and land-based establishment in the New World; that they resulted in important advances in navigation, geography, and anthropology; and that the organization and joint-stock financing of the voyages were prototypes for later English exploration and settlement in the New World: all are completely or largely unknown to scholars and the public. Frobisher is the best-kept secret of the Quincentennial era.

From an anthropological point of view, the Frobisher voyages provide a time-capsule and an easily recognized archaeological horizon of European contact which can be used to trace the development of Inuit culture and European-Inuit contact in the Eastern Arctic. By virtue of their short duration, geographic isolation, and precise location, the voyages offer an opportunity to study virtually the first European contact with Inuit culture (apart from sporadic and imprecise Norse contacts) under relatively controlled conditions. No other sixteenth century New World contacts provide such an ideal landscape for research on early European-Native interaction. From the point of view of European history, Kodlunarn's geographic isolation also facilitates archaeological study of little-known sixteenth century European mining, assaying, and metallurgical technology. Such a discrete and precisely-dated study would be impossible to conduct given the archaeological record in Britain. Finally, research on these voyages allows us to test, corroborate, and refine information from a vast array of historical documentation by comparison with the material archaeological record. As we have learned at Red Bay and elsewhere, written history tells only part of the story.

While our early work concentrated on Kodlunarn Island [Fitzhugh and Olin 1993], recent field work has combined survey and excavation strategies to expand our knowledge of regional systems and to gather detailed information on Inuit culture history from ca. A.D. 1500 to the present. This period is almost completely unknown in southeast Baffin. Previous work has been directed almost exclusively at prehistoric Eskimo/Inuit development [Collins 1950; Maxwell 1988, 1985; Sabo 1991; Schledermann 1975; Stenton 1987, 1989] in the Iqaluit and Lake Harbour regions. Our research has focused on the outer coast not previously accessible to archaeologists and concentrates on the period after European contact became a significant factor in Inuit history post-1550.

In approaching this problem we can be somewhat guided by trends in contact history that have specific consequences for archaeology. Viewed from this perspective, the last five hundred years of culture history provisionally can be divided into several phases: 1) pre-contact Developed Thule (before 1576); 2) a short period of direct Frobisher contact and influence (1576-1578); 3) some years of indirect but significant impact resulting from scavenging Kodlunarn Island materials (ca. 1578-1600); 4) a long period of attenuating Frobisher material culture influence and sporadic European contacts (ca. 1600-1830); 5) the whaling/fur trade era (1830-1940); and 6) the modern era, dominated by airbase and government activities. As each of these stages has predictable material correlates, this sequence serves as a provisional model for archaeological testing. A similar method has been used in studying Labrador Inuit culture change in the historical period [Kaplan 1983].

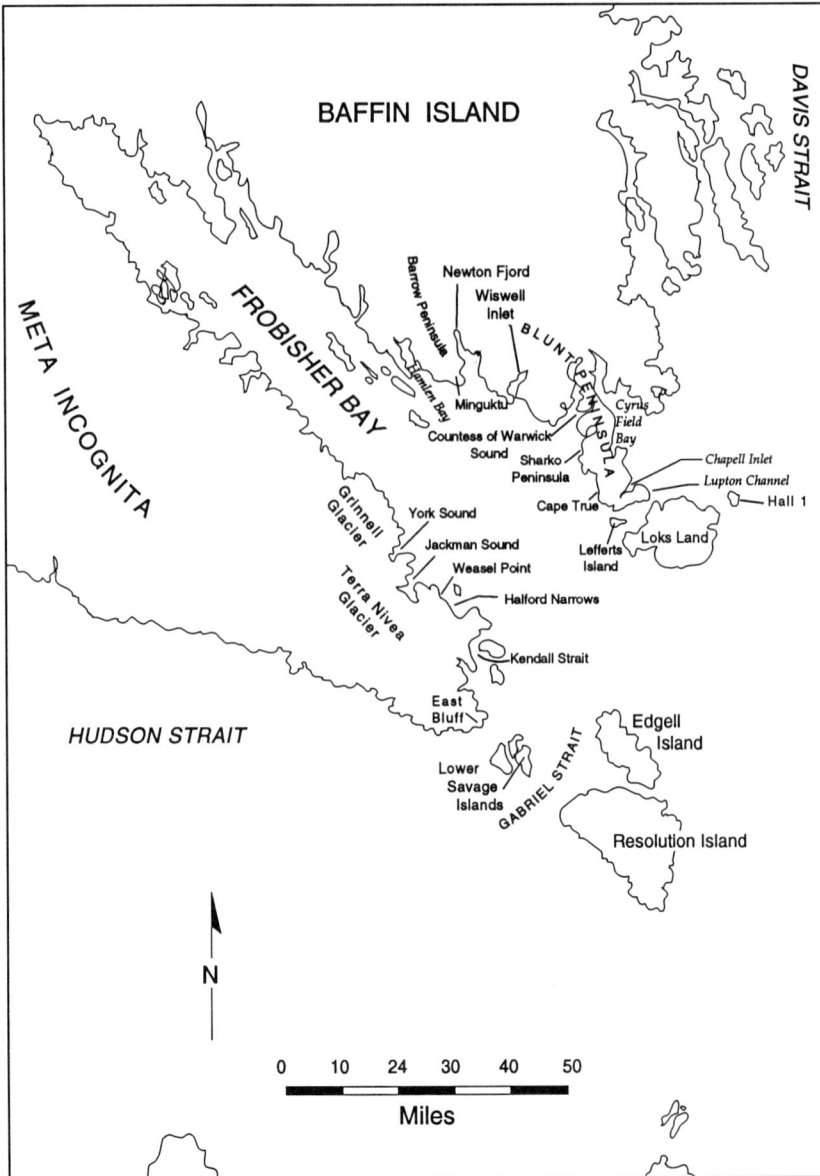

Figure 4: Map of Frobisher Bay, Southeast Baffin Island, N.W.T.

However, investigation of European influences, contact dynamics, and Inuit cultural response is not the only focus of this project; European impacts are only part of the story of recent Inuit culture history. Attention will be directed to exploring aspects of Inuit culture development not related to European contact, including settlement and subsistence patterns, stylistic change, adaptation to changing environmental and climatic conditions, and other factors contributing to cultural identity and persistence of Inuit traditions [Jacobs 1985; Jacobs and Stenton 1985; Jacobs et al. 1985; Stenton 1991]. Finally, the project seeks information for comparative study with Inuit contact history in Greenland, Labrador, the Central Arctic, and Alaska; from this we may eventually derive understanding of cultural processes operating in northern regions in diverse cultural, historical, and environmental contexts.

Field Results

1990 Field Work

The 1990 season of the Frobisher project required the relocation of the research vessel *Pitsiulak* and field gear from Newfoundland to Frobisher Bay; this was accomplished in July. During August site survey in outer Frobisher Bay (*Fig. 4*) was begun; our team of Canadian and American researchers, including geologists, located in the outer bay region forty-six sites with Pre-Dorset (1), Dorset (13), Thule (11), or Recent Inuit (35) components (Table 1, *Fig. 5*). Five previously undiscovered Frobisher mines and a second possible Frobisher habitation/workshop site (at Anvil Cove, Willows Island) were found [Fitzhugh 1990b].

These surveys produced evidence of Frobisher mines at Newland Island, Judy Point, Kodlunarn Island, Tikkoon, and Countess of Sussex. Mine excavation trenches were identified and samples of ore were secured. Coal dumps were noted at Newland, Judy Point, and Kodlunarn. These dumps were invariably associated with pebbles of English flint, probably a result of mixing of coal and flint ballast in the holds of the ships. No identifiable Frobisher structures or features were found.

Among conclusions reached concerning Inuit culture history were: 1) scarcity of early Paleoeskimo (Pre-Dorset and Transitional, and Early Dorset) sites, due to loss from submergence and coastal erosion; 2) abundance of Middle-Late Dorset sites (sod-house middens and spring/fall settlements), many of which are also damaged and threatened by erosion; 3) relative scarcity of early Thule sites; 4) abundance of Late Thule or Historic

Inuit winter villages from the period A.D. 1400-1900; and 5) abundance of Recent Inuit sites and camps of all kinds.

Economically, the subsistence base of Inuit occupations was found to be primarily caribou, seal, and walrus. Late Thule/Early Inuit sites, however, often contain significant amounts of whalebone and baleen. The absence of parallels in artifact types and house forms, and absence of exchange of raw materials, suggest that early Inuit groups of southeast Baffin, throughout their four thousand year history, had little or no contact with groups south of Hudson Strait in Labrador and Ungava. Dorset sites in particular were found to have western rather than southern connections and contained no Ramah chert or Labrador Dorset tool styles. In 1992 small amounts of Ramah chert tools and flakes were found in Dorset deposits at Kamaiyuk and Willows Island 4.

The 1990 field work produced important information on historic-period Inuit sites occupied during or shortly after the Frobisher period. Several large Inuit sites found near Kodlunarn Island contained a sequence of occupations from Developed Thule times to the present. The largest of these, Kuyait, consists of twelve structures, most of them semi-subterranean, two-room sod houses. The smaller site, Kamaiyuk, has six multi-room sod houses. Both sites contained faunal remains and Inuit material culture, with significant admixtures of Frobisher tile and other ceramics, English flint, glass, and slag. Some houses at these sites contained traces of later European contact. The large amount of early European materials that could be linked definitely to the Frobisher voyages suggests Kamaiyuk was occupied during or shortly after the expeditions.

In addition to sod-house villages, tent and igloo campsites were found throughout Countess of Warwick Sound, Cyrus Field Bay, and other locations. The most important of these is Tikkoon, a large settlement area only a few hundred metres from Kodlunarn Island; there we noted many tent rings with fragments of Frobisher tile and brick, flint, and in one a "bloom-like" chunk of iron [see Ehrenreich and Wayman, this volume]. On Kodlunarn Island itself many Inuit tent camps were found to contain Frobisher brick, tile, and flint. An iron arrow point, probably of Frobisher origin, was found at one of these sites.

The most important find in 1990 - an iron bloom similar to those found on Kodlunarn in 1981 - was made in a large Neoeskimo spring camp on what is probably the island named by Hall "Lookout Island", in Cyrus Field Bay. Here we literally stumbled upon a 17.5 lb. iron bloom in an Inuit tent ring that was half eroded into the sea. The Lookout Island bloom is noteworthy because in 1861 one of Hall's Inuit informants told him he had taken an iron bloom from the Kodlunarn Island area to Cyrus Field Bay only a few years earlier. Our find may in fact be this same bloom. It may also be the one that Hall reported finding in 1861, and which he stated as having "collected for science", although there is no record of this bloom in his list of specimens donated to the Smithsonian and the Royal Geographical Society.

Together, these finds suggest that considerable evidence of European-Inuit contact exists at outer Frobisher Bay Inuit sites, and that Inuit interaction with the Frobisher expeditions and material remains was more extensive than noted in the historical accounts. This material offers great potential for European-Inuit contact studies, including indirect effects of European contact on Inuit political, economic, and demographic systems.

Finally, we noted that most of the Neoeskimo winter villages found in 1990 date to the period *ca.* A.D. 1400-1900, and that they contain houses both with and without historic materials and with architectural features ranging from single-room "Thule" structures to multiple-room "clover-leaf" forms. At Kamaiyuk we found one house resembling the large Greenland or Labrador-style rectangular "communal" house. The 1990 season also brought us into close contact with the community of Iqaluit, which showed strong interest in our project. In addition we established working relationships with Inuit families who hunt in the outer bay region and found them very enthusiastic about the project.

We found everywhere that coastal submergence and site erosion has destroyed much of the outer coast archaeological record, with the greatest damage sustained by the earliest sites; even recent sites are eroding at an alarming rate. Pre-Dorset and early Dorset sites were preserved only occasionally as remnants, while Thule and historic period sites (especially at Kamaiyuk) were also heavily damaged and eroding rapidly.

Laboratory Research

Over the winter, research was conducted on materials collected during the 1990 field season. Preliminary results are available on studies of iron objects [Wayman and Ehrenreich 1993; Ehrenreich and Wayman, this volume] and ceramic samples [Auger 1993; Auger et al., this volume]. No studies have yet been undertaken on the Lookout Island iron bloom. A review of research options concerning this bloom and the three recovered from Kodlunarn Island in 1981 is currently underway.

Considerable progress has been made on radiocarbon dating of Kodlunarn Island samples collected in 1981 and Inuit site samples from 1990-91. In addition to a previous series of Kodlunarn Island dates [Fitzhugh and Olin 1993], results from two recent submissions of 1981 samples have been obtained. One sample from the assay shop (S2, TP1) consisting of 2.8 g of oak charcoal produced a date of 320±90 B.P. (A.D. 1446-1656, calib., Beta-42659). A sample of 3 g of oak charcoal from the smithy (S1, TP1) produced a date of 510±80 B.P. (A.D. 1347-1351, 1391-1442, calib., Beta-42660). The assay shop date seems on target, but the smithy date is early, similar to dates obtained from the iron blooms, and raises similar questions. Is this date a reliable indication of the site's age; is it a heartwood sample from the core of an old English oak; or might it be contaminated with coal, which is present in large quantities in the smithy? [See Fitzhugh 1993a for a full report of Kodlunarn Island dating and description.

Dates on our Kuyait and Kamaiyuk excavations are reported in this volume in papers by Gullason et al. and Laeyendecker.

1991 Field Work

The 1991 season was dedicated to expanding our preliminary survey of the outer Frobisher Bay and to excavation of Inuit houses at the historic winter village sites of Kuyait and Kamaiyuk, with the aim of gathering data on European-Inuit contact and culture change.

Field work took place between 4 July and 10 September. While the *Pitsiulak* crew remained in Iqaluit to prepare the vessel, the excavation team flew to Gold Cove on 9 July. Favoured by good weather throughout the summer, we completed most of our major goals, conducting three weeks of work at Kuyait before moving to Kamaiyuk, near Kodlunarn Island. While work proceeded at Kamaiyuk, surveys were conducted with the *Pitsiulak* in Countess of Warwick Sound, Beare Sound, Chapell Inlet, and on the south side of Frobisher Bay from York Sound to East Bluff. Heavy ice pack prevented surveys in Loks Land and Cyrus Field Bay throughout August; however, we were able to visit Cyrus Field Bay sites by helicopter briefly at the end of the season.

Archaeological Results

Archaeological work was undertaken at thirty-two sites (Tables 2, 3; *Fig. 5*). Twenty-three of these are new discoveries, the remainder consisting of revisits to sites found in 1981 and 1990. Except at Kuyait and Kamaiyuk, most sites were visited only briefly to gather basic documentation on location, features, cultural components, depth, age, and extent of deposit. Representative samples of tools, materials, fauna, and botanical remains were made from the surface, test pits, and eroding deposits. Since many sites had been impacted by marine erosion, attention was given to assessing site significance with respect to conservation and preservation.

Little survey work was done in July because the coast was ice-blocked, but with open water in August we succeeded in expanding survey coverage beyond our 1990 limits and included areas featured in the Frobisher records. The results add much to data on settlement patterns of both prehistoric and historic periods. The major effort went toward excavation of the village sites at Kuyait and Kamaiyuk, since it was here that we expected to find our best evidence of Frobisher and later European contact. A large crew worked at these sites throughout the summer under the direction of Lynda Gullason and Anne Henshaw.

1991 Survey Sites

KUYAIT 1 (KfDf-2)   This large winter village site, located on the south tip of the Wiswell Inlet Peninsula, and first identified in 1990, contains at least twelve recognizeable house foundations and the remains of many other tent rings, caches, and other structures. Neoeskimo components are spread about on several hundred square metres of peat-covered raised beaches and rock outcrops. Shoreside locations, which are undergoing extensive slumpage and marine erosion, contain Dorset middens; Dorset artifacts, debitage, and burned slabs can be collected all along the eroding face and exposed beach area. Test pits were excavated in a number of the Neoeskimo house pits and in other promising locations to determine the age and extent of Neoeskimo and Dorset deposits. [Further details on this site are in Gullason et al., this volume].

SUMNER ISLAND 2 (KfDf-5)   The island opposite Kuyait 1 has a group of four small sod houses (L2) and several clusters of spring tent ring camps (L1,3,4). House 1, the northernmost, was half eroded into the sea; H2 was a small bilobate house with entrance lintel rocks; H3 had a single gravelly platform and a grassy entrance way; and H4, the southernmost, also bilobate, was grassed over and had been used as a recent rubbish dump. Walrus bones were strewn about, and a raven's nest and ancient midden occupied the ledges on the west side of the beachpass. No testpits were excavated, but the sod houses appeared to date to the twentieth century. Further survey in 1992 indicated that this site was larger and contained several other twentieth century sod houses and a group of four large, bilobate winter houses dating to seventeenth/eighteenth centuries, located about a hundred metres south of the northern house cluster.

CAPE SARAH 1 (KeDe-11)   This site appears to have been used as a spring walrus-hunting camp and is marked by prominent, large, iron, storage tanks similar to those at the Cape Haven whaling site, Kuyait, and Minguktoo. It has many tent ring camps and several qarmat-type structures. Most occupations appear to date to the nineteenth/twentieth centuries. No subsurface testing was done. Iron strap and large sheets of copper were noted on the surface. A broken walrus harpoon blank of antler was found in the southern area of the site. Whalebones were found in caches in the nearby cliffs.

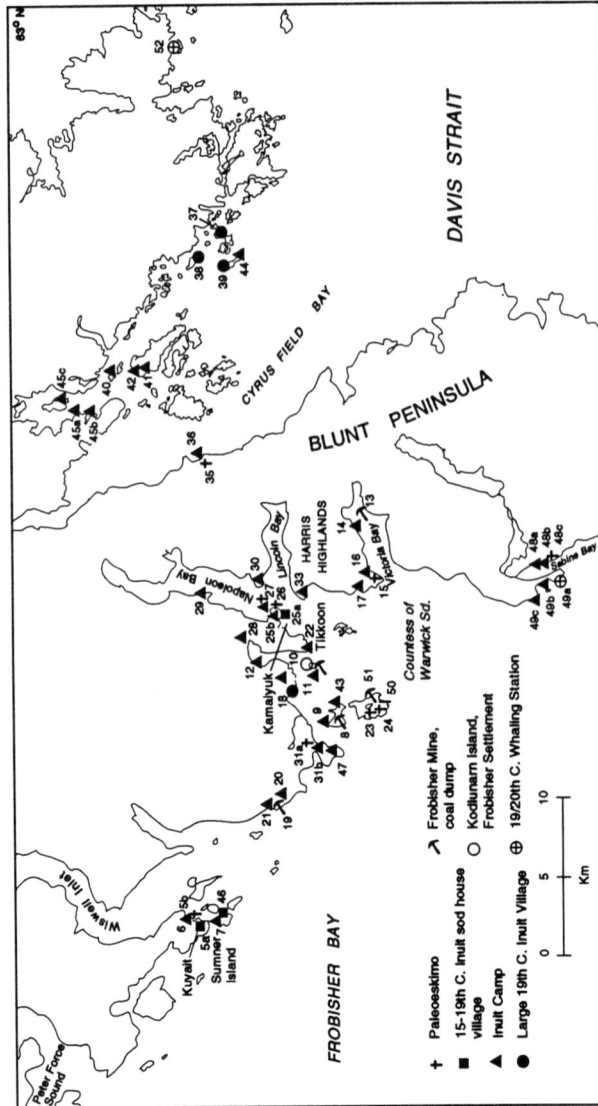

Figure 5a: Map of archaeological sites found in 1990 and 1991 in Countess of Warwick Sound region (for key, see Table 1).

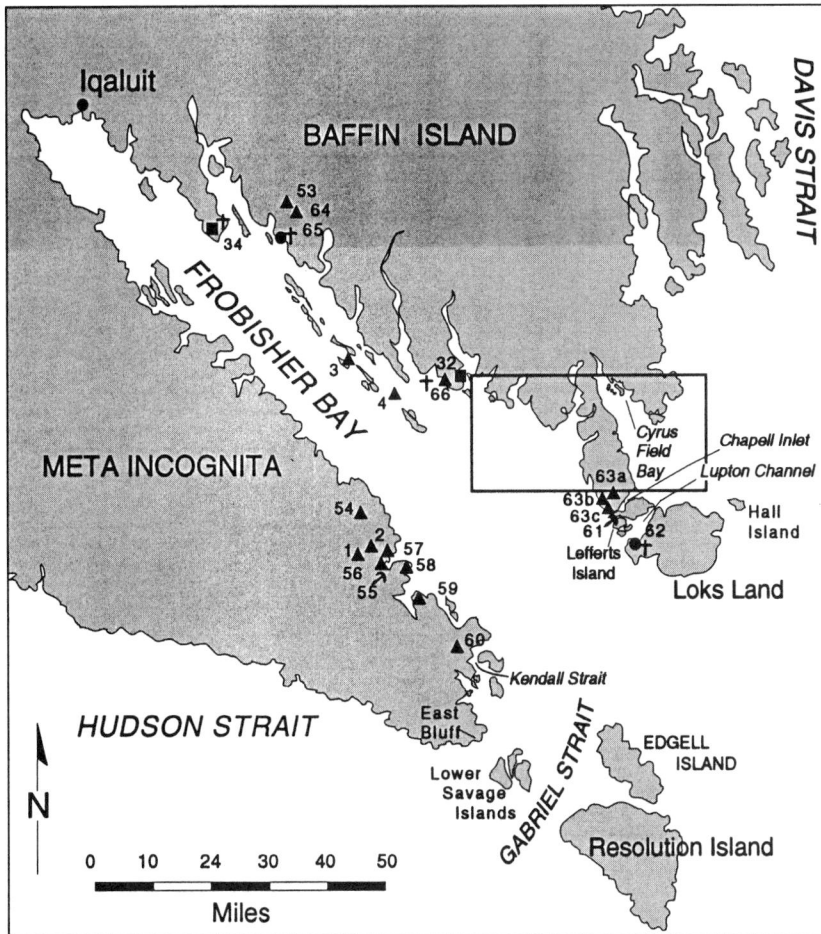

Figure 5b: Map of archaeological sites found in 1990 and 1991 in Frobisher Bay (for key, see Table 1).

Table 1 *Archaeological sites recorded in 1981, 1990, and 1991*

Site name	Map code	Culture*
KINGAIT COAST:		
York Sound 1	54	Bloody Point Inuit camp
Jackman Sound 1	1	Recent Inuit
Jackman Sound 2	2	Recent Inuit
Jackman Sound 3	55	Frobisher "silver" mine
Jackman Sound 4	56	Inuit tent-ring camps
Jackman Sound 5	57	Inuit tent-ring camps
Weasel Point 1	58	Inuit tent-ring camps
Halford Island Narrows	59	Inuit tent-ring camps; Cesna crash
Kendall Strait	60	Inuit pinnacles
LOWER FROBISHER BAY:		
Idlaulitoo Outpost Camp	53	Modern Inuit outpost
Tongue Cape 1	64	Dorset/Neoeskimo camp
Tongue Cape 2	65	Modern Inuit field camps
Ikkerasukudunuk 1	3	Neoeskimo/Recent Inuit
Minguktoo 1	32	Thule/Neoeskimo sod-house village
Minguktoo 2	66	Dorset/Neoeskimo tent-ring camps
Imilik 1	34	Dorset/Neoeskimo sod-house village
Gabriel Island	4	Neoeskimo camp
Kuyait 1	5a,b	Dorset/Thule/Neoeskimo village
Kuyait 2	6	Neoeskimo tent-ring camps
Sumner Island 1	7	Neoeskimo tent-ring camps
Sumner Island 2	46	Inuit sod-house village
Newland Island 1	8	Frobisher mine and coal dump
Newland Island 2	9	Neoeskimo tent-ring camps
Newland Island 3	43	Neoeskimo tent-ring camp
Kodlunarn Island 1	10	Frobisher sites
Kodlunarn Island 2	11	Neoeskimo camps
Diana Marsh Outcrop	12	Neoeskimo grave site
Judy Point 1	13	Frobisher coal dump
Judy Point 2	14	Neoeskimo tent camps/structures
Victoria Bay 1	15	Dorset camp
Victoria Bay 2	16	Neoeskimo tent camps
Victoria Bay 3	17	Neoeskimo cave site
Hall Peninsula 1	18	Recent Inuit spring camp
Countess of Sussex 1	19	Frobisher mine
Countess of Sussex 2	20	Dorset camp
Countess of Sussex 3	21	Neoeskimo camps
Tikkoon Point 1	22	Frobisher(?)/Neoeskimo structures
Willows Island 1	23	Dorset midden/Thule/Neoeskimo camps
Willows Island 2	24	Dorset midden
Willows Island 3	50	Dorset midden and winter village

(Table 1 cont.)

Site name	Map code	Culture[*]
Anvil Cove 1	51	Frobisher coal dump; Inuit camps
Napoleon Bay 1 (Kamaiyuk)	25a,b	Dorset midden/Thule/Neoeskimo village
Napoleon Bay 2	26	Dorset/Thule/Neoeskimo camps
Napoleon Bay 3	27	Dorset/Thule/Recent camps
Napoleon Bay 4	28	Recent Inuit camps
Napoleon Bay 5	29	Caribou blind
Lincoln Bay 1	30	Neoeskimo camps
Harris Point 1	33	Recent Inuit
Cape Sarah Neck 1	31a,b	Paleoeskimo (Transitional)
Cape Sarah 1	47	Thule/Inuit qarmat and tent site
Sabine Bay 1	48a,b,c	Dorset/Neoeskimo tent sites
Sharko Peninsula 1	49a,b,c	Thule/Inuit/European whaling station
Beare Sound 1	62	Dorset/Neoeskimo TR village
Lefferts Island 1	61	Frobisher mines and Inuit camps
CYRUS FIELD BAY:		
Itilikjuak 1	35	Dorset village/Neoeskimo tent camps
Itilikjuak 2	36	Caribou drive system
Chappell Inlet 1	63a	Old Inuit tent ring
Chappell Inlet 1	63b	Neoeskimo caribou drive system
Chappell Inlet 3	63c	Neoeskimo tent ring camps
Cyrus Field Bay 1 (Lookout I.)	37	Historic and Recent Inuit camps
Cyrus Field Bay 2	38	Paleoeskimo/Neoeskimo camps
Cyrus Field Bay 3	39	Thule/Neoeskimo/recent Inuit camps
George Henry Island 1	40	Recent Inuit
George Henry Island 2	41	Thule/Neoeskimo camps
George Henry Island 3	42	Thule/Neoeskimo camps
Island-95 1	43	Unknown stone structure
Island-95 2	44	Neoeskimo camps
Cyrus Field Bay Survey	45a,b,c	Recent Inuit (inner bay surveys)
Cape Haven 1	52	European whaling station

[*] Recent Inuit = 19/20th century; Neoeskimo = undatable but of Thule/Inuit tradition; Thule = prehistoric Neoeskimo, ca. A.D. 1000-1550; Early Historic Neoeskimo = A.D. 1550-1800; Dorset = 2500-1000 B.P.; Transitional Paleoeskimo = ca. 3000-2500 B.P.; Pre-Dorset = ca. 4000-2800 B.P.

Table 2 *Archaeological sites recorded in 1991*

FROBISHER BAY:

Kuyait 1	KfDf-2	Dorset, Thule, Inuit winter vill.	3 houses excavated
Sumner Island 2	KfDf-5	19/20th C. Inuit village	surveyed, 4 loci
Cape Sarah 1	KeDe-11	Thule/Inuit qarmat and tent site	surveyed, several loci
Kamaiyuk	KfDe-5	Dorset, Thule, Inuit winter vill.	1.5 houses excavated
Sabine Bay 1	KeDd-6	Dorset, Neoeskimo tent sites	surveyed, 6 loci
Skarko Peninsula 1	KeDd-7	Thule, Inuit, European whaling station	surveyed, 7 loci
Chapell Inlet 1	KdDd-2	Old Inuit tent ring	surveyed
Chapell Inlet 2	KdDd-3	Neoeskimo caribou drive system	surveyed, 4 loci
Chapell Inlet 3	KdDd-4	Neoeskimo tent ring camps	surveyed, 4 loci
Beare Sound 1	KcDc-1	Dorset, Neoeskimo TR and winter vill.	surveyed, 3 loci
Lefferts Island 1	KdDd-5	Frobisher mines and Inuit TR camps	surveyed 4 loci
Victoria Bay 1	KeDd-3	Dorset camp	surveyed, tested 2 loci
Victoria Bay 3	KeDd-5	Cave site Neoeskimo structures	mapped and tested
Tikkoon Point	KeDe-4	Dorset, Neoeskimo camps	mapped, tested 4 loci
Lincoln Bay 1	KfDd-1	Neoeskimo tent rings	excavated A1 locus rings
Willows Island 2	KeDe-8	Dorset house midden; walrus feature	tested
Willows Island 3	KeDe-12	Dorset village site and midden	surveyed and tested
Anvil Cove 1	KeDe-13	Frobisher coal dump; Neoeskimo camps	surveyed, tested 3 loci
Yorke Sound 1	KcDh-3	Inuit camp attacked by Frobisher	surveyed 4 loci
Jackman Sound 3	KbDg-1	Frobisher "silver" mine	surveyed and sampled
Jackman Sound 4	KbDh-1	Inuit TR camps	surveyed
Jackman Sound 5	KcDh-4	Inuit TR camps	surveyed 2 loci
"Weasel" Point	KbDg-2	Inuit TR camps	surveyed 8 loci
Halford Island Narrows	KbDg-3	Inuit TR camps and Cessna crash	surveyed 3 loci
Kendall Strait	------	Inuit pinnacles	surveyed
Minguktoo 1	KfDg-1	Inuit sod-house village	tested two structures
Minguktoo 2	KfDg-2	Dorset and Neoeskimo TR camps	surveyed 8 loci
Idlaulitoo Outpost	------	Modern camp and sod house	surveyed
Tongue Cape 1	KhDj-1	Dorset and Neoeskimo camp	surveyed
Tongue Cape 2	KhDi-1	Modern Inuit camps	surveyed several loci

CYRUS FIELD BAY:

C. Haven 1	KfDb-1	Whaling Station ("Singaijaq")	surveyed
Island 95	KfDc-3	Large Inuit campsite	surveyed

Table 3 *1991 sites by affiliation and function*

NEOESKIMO/INUIT

sod-house villages:	*Kuyait* (3 houses excav.), *Kamaiyuk* (1.5 houses excav.), Minguktoo 1, Sumner Island 2
snowhouse village:	Anvil Cove 1, Tikkoon, Beare Sound 1, Island 95, Tongue Cape 1
large tent camps:	Island 95-1, Cape Sarah 1, Minguktoo 1-2, *York Sound 1*, Beare Sound 1, Weasel Point 1, Halford Island Narrows, Tongue Cape 2
isolated camps:	Sabine Bay 1, Sharko Peninsula 1, Chapell Inlet 1, Chapell Inlet 3, Victoria Bay 3 (cave), Lincoln Bay 1, Jackman Sound 4-5
caribou drive:	Chapell Inlet 2

PALEOESKIMO

large sites/middens:	Kuyait, Kamaiyuk, Beare Sound 1, Willows Island 2-3
small sites:	Victoria Bay 1, Minguktoo 2

WHALING STATIONS

	Sharko Peninsula 1 (1850s), Cape Haven 1 (late nineteenth century)

FROBISHER

black ore mine:	Lefferts Island 1 mine (Beare Sound/Sussex Island mine)
silver mine:	Jackman Sound 3
coal dump:	Anvil Cove 1

(*italic* = Frobisher contact site)

Table 4 *Conservation status of 1991 sites*

FROBISHER BAY:

Kuyait 1	KfDf-2	extensive erosion of Dorset middens
Sumner Island 2	KfDf-5	research priority high, conserv. priority low
Cape Sarah 1	KeDe-11	stable; low priority
Kamaiyuk 1	KfDe-5	serious erosion; high research and conserv. priority
Sabine Bay 1	KeDd-6	mostly stable; low priority
Skarko Peninsula 1	KeDd-7	stable; low priority, except L4 ceremonial house
Chapell Inlet 1	KdDd-2	stable; low priority
Chapell Inlet 2	KdDd-3	stable; low priority
Chapell Inlet 3	KdDd-4	stable; low priority
Beare Sound 1	KcDc-1	extensive erosion of Dorset midden; moderate priority
Lefferts Island 1	KdDd-5	erosion of mine underway; high priority
Victoria Bay 1	KeDd-3	stable; low research and conserv. priority
Victoria Bay 3	KeDd-5	stable; low priority
Tikkoon Point	KeDe-4	stable; high research priority
Lincoln Bay 1	KfDd-1	stable; work completed
Willows Island 2	KeDe-8	extensive erosion; high research and conserv. priority
Willows Island 3	KeDe-12	stable; high research priority
Anvil Cove 1	KeDe-13	eroding; high research and conserv. priority
Yorke Sound 1	KcDh-3	stable; high research priority
Jackman Sound 3	KbDg-1	stable; little potential for research
Jackman Sound 4	KbDh-1	stable; low research potential
Jackman Sound 5	KcDh-4	stable; low research potential
"Weasel" Point	KbDg-2	stable; moderate research potential
Halford Island Narrows	KbDg-3	eroding, but low research potential
Kendall Strait	------	eroding, but no sites!
Minguktoo 1	KfDg-1	stable; high research potential
Minguktoo 2	KfDg-2	eroding; high research and conserv. priority
Idlaulitoo Outpost	------	stable; low research potential
Tongue Cape 1	KhDj-1	stable; high research potential
Tongue Cape 2	KhDi-1	stable; low research potential

CYRUS FIELD BAY:

C. Haven 1 (Singaijaq)	KfDb-1	seriously endangered; high research/conserv. priority
Island 95	KfDc-3	stable; moderate research potential

Figure 6: A Dorset soapstone figure found in House 2 deposits at Kamaiyuk.

Figure 7: Kooyoo Sageatook inspects a large ceremonial ring structure at Sharko Peninsula 1, L3. Stone benches line the ring interior, and a ring-shaped enclosure is at rear.

Figure 8: Chapell Inlet 2, L3 caribou hunting blind, one of many such features constructed at the termination of a large drive system at this location.

Figure 9: Lefferts Island hornblende outcrop No. 2 (on the east side of the island), a possible location of Frobisher's Sussex Island mine.

KAMAIYUK 1 (KfDe-5)   This large Neoeskimo site, 3 km northeast of Kodlunarn Island, existed at the time of the Frobisher visit, when it was described by George Best [Stefansson and McCaskill 1938, 1:64], making it the first Inuit village and archaeological site to appear in western literature. Kamaiyuk has four large and two small sod-house structures which had been excavated into Thule and earlier Dorset houses and middens (*Fig. 6*). The entire site is severely damaged by marine erosion and received major attention in our 1991 excavation programme [see Gullason et al., this volume].

SABINE BAY 1 (KeDd-6)   A survey of the east shore of Sabine Bay revealed the presence of seven tent camp clusters. Today this area is used for summer caribou hunting in the nearby lowlands. Two locations (L1,4) had Paleoeskimo remains. L1, a slab pavement associated with flakes of limey chert from the limestone beds at the bottom of Frobisher Bay, was under active erosion. L4 was a cluster of Dorset structures where we found a quartz crystal microblade core. Other structures appeared to be twentieth century Inuit hunting camps spanning a range of time - some occupied in the last few years.

SHARKO PENINSULA 1 (KeDd-7)   Surveys on the west side of the peninsula across from Sabine Bay identified a string of Neoeskimo camps dating from early historic times to the twentieth century. L1 at the southern end of the peninsula may be the remains of the abandoned whaling station. L3 is an historic period Inuit tent village associated with a probable ceremonial tent or enclosure ringed with stone benches and an inner "performer's ring" (*Fig. 7*). Other locations contained historic tent ring clusters, of which the largest, L7, contained a huge circular stone ring and an inukshuk system.

CHAPELL INLET 1 (KdDd-4)   A heavy stone tent ring with associated caches was found in a protected ravine on the north shore of Chapell Inlet. Wood remains appear to have been cut with iron tools.

CHAPELL INLET 2 (KdDd-5)   The lowland isthmus at the head of Chapell Inlet has been used to construct a series of caribou drive systems through which caribou travelling toward Loks Land must pass. Inukshuks, blinds, boulder alignments, and caches, probably dating to different periods, are found in four locations. The L3 blinds (*Fig. 8*) are the most extensive and must have been a cooperative enterprise of a large group of hunters. Caribou hunting and driftwood collecting appear to have been important activities in this area.

CHAPELL INLET 3 (KdDd-6)   A group of early historic Inuit tent rings (L1) was found at the stream outlet from the isthmus pond into Chapell Inlet, associated with the Line 2 caribou drive system (above). L2 includes scattered groups of recent tent ring camps found along the southeastern shore of Chapell Inlet and the nearby shore of Beare

Sound. Some of these caribou hunting and transit camps have been occupied in recent times by relatives of our crew-member Juta Ipeelie. Formerly, skin and light wood boats were carried across the isthmus between Beare Sound and Chapell Inlet to avoid ice and dangerous currents in Lupton Channel.

Surveys in Chapell Inlet found its shores strewn with windrows of driftwood: weather-beaten logs of potentially old Arctic drift, together with lighter materials of less distant origin discarded recently by deep-sea vessels. The submergent nature of the coast has concentrated driftwood of different ages along the current storm tide line. The entire Loks Land coast seems to receive large volumes of driftwood, which may have been a principal attraction in prehistoric and early historic times. Best observed large amounts of driftwood during Frobisher's approach to Baffin Island in 1576. Dosia Laeyendecker sampled some of the older logs for species identification and age determination but eventually was overwhelmed by the volume. The age and origin of local driftwood is of interest in connection with the Frobisher iron blooms, whose anomalously early radiocarbon dates could have resulted from the blooms having been smelted with charcoal made from old Arctic driftwood.

BEARE SOUND 1 (KcDc-1)   Three site locales were found on a boulder spit projecting eastwards into the extension of Beare Sounde south of Matlack Island. L3 contained small clusters of tent rings, caches, and hunting blinds. L2 was a group of paved snowhouse floors associated with surface bone and wood deposits where we found a wood leister fragment. L1 was a grassy terrace of several hundred square metres in extent with numerous tent rings and caches. Tests revealed Neoeskimo bone middens and wood remains in a thick, peaty sod, while Dorset deposits were found eroding from the bank. No semi-subterranean houses were noted; the nearby ledges contained caches and blinds. This site has Dorset, Thule, and historic Inuit occupations and seems to be one of the few long-term settlement areas in the Beare Sound region.

LEFFERTS ISLAND 1 (KdDd-5)   A detailed foot survey was made of the east and north shores of Lefferts Island. Tent rings dating predominantly to the twentieth century occur along the Beare Sound shore, but no large camps or early sites were noted. In four locations we found small outcrops of "black ore" (hornblende) and one of these, Ore Source 2, appears to have been mined (*Fig. 9*). This outcrop was perched above a narrow cleft that facilitated boat loading. In addition to a thin scatter of mine tailings, we found a chunk of possibly European chert. No coal or other Frobisher remains were found. Today the sea washes over this site at high tide. One wonders if this outcrop is large enough to have produced the 330 tons of ore Frobisher took from his Sussex Island mine in Beare Sound. Some of the other outcrops along the north side of Lefferts Island may have been mined, but evidence of working is not obvious today.

VICTORIA BAY 1 (KeDd-3)   A return visit was made to this site on a low point at the northwestern entrance of Victoria Bay. Dorset flakes and artifacts are found in a thin scatter around the crest of a hillock. Two locales were tested and contained *in situ* Dorset material. L1 also has a Neoeskimo component consisting of small oval boulder rings and caches. The site is only of moderate interest but could yield a tightly defined Dorset assemblage and charcoal for dating. The hillslope to the northeast of the site contains Neoeskimo tent ring camps, caches, and caribou fences.

VICTORIA BAY 3 (KeDd-5)   This large conspicuous cave on the hillside at the north entrance of Victoria Bay was inspected in 1990. A brief visit was made in 1991 to check for buried cultural deposits. Test pits in the grassy apron in front of the mouth and inside the drip line revealed no traces of occupation. The cave and its cultural features, which include two cache or shelter boulder structures, were mapped. Seal bones on the floor were remains of polar bear kills. No artifacts or bones were associated with the cave's boulder features.

TIKKOON POINT (KeDe-4)   Réginald Auger tested several structures (noted by Walter Kenyon and us in previous surveys) that suggested possible Frobisher connections. These included three stone foundations along the side of the northern hillslope, S4, S20, and S21, and a group of tent rings (S14,17) containing Frobisher ceramics. Auger's excavations at the hillside pavements produced sled runners and historic Inuit materials that suggest these structures to be stone floors and sleeping platforms for snowhouse dwellings (*Fig. 10*). Excavation of the S14 tent ring produced Elizabethan roof tile, a fragment of brass, and faunal remains. It remains to be seen if Frobisher settlements exist at Tikkoon; if so, they may be difficult to find in the thick sod cover in the western beach. No work was done on S7 where the cast iron chunk was recovered in 1990.

LINCOLN BAY 1 (KfDd-1)   Two tent rings found in 1990, one with a large fragment of early yellow-glazed ceramic, were excavated to determine their age and possible Frobisher association. Nothing else was found in either structure apart from bone and wood fragments.

WILLOWS ISLAND 2 (KeDe-8)   Three 50 cm test pits were excavated in this small, rapidly eroding, and extremely productive late Dorset midden at Opingivik Island, tested in 1990. At that time we believe the site to nearly completely eroded out. Tests in 1991 revealed about a hundred square metres of the site's 20-40 cm thick midden to be intact, stratified below a Neoeskimo level. We reinspected a peculiar alignment of walrus mandibles found in 1990 on the beach ridge to the south, partially buried in the soil (*Fig. 11*). Part of the mandible alignment, which is oriented east-west and is perpendicular to the hillslope, was exposed. The line is composed of twenty-five mandibles, nested tightly, tooth side up, and extends for a distance of 5 m.

Figure 10: Tikkoon Point, Structure 4, the view to the east with gull cliff in the background - there, according to Inuit accounts, Frobisher's men masted a boat in which they tried to escape. This structure was tested by Réginald Auger, who found sled runner fragments and other evidence of winter occupation. The slab pavements appear to be sleeping platforms of snowhouses.

Figure 11: A row of walrus mandibles nested tooth side up, part of a 5-metre long (ceremonial?) alignment at Willows Island 2. Both Dorset and Neoeskimo components are present nearby. Dates are pending on a jaw sample.

Figure 12: "Ig-loos or snow village at Oopungnewing" [Hall 1865]. This igloo village on the southern end of Willows Island, visited by Hall in 1862, was probably located at the site of Anvil Cove 1, L2. Note the walrus heads on the igloo roof.

Figure 13: The walrus mandible alignment at Anvil Cove 1 at a snowhouse village site. About a hundred mandibles nested tooth side down form a 25-metre long alignment, roughly 0.5 km across the ridge from a corresponding alignment on the other side of Willows Island.

Figure 14: Quarried blocks of quartz at the probable location of the Smithe's Island "silver" mine tested by Frobisher's party in Jackman Sound in 1577.

Figure 15: Modern sod-house construction at Idlaulitoo outpost camp, Wadell Bay, showing sod wall construction technique, the method of joining roofing (roof carpet), and hold-down stones.

Figure 16: The remains of building foundations and iron tanks at Cape Haven whaling station. Tent camps here were used by Inuit employees and by others who periodically visited later to scavenge European materials after the station closed in the early 1900s.

Figure 17: An iron nauluk and a worked walrus tusk fragment, taken from eroding shoreside deposits at Cape Haven station.

WILLOWS ISLAND 3 (KeDe-12)   A large Dorset midden was found on the sloping grassy hillside at the extreme southern end of Willows Island. The site is unusual in that it is one of the few Dorset sites we found that was not being actively eroded. Three 50 cm test pits produced late Dorset implements, preserved faunal remains, and charred slabs in a 20-30 cm thick deposit. A marshy gully north of the site contained thick deposits of wood, walrus hide, baleen, and other faunal remains. Whether this material is Dorset or Neoeskimo was not determined.

ANVIL COVE 1 (KeDe-13)   Surveys across the southern end of Willows (Opingivik) Island in Anvil Cove identified numerous tent ring sites along its shores, two locations of which were given site designations. At L1 we found an historic Inuit tent ring camp with caches and hearth features above a 1-2 cm thick lens of coal, which was eroding at the shore for a distance of 10 m. Tests indicated the coal lens was a remnant of a larger shoreside dump. Caramel-coloured English flint was found with the coal. As in 1981, we searched the shore without success for the lost Frobisher anvil.

The L2 site location covers several hundred square metres of terrace below the east side of the hillside. Here we found faunal remains embedded in the wet moss, caches, and a possible Paleoeskimo mid-passage floor. The bone deposit contained butchered walrus, seal, small whales, and caribou. Wood was occasionally preserved. The site setting, the dispersed and unburied nature of the bone deposit, and the absence of tent rings suggest the area had been used as a snowhouse village (*Fig. 12*).

At the northeast end of L2 we found another alignment of walrus mandibles (L3) buried in the sod. But, unlike the walrus jaw feature found at Willows Island 2, the L3 feature was much larger, extending 25 m in an easterly direction, and its mandibles were all nested tooth side down (*Fig. 13*). All teeth had been removed from the jaws. We estimated about ninety-five mandibles present. Such an alignment of walrus jaws was noted by Hall in 1861, but his notes speak of jaws placed two feet apart extending over the top of the hill at the *north* end of the island. Our feature was at the south end of Willows/Opingivik and did not extend over the hill. Perhaps Hall misidentified the location. Neither Hall nor his Inuit companions knew the function of the feature. A hunting ceremonial function seem likely.

YORK SOUND 1 (KcDh-3)   On the Kingait (south) side of Frobisher Bay we located a large tent campsite on the north shore of York Sound; this can hardly be other than the Inuit village attacked by Frobisher's exploring parties in the early summer of 1577. Earlier, the Elizabethans had visited a York Sound fishing camp from which the Inuit had abandoned upon their approach; here Frobisher's men discovered clothing belonging to the sailors lost in 1576 [see Auger et al., this volume]. This site would have been on the gravel beach at the mouth of the York River, which is merely a storm bar regularly swept over by the sea. No traces of sites, old or recent, were found here or along the adjacent beaches and high sand terrace.

According to the records, the Frobisher men found the Inuit had moved to another location on a point farther out on the north shore. York Sound 1 must be this location, as it is the only possible place to camp on this steep shore. Here, against a dramatic backdrop of mountains and glaciers, we identified four separate settlement loci, of which L1,2,3 are of early historic age. These sites consist of tent ring clusters, caches, stone enclosures, and possible remains of kayak supports. The dwelling sites are covered with a thin moss and no artifacts were visible. A short distance to the east is a rocky promontory answering the description of "Bloody Point", where the fleeing Inuit were overtaken and attacked.

JACKMAN SOUND 1 (KcDh-1)   A short return visit to this site, found in 1990, confirmed it as a relatively late Inuit camp. A sample of hornblende from an outcrop along the south shore of the point, resembling the Frobisher "black ore" from Kodlunarn, was collected. This is probably the source of the black ore mined by the Frobisher crew and loaded into the *Ayde* early in the 1577 season, before Frobisher had discovered Kodlunarn Island.

JACKMAN SOUND 3 (KbDg-1)   On a small island in the narrow southern extension of Jackman Sound we found a conspicuous quartz outcrop bearing evidence of quarrying (*Fig. 14*). This site answers the description by George Best: "Upon a small island, within this [i.e. Jackman] sounde, called Smithes Island (because he first set up his forge there) was found a mine of silver, but was not won out of the rocks without great labor" [Stefansson and McCaskill 1938, 1:61]. Despite the small size of the outcrop, only several square metres in area, we found no other outcrop that might have been taken by Elizabethans as a potential silver mine.

JACKMAN SOUND 4 (KbDh-1)   Several tent rings and the skeleton of a polar bear (a recent hunter's kill) were found on a low peninsula midway down the east shore of the Sound. Most camps appeared to be of recent origin and little interest.

JACKMAN SOUND 5 (KcDh-4)   Surveys at the rocky point on the south side of the Sound revealed two tent camp loci and several rock pinnacles on the crest of the ridge.

"WEASEL" POINT 1 (KbDg-2)   A low peninsula with a shallow but protected harbour complex, 5 km south of the entrance to Jackman Sound, has been used extensively for summer hunting camps. Eight loci were identified, some of which contained as many as 8-10 tent rings. The camps all appear to date to a distinct early historic period during which U-shaped hearths were used. Shreds of canvas were noted, and in one location a cache was discovered containing a dowel-pinned section of ship's timber (oak) and cold-hammered iron spikes.

HALFORD ISLAND NARROWS (KbDg-2)   Several small campsites containing tent rings and caches were found on the mainland (west) side of Halford Island Narrows. An isolated find of a Paleoeskimo biface fragment was also made, the only Paleoeskimo sign we found during our survey from York Sound to East Bluff. Equally unusual was the discovery of the hulk of a Cessna 185 airplane flipped on its back in the middle of a bog. The crash probably occurred about 10-15 years ago. Parts of the plane have been scavenged. No human remains or loose articles were present.

KENDALL STRAIT (no Borden assignment)   We spent one afternoon surveying the channels and islands on the north side of Kendall Strait and south among the small islands west of Gross Island. Surprisingly few settlement traces were found in this area. We had expected Inuit activity to pick up as one approached the southeastern tip of Baffin Island, known for its strong currents and tidal mixing. However, other than a few isolated tent rings and stone pinnacles, there were few Inuit sites. Another surprise, considering the rocky nature of East Baffin (Norse "Helluland", or flatstone land), was the extensive deposits of sand in the form of huge kame terraces along the hillsides, sand-filled valleys, and bridging sand-bars between islands. While our surveys here were not thorough enough to be definitive, there seems to have been only light Neoeskimo occupation in this region. Paleoeskimo sites were not noted, probably due to erosion loss. Infrequent Inuit use of this area is probably related to poor hunting potential. Today, the outer reaches of the eastern Meta Incognita shore are rarely visited by Inuit although, in the past, early summer beluga and walrus hunts were conducted here. We saw few signs of caribou and little evidence of seal, walrus, or whale.

Time did not allow us to extend our survey to the Lower Savage Islands and the Resolution/Edgell Island region, which we had hoped to reach.

MINGUKTOO 1 (KfDg-1)   Further reconnaissance was made at this large historic period sod-house village at the tip of Brewster Peninsula. Test pits were excavated in two of these structures. The pit in the west edge of the sleeping platform of H12, a bilobate structure similar to Kuyait H8 and Kamaiyuk H2, produced caribou bone but no cultural materials. Tests in two houses produced a large sample of nineteenth century European materials.

MINGUKTOO 2 (KfDg-2)   Inspection of the western arm of Brewster Point revealed numerous recent and some early historic Inuit tent camps. In addition, we found seven loci along the shore where Dorset collections were eroding. Most appear to be remnants of small summer camps rather than midden or winter sites. Collections from these sites indicate Early Dorset, Transitional, and Late Dorset occupations.

IDLAULITOO OUTPOST CAMP (no Borden assignment)   This modern settlement site at the mouth of Waddell Bay contains a large building whose sod wall and roof provided interesting parallels for interpreting early sod-house construction techniques

(*Fig. 15*). The walls consisted of a tapered foundation of sods one metre high; the roof, of floor carpet - a good replacement for scarce and smelly walrus hide - was secured down on top of the wall with large flat-sided boulders. The collapse of such a structure results in the walls and perched rocks falling inwards onto the floor, filling the house with a thick level of wall sods and angular boulders.

TONGUE CAPE 1 (KhDj-1)   A grassy ledge perched above the southern tip of Tongue Peninsula, at the southern entrance of Waddell Bay, contains numerous tent rings, multi-tiered snowhouse floor pavements, and other features of historic Inuit origin. A test pit near the edge of the bank produced old iron, bone, and wood above a Dorset horizon. This is a promising site.

TONGUE CAPE 2 (KhDi-1)   The north side of the cape has been used as a camping place for many years. Several large tent ring clusters were noted, some with 20-30 rings dating to recent times. Some of the smaller clusters appear to date to the nineteenth or early twentieth centuries. These sites are situated on gravel and contain few material culture remains.

CAPE HAVEN WHALING STATION (KfDb-1)   The whaling and trading station known to Inuit as *Singaijaq*, on the south side of William Peninsula near Cape Haven, Cyrus Field Bay, was visited briefly at the end of August in a helicopter survey. This site was inspected several years ago by Douglas Stenton, accompanied by Iqaluit elders. Our visit provides further documentation of this important site, which was occupied by various Scottish and English whaling concerns during the late ninteenth and early twentieth centuries. The site covers several hundred square metres of bedrock barely above sea level between a small pond and the sea. Its most obvious features are three huge iron tanks, two large iron kettles, machinery parts, pipes, barrel hoop iron of various sizes, and heavy chain. A large building foundation with several construction stages and adjacent slab pavements occupy the centre of the site, flanked by smaller slab and boulder features. A boulder platform has been built up as a high tide dock. European objects of all descriptions and sizes - industrial and domestic - are strewn over the barren bedrock surface, at the bottom of ponds, and in shallow turf deposits in the central occupation area. Most are of European materials and types; but some, like an Inuit-style iron walrus harpoon found on the wave-washed face of the ledge, indicate Inuit influence, if not Inuit origin. The site is covered with wood, consisting of lumber derived from the station buildings and from driftwood, whose deposition pattern suggests that storm seas periodically overwash the site. Great volumes of bone materials, mostly of seal and walrus, but also of whale and caribou, are found throughout the site. The site is extremely productive archaeologically. Our activities were confined to mapping, testing, and sampling small finds. In addition to the European remains, Inuit-style tent rings are found (*Fig. 16*), some of which appear to be outbuildings to the main foundation and may have been occupied by Inuit station employees; other tent rings that occur in the middle of the station "plaza" seem to be post-European Inuit occupations. These rings also contain rich deposits of bone and European artifacts, including trade beads (*Fig. 17*).

As a small, well-preserved whaling station, Cape Haven offers excellent potential for archaeological research, both into the operation of a European commercial establishment and as a locus for European-Inuit contact and cultural exchange. Its value as a research site is greatly enhanced by its small size. Unlike the huge whaling station of Kekkerton, Cape Haven presents a manageable archaeological project and should be excavated in the near future before it is destroyed completely by erosion and submergence. The increasingly rapid rate of erosion of its exposed and thinly buried deposits requires urgent archaeological attention.

Discussion

The 1991 survey programme produced important evidence for Inuit culture history and settlement patterns, new Frobisher mines and coal dumps, and environmental data. The surveys provided an opportunity to determine conservation status and research priority in relation to the goals of the Frobisher project. These results are summarized in the following paragraphs.

Culture History

The new site inventories provide our first view of the history of Inuit occupations in outer Frobisher Bay. In broad profile, this regional history is similar to that known elsewhere in the Eastern Canadian Arctic. Early Paleoeskimo (Pre-Dorset) people probably appeared here first about four thousand years ago. Now their traces are barely detectable, as they consist mainly of eroding remnants of larger sites. The only Pre-Dorset finds recovered are limited to burins from Willows Island 1, Kuyait 1 (H12), and Kamaiyuk (H2). Although the early components of most of these sites have been destroyed by the severe coastal erosion occurring in the East Baffin region over the past several thousand years, finds from Kuyait H12 suggest that intact Pre-Dorset components will eventually be found away from the active shoreline.

Evidence of the transition from Pre-Dorset to Dorset is also noted. In addition to the Cape Sarah Neck 1 site [Fitzhugh 1993b], Minguktoo 2 and Kuyait 1 contain ground and spalled burin-like tools dating to the Independence II/Groswater Dorset period *ca.* 3000-2500 B.P. From slightly later times, Early Dorset finds (ca. 2500-2000

B.P.) occur at a small but growing number of sites (Kuyait, Kamaiyuk, and Minguktoo). These collections are stylistically more closely related to Central Arctic Southampton Island T1 Early Dorset than to Labrador Early Dorset.

Middle Dorset sites of the period 2000-1500 B.P. are rare, judging from the complete absence of "type-fossils" like tip-fluted endblades and nephrite burin-like tools. However, during Late Dorset times, outer Frobisher Bay had a large Dorset population whose economy included caribou, walrus, seal, and possibly whale; baleen is frequently found in Dorset middens of this period. In addition to occasional large concave-base bifacial endblades, Late Dorset sites display a high frequency of small, delicate, serrated-edge points and have a delicate, miniaturized lithic industry. Although as yet undated radiometrically, the Late Dorset component appears to date to *ca.* 1500-800 B.P. Stylistically and in terms of lithic usage, these collections relate more closely to the Central Arctic than to Labrador. In all the Dorset material collected in 1991 only one flake of Labrador Ramah chert was found. All the burins in these assemblages were standard unspalled Late Dorset notched and ground forms.

Early Thule culture remains are present at Kuyait (H3, 8, 12) and Kamaiyuk (H1, 2). Our collections from these houses contain many Thule finds, but only from secondary context; the only Thule horizon identified was a disturbed remnant of an early floor in Kuyait H3. To date, no intact sod houses of Thule age have been located; nor have we identified any clearly prehistoric Thule summer or fall camps. Although Thule was present in the outer bay, apparently in smaller numbers than in Iqaluit (where whale hunting was more productive), this occupation intensity is difficult to assess because its winter sites have been disturbed by subsequent building phases. Lacking positive geological uplift and an abundance of site locales with adequate sod and turf development, outer bay Inuit have had a long tradition of reoccupying and remodelling older house pits whose thick anthropogenic turf and existing sod and rock walls facilitated house construction.

Yet, even considering the remodelling of Thule settlements, the lack of prehistoric Thule middens and summer camps gives the appearance of an increase in the size and number of houses beginning in the early historic period, *ca.* sixteenth/seventeenth centuries. This suggests a Thule population expansion of Inuit settlement in the outer bay about the time of the Frobisher voyages. Best documented the Inuit sod-house village at Kamaiyuk in 1578. Nearly all the historic period sod houses sampled at Kuyait and Kamaiyuk contain Frobisher remains - most commonly roof tile, flint, coal, and green-glazed stove tile scavenged from Kodlunarn Island, and small amounts of scrap iron. The latter may have been obtained as drift from the Davis Strait whale fishery. Inuit continued to live in the area from the sixteenth century to the present, even continuing to occupy single and bilobate earth-covered winter dwellings into the twentieth century. This is despite the fact that, for a period in the late nineteenth century, Hall reported sod houses had gone out of fashion and only snowhouse winter dwellings were being used. Throughout this period Inuit maintained their traditional life, primarily as walrus, seal, and caribou hunters. Whales rarely visit this area of Frobisher Bay. The relative scarcity of trade goods suggests little contact with Europeans in outer Frobisher Bay from the late sixteenth to mid-nineteenth century.

The supply of European goods reaching Frobisher Bay seems to have been extremely limited throughout this period. This pattern did not change until after 1850, when whalers, including the *George Henry*, (and Hall) began providing Inuit with massive amounts of foreign goods. This impact is clearly seen in our collections from Kuyait H12, Hall Peninsula 1 (Kussejeerarkjuan), and George Henry Island 1. These goods were obtained both through direct contact and employment at whaling stations (e.g. Singaijak/Cape Haven 1). Sabine Peninsula 1 and Cape True (which we were unable to visit in 1991) also provided access to whaling contacts. After the departure of the whalers, these stations continued to supply Inuit with European goods until the present-day.

Frobisher sites

Our 1991 work located several new sites that we attribute to the Frobisher voyages, and expanded knowledge of others. Donald Hogarth's work at the Countess of Sussex Mine documents the geology and mining of this large Frobisher mine. Re-survey of the Dyers Sound Mine (Judy Point) added knowledge of this location and its extensive coal/flint deposit but failed to pinpoint its ore source, which may be buried in talus. At Willows (Opingivik) Island we found the remnant of a small coal dump in Anvil Cove which may mark the presence of an unrecorded mine or furnace site. We also found the probable source of the Sussex Island Mine in Beare Sound. Finally, we located the probable source of Frobisher's Smithe Island "silver" mine and the early 1577 black ore mine in Jackman Sound.

Frobisher-Inuit Contact

Even definition of the concept "Frobisher-Inuit contact" is a complicated issue. Clearly there may be relatively little chance of discovering evidence of face-to-face contact, unless we discover the land site occupied by Frobisher's lost sailors of 1576, Inuit victims of the 1577 Bloody Point encounter, or the Englishmen Inuit say were abandoned on Kodlunarn in the fall of 1578. Evidence of "contact" may be defined at several levels: 1) identification of sites where contact occurred; 2) verification of historical records of contact; 3) recovery of data bearing on unrecorded contacts; 4) evidence of Inuit occupations and activities at Kodlunarn or other Frobisher sites (i.e. scavenging and collecting); and 5) recovery and interpretation of Elizabethan materials found in Inuit site contexts. To date, our work has contributed largely to 1) and 5).

In the first category, we have located (but not archaeologically tested) the Bloody Point site in York Sound. This site and the adjacent headland should be investigated, for it might amplify records of that deadly Frobisher-Inuit encounter. While we are not likely to find the boots and arrow-pierced doublets of the "murdered" sailors, nor perhaps anything Elizabethan, the importance of this event is such that this should be pursued. Excavations would also provide information on an early historic Inuit summer camp; such sites are often passed over, as being less productive of artifacts than winter dwelling areas.

The Kuyait and Kamaiyuk excavations provided information on the incorporation of Frobisher materials into Inuit sites and behavioural systems (i.e. point 5). While our excavations to date do not seem to represent intact Frobisher-period house floors, midden levels, or sealed features, a definite pattern has emerged as to kinds of Elizabethan materials present in early historic Inuit houses and their conditions of use and discard:

* No evidence has been found attributable to direct Frobisher-Inuit trade or contact (i.e. intact large items like whole pots, guns, swords, clothing, boat parts, etc.).

* Presence of small finds (consisting of ceramic roof tile, glazed stove tile, European wood, bits of metal, and other items) suggests that the floors excavated post-date the period of direct encounter and Frobisher materials therein result from Inuit scavenging.

* Adaptation to, rather than transference of, European technology and materials is indicated by the uses to which Frobisher materials have been put; e.g. grindstones, polishers, hardwoods to replace traditional softwood implements made of driftwood, and metal to replace stone blades, etc.

* Scavenging of Frobisher sites after 1578, until the virtual exhaustion of all surface finds on Kodlunarn, apparently supplied Frobisher Inuit for years, even centuries. This process continues. In 1981 we met an Inuit group bound for Iqaluit with a boatload of whalebones and grave-goods obtained from early Inuit sites.

* Adaptation to attenuating Frobisher resources is evident as a time-dependent process, in that later house floors appear to have smaller pieces of stove and roof tile than earlier floors. Inuit seem to have lost or discarded larger pieces of these

materials, used mainly for polishing metal ornaments, in early post-Frobisher times than in later times when these materials became scarcer and more difficult to find at Kodlunarn.

From our present data it appears that Frobisher Bay Inuit were introduced at a very early time to European goods and materials; they were also introduced, to a lesser extent, to European ways of behaviour: exploring and mining; brief summer encounters rather than permanent settlement; and interactions characterized by trading, hostage-taking, and fighting. Written evidence suggests that avoidance, not intensive interaction, was the pattern of conduct when the Englishmen were present. Upon their yearly departure, and continuously after 1578, the primary source for the Inuit of European materials - such as abrasive ceramics, hardwood, flint, and coal - seems to have been the caches, house, shops, and other Elizabethan deposits on Kodlunarn Island. Strangely, the abundant deposits of coal, some of which found its way into Inuit sites, apparently were not sources of fuel or ornamentation.

The absence of large objects of Frobisher material culture in the Inuit sites probably results from recycling and attrition of the Frobisher deposits over the years. We may also expect that the larger of the choice materials obtained during, or immediately after, the Frobisher voyages were recycled, re-used, and cannibalized "in hand" or "off site" rather than being discarded in original form in house or midden deposits. The iron blooms are a flagrant exception, probably because bloomery iron in this non-malleable state is virtually useless as a raw material.

Absence of many Frobisher items from Inuit assemblages may also result partly from natural corrosion and decay. Much of the most useful material obtained from trade or scavenging also preserves poorly. Iron (unless thick), wood, bone, leather, and articles of cloth, are all subject to decay; few of these materials were preserved in Frobisher Bay's ubiquitously permafrost-free winter village sites.

Finally, larger regional and social processes, such as trade and exchange, have to be considered in evaluating Frobisher materials recovered at archaeological sites like Kuyait and Kamaiyuk. Many Elizabethan materials obtained by Inuit would have moved rapidly outside the zone of primary acquisition into other regions of Frobisher Bay, and beyond, as Inuit proceeded through their yearly cycle and traded or exchanged materials with other groups. Douglas Stenton recovered fragments of Frobisher stove tiles from Thule villages near Iqaluit. Since showy as well as ordinary materials (like roof tile fragments) would have entered the Inuit social and economic network, the role of outer bay Inuit as middlemen or dealers initiating these transfers has to be considered. Did the availability of Elizabethan material culture create a "bonanza" for Inuit who controlled access to these materials? What new or exotic materials could local Inuit have acquired in exchange for European goods? An immediate question raised by our excavations is whether the apparent increase in population in the outer bay, which seems to begin in the sixteenth century, is related to the Frobisher presence or existence of accessible European material remains at Kodlunarn. These issues call for consideration of the impact of the Frobisher voyages and their aftermath on Inuit society and cultural development in larger regional settings of the Eastern Arctic.

The process of cleaning, conserving, identifying, and analyzing the collections from 1991 should allow us to test these preliminary conclusions. It is premature to judge results from the field until this work has been accomplished. But, by any measure, the 1991 field programme has greatly advanced our ability to study Frobisher and post-Frobisher European-Inuit interaction, culture change, and human-environment interactions.

Climate, Environment, and Subsistence

An important component of the research programme is to use analysis of environmental and ecological data to increase understanding of European-Inuit interaction. Conducted by Anne Henshaw, this work employs systematic examination of "ecofactual" information from sites representing different phases of contact history, *ca.* A.D. 1500 to the present, to monitor Inuit cultural continuity and change through time. Several types of information will be used to study: historical change in Inuit subsistence; procurement strategies; settlement patterns; changes in Inuit bone modification techniques resulting from acquisition of European metal tools, and new hunting methods; and paleoclimate. While most archaeological studies of culture contact have emphasized artifact remains, this work integrates environmental analysis with traditional studies of cultural change and provides a method to examine the different channels through which the acculturation process filters. The study also utilizes local Inuit expertise and knowledge pertaining to human-animal relations and establishes links with Inuit ethnography, oral history, and cultural heritage. The inclusion of a paleoclimate programme involving biological and geophysical studies will provide information on the historical and cultural impact of the Little Ice Age (in which the Frobisher voyages took place) and will shed light on larger questions of culture-climate interaction. [Further discussion of this research is found in Gullason et al., this volume].

Communal House Problem

One of the long-standing problems in the development of recent Inuit culture relates to construction of large communal houses, which are a prominent feature of Labrador and West Greenland archaeological sites. Given the distribution and approximately equivalent dates of Greenland and Labrador communal houses (seventeenth to eighteenth century), their absence in East Baffin [Schledermann 1976] has raised questions about the possibility of a different culture history for East Baffin Inuit. At issue is whether the East Baffin Inuit, who used double- and triple-room winter dwellings, were in communication with Labrador and Greenland Inuit during this period, and whether they participated to the same extent in European contacts that have been proposed as a possible cause for the development of large multi-family domestic organization elsewhere [Taylor 1976; Jordan 1978; Jordan and Kaplan 1980; Kaplan 1983]. Put another way, why is cultural stability in architectural (and possibly social and economic) sectors a distinctive feature of Baffin Inuit in contrast to a more dynamic Greenland and Labrador Inuit history?

In 1990 we tentatively identified Kamaiyuk House 1 as a Labrador-style communal house and in 1991 began excavation there. While this work has not yet been completed, H1 does not appear to be a typical Labrador-style communal structure, i.e. having a continuous multi-family sleeping bench along the rear and sides of the house. Rather, the "communal house" appearance may simply be the result of an atypical construction in which family dwelling alcoves were placed along the rear and side wall of a large rectangular dwelling, rather than in the typical East Baffin double- or triple-room form. These changes may simply reflect the availability of long timbers and roof beams rather than different economic or sociological structure. Further investigation of this problem was to continue in 1992.

Site Conservation Issues

As noted previously, the entire outer region of Frobisher Bay is undergoing gradual geological submergence as a "hinge-effect" related to isostasy following the melting of continental glaciers. The rapidity of submergence in the outer coast is striking and seems to be accelerating. Witness to this effect is everywhere apparent. Artifacts like the Lookout Island bloom were about to be washed into the sea from a campsite occupied in 1860. Even recently occupied twentieth century sites are affected.

Conservation status of the sites studied in 1991 is indicated in Table 4. Such designations are difficult to assign because priorities vary according to site potential, uniqueness, and the research mission at hand. In terms of the Frobisher project goals, the most serious erosional problems are at Kodlunarn Island (due to uniqueness; *Fig. 18*) and at Kamaiyuk, which has the greatest potential for recovering artifacts and materials relating to Frobisher-Inuit relationships, but is being severely eroded by wind, ice, and waves (*Fig. 19*). Part of this site is now underwater at high tide, and the sea has destroyed the entrance passages and much of the front walls of all six houses. Evidence of vandalism was also noted.

Figure 18: Remains of a recent historic Inuit tent ring at the northwest edge of "Best's Bulwark" show the rapid pace of erosion on the exposed south side of Kodlunarn Island. Nearby, midden remains from the Frobisher smithy structure have been under active erosion for years.

Figure 19: Winter ice and fall storms, combined with coastal submergence, have destroyed the entrance passages and parts of the house fronts at Kamaiyuk (visited and described by George Best in 1577). Excavation in the interiors of these houses was completed in 1992.

Other unique or extremely important sites that are threatened include the Cape Haven whaling station, the Lookout Island bloom site, the early Dorset components at Minguktoo 2, and the late Dorset site Willows Island 2. Frobisher sites threatened, in addition to those on Kodlunarn Island, are the Anvil Cove coal deposit (which may contain other Frobisher materials) and the (Sussex Island?) mine site newly-found at Lefferts Island in Beare Sound.

With these comments in mind and recognizing that the outermost coast is sinking most rapidly, future surveys are needed in the vicinity of Hall Island, Osbon Bay, Kane Channel, and other locations in eastern Loks Land where Frobisher may have made landfall and first contact with Inuit. Loks Land was a favourite Inuit settlement area which, according to oral history given to Hall, was abandoned by the Inuit after their villages there were destroyed and people died in a natural disaster - most likely an earthquake and tidal wave that probably occurred in the early 1800s. This area could not be approached by boat in 1991 because of heavy pack ice.

ACKNOWLEDGEMENTS: Project personnel in 1991 included eleven members of the scientific team and five others whose main responsibilities were to operate the *R. V. Pitsiulak* and support the surveys and shore camp activities. Lynda Gullason and Anne Henshaw co-directed excavations at Kuyait and Kamaiyuk. Other members of the scientific team included Réginald Auger, Michael Bradford, Kim Gardner, Dosia Laeyendecker, Daniel Odess, Patrick Saltonstall, Edmund Searles, and Jeanette Smith. This "land crew" was assisted by Ooleetoa Pishuktie of Iqaluit. The "boat crew" of Perry Colbourne, Sophie Morse, Pauloosie Pishuktie, and Juta Ipeelie performed major and minor miracles that ensured project success and safety. Adjunct scientific personnel also made important contributions. Donald Hogarth and Davin Ala spent most of August researching Frobisher mines and assisting the site excavations. Darrell Kaufman and Bill Manley conducted quaternary geological surveys. Important logistic and material assistance was provided by the Iqaluit Research Centre directed by Bob Longworth. Bill McKenzie provided equipment storage, transportation, materiel, and advice. Community support and logistics were provided: by Mary Ellen Thomas, Christina Tikivik, Jacoboosie Peter, Harry Kilabuk, Brian Faddegon, Brian Pearson; by Arctic College staff Trish Lewis, Lynne Mauss, Bert Rose, and Douglas Stenton; and by Denise Bekkema of the Nunatta Sunaqutangit. Media representatives Ted Timreck and Will Goetzman assisted with film documentation, and Malcolm Billings prepared a BBC World Service report. Inuit visitors provided much valuable information and assistance.

Funding support for the project came from a variety of sources. The Scholarly Studies Program of the Smithsonian provided a major grant, which was supplemented by support from the Arctic Studies Center. The Smithsonian also provided field equipment, lab facilities, radiocarbon dating, photographic, and other research services. The

University of Massachusetts, through the offices of Stearns A. Morse, maintained the loan of the *Pitsiulak* to the project. Material support also came in the form of field equipment and shipping from the Canadian Museum of Civilization. CMC also provided funding assistance to Lynda Gullason, Réginald Auger, Donald Hogarth, and Susan Rowley. Polar Continental Shelf donated an air charter flight; Canada Manpower, funds for hiring Kim Gardner. Field work grants were provided to Anne Henshaw by the Canadian Embassy in Washington, Wenner Gren Foundation, and Harvard University. As noted above, important support was received from the Iqaluit Research Centre, the Iqaluit Town Council, and many other institutions, groups, and individuals in Iqaluit.

References

Auger, Réginald
  1991   *Labrador Inuit and Europeans in the Strait of Belle Isle: from the Written Sources to the Archeological Evidence.* N. 55, Collection Nordicanal, Centre d'études nordiques. Québec: Université Laval.

  1993   Sixteenth century ceramics from Kodlunarn Island. In *Archeology of the Frobisher Voyages*, ed. W. Fitzhugh and J. Olin, 147-54. Washington: Smithsonian Institution Press.

Best, George
  1578   *A True Discourse of the Late Voyages of Discoverie ... Under the Conduct of Martin Frobisher Generall ....* London. (Reprinted in Stefansson 1938)

Boas, Franz
  1888   The central Eskimo. *Sixth Annual Report of the Bureau of Ethnology*, 399-666. Washington: Smithsonian Institution, Bureau of Ethnology.

Cheshire, Neil, Tony Waldron, Alison Quinn, and David Quinn
  1980   Frobisher's Eskimos in England. *Archivaria* 10:23-50.

Collins, Henry B.
  1950   Excavations at Frobisher Bay, Baffin Island, N.W.T.: a preliminary report. In *Annual Report of the National Museum for the Fiscal Year 1948-1949.* National Museum of Canada Bulletin 118:18-43.

Collinson, R., ed.
  1867   *The Three Voyages of Martin Frobisher in Search of a Passage to Cathaia and India by the North-west, A.D. 1576-8.* Hakluyt Society Publications, 1st ser., vol. 38.

Ellis, Thomas
   1578   *A True Report of the Third and Last Voyage into Meta Incognita: Achieved by the
               Worthie Capteine, M. Martine Frobisher Esquire, Anno 1578.*   London.
               (Reprinted in Stefansson 1938)

Fitzhugh, William W
   1985a   Early contacts north of Newfoundland before A.D. 1600.   In *Cultures in
               Contact*, 23-44. Washington: Smithsonian Institution Press.

   1985b   *Cultures in Contact: the Impact of European Contacts on Native American
               Cultural Institutions, A.D. 1000-1800.*   (editor). Washington: Smithsonian
               Institution Press.

   1989   Archeology of the Frobisher voyages: Kodlunarn Island and European-Inuit
               contact (I). Proposal to Smithsonian Scholarly Studies Program.

   1990a   Archeology of the Frobisher voyages ... (II). Proposal to Smithsonian Scholarly
               Studies Program.

   1990b   Archeology of the Frobisher voyages: field report for 1990. Arctic Studies
               Center, Smithsonian Institution. October.

   1993a   Archeology of Kodlunarn Island. In *Archeology of the Frobisher Voyages*, ed.
               W. Fitzhugh and J. Olin, 58-97. Washington: Smithsonian Institution Press.

   1993b   Field surveys in Outer Frobisher Bay. In *Archeology of the Frobisher Voyages*,
               ed. W. Fitzhugh and J. Olin, 98-136. Washington: Smithsonian Institution
               Press.

Fitzhugh, William W. and Jacqueline Olin, eds.
   1993   *Archeology of the Frobisher Voyages.* Washington: Smithsonian Institution
               Press.

Gullov, Hans Christian
   1985   Whales, whalers, and Eskimos: the impact of European whaling on the
               demography and economy of Eskimo society in West Greenland. In: *Cultures
               in Contact*, ed. W. Fitzhugh, 71-96. Washington: Smithsonian Institution Press.

Hall, Charles Francis
   1865   *Arctic Researches and Life Among the Esquimaux.* New York: Harper and
               Brothers.

Harbottle, Garman, Richard Cresswell, and Raymond W. Stoenner
   1993   Carbon-14 dating of the Kodlunarn Island iron blooms. In *Archeology of the
               Frobisher Voyages*, ed. W. Fitzhugh and J. Olin, 173-80. Washington:
               Smithsonian Institution Press.

Hogarth, Donald
1989   The *Emanuel* of Bridgewater and discovery of Martin Frobisher's "black ore" in Ireland. *The American Neptune* 49(1): 14-20.

Hogarth, Donald, and W.A. Gibbins
1984   Martin Frobisher's "gold mines" on Kodlunarn Island and adjacent Baffin Island, Frobisher Bay, NWT. *Contributions to the Geology of the Northwest Territories*, 1, INAC, EGS 1984-6, pp. 69-78.

Hogarth, Donald, and J. Loop
1986   Precious metals in Martin Frobisher's "black ores" in Frobisher Bay, Northwest Territories. *Canadian Mineralogist* 24:259-263.

Hogarth, Donald, and J.C. Roddick
1989   Discovery of Martin Frobisher's Baffin Island "ore" in Ireland. *Canadian Journal of Earth Sciences* 26:1053-60.

Jacobs, John D.
1985   Environment and prehistory, Baffin Island. In *Quaternary Environments: Baffin Island, Baffin Bay, and West Greenland*, ed. J. Andrews, 719-40. Winchester (Mass.): Allen and Unwin.

Jacobs, John D., W. N. Mode, C.A. Squires, and G.H. Miller
1985   Holocene environmental change in the Frobisher Bay area, Baffin Island, N.W.T.: deglaciation, emergence, and the sequence of vegetation and climate. *Geographie Physique et Quaternaire* 39(2): 151-162.

Jacobs, John D., and Douglas Stenton
1985   Environment, resources, and prehistoric settlement in upper Frobisher Bay, Baffin Island. *Arctic Anthropology* 22(2): 59-76.

Jordan, Richard H.
1978   Archeological investigations of the Hamilton Inlet Labrador Eskimo: social and economic responses to European contact. *Arctic Anthropology* 15(2): 175-85.

Jordan, Richard H. and Susan A. Kaplan
1980   An archaeological view of the Inuit/European contact period in Central Labrador. *Etudes/Inuit/Studies* 4(1-2): 35-45.

Kaplan, Susan A.
1983   Economic and social change in Labrador Neo-Eskimo culture. Ph.D. diss., Department of Anthropology, Bryn Mawr College.

1985   European goods and socio-economic change in early Labrador Inuit society. In *Cultures in Contact*, ed. W. Fitzhugh, 45-69. Washington: Smithsonian Institution Press.

Kenyon, Walter A.
1975a   "All is not golde that shineth". *The Beaver*, Summer, 40-46.

1975b   *Tokens of Possession: the Northern Voyages of Martin Frobisher*. Toronto: Royal Ontario Museum.

1980/81   The Canadian Arctic journal of Capt. Edward Fenton, 1578. *Archivaria* 11:171-203.

Maxwell, Moreau
1985   *Prehistory of the Eastern Arctic*. Orlando: Academic Press.

1988   The Crystal II site: the Dorset component. Frobisher Bay, Baffin Island, N.W.T., Canada. Manuscript.

McFee, William
1928   *The Life of Sir Martin Frobisher*. New York and London: Bodley Head.

Rowley, Susan
1993   Frobisher *miksanut*: Inuit accounts of the Frobisher voyages. In *Archeology of the Frobisher Voyages*, ed. W. Fitzhugh and J. Olin, 27-40. Washington: Smithsonian Institution Press.

Sabo, George
1991   *Thule Culture Adaptations on the South Coast of Baffin Island, N.W.T.* New York and London: Garland Press.

Sayre Edward V., Garman Harbottle, Raymond W. Stoenner, Wilcomb Washburn, Jacqueline S. Olin, and William Fitzhugh
1982   The carbon-14 dating of an iron bloom associated with the voyages of Martin Frobisher. In *Nuclear Dating Techniques*, ed. L. Currie, 441-51. ACS Symposium Series, 1976. Washington: American Chemical Society.

Schledermann, Peter
1975   *Thule Eskimo Prehistory of Cumberland Sound, Baffin Island, Canada*. National Museum of Man, Mercury Series, Archaeological Survey of Canada Paper 38.

1976   The effect of climatic/ecological changes on the style of Thule culture winter dwellings. *Arctic and Alpine Research* 8(1): 37-47.

Settle, Dionyse
1577   *A True Reporte of the Laste Voyage into the West and Northwest Regions, etc.
            1577, Worthily Achieved by Capteine Frobisher of the Sayde Voyage the First
            Finder and Generall.* London. (Reprinted in Stefansson 1938)

Skelton, R.A., Thomas Marston, and George D. Painter
1965   *The Vinland Map and the Tartar Relation.* New Haven and London: Yale
            University Press.

Smithsonian Institution
1873   [Report on Charles Francis Hall research] Report of the Secretary. *Smithsonian
            Institution Annual Report for 1871*, p. 32.

Stefansson, Vilhjalmur, and Eloise McCaskill, eds.
1938   *The Three Voyages of Martin Frobisher in Search of a Passage to Cathay and
            India by the North-west, A.D. 1576-8.* 2 vols. London: Argonaut Press.

Stenton, Douglas
1987   Recent archaeological investigations in Frobisher Bay, Baffin Island, N.W.T.
            Canadian Journal of Archaeology 11:13-48.

1989   Terrestrial adaptations of Neo-Eskimo coastal-marine hunters on southern Baffin
            Island, N.W.T. Ph.D. diss., University of Alberta.

1991   Caribou population dynamics and Thule culture adaptation on southern Baffin
            Island, N.W.T. *Arctic Anthropology* 28(2): 15-43.

Strong, Duncan
1927-29   Rawson-MacMillan expedition field notes, Aug. 23-4, 1927. National
            Anthropological Achives, Smithsonian Institution.

1927   The Rawson-MacMillan arctic expedition of Field Museum, *Science* 66(30 Sept.):
            295

1929   [Report of Duncan Strong concerning Kodlunarn Island and Labrador research],
            Annual Report of the Director for Year 1928, FMNH Bulletin 7(3): 417-423

Sturtevant, William C. and David B. Quinn
1987   This new prey: Eskimos in Europe in 1567, 1576, and 1577. In: *Indians and
            Europe: an Interdisciplinary Collection of Essays*, ed. C. Feest, 61-140. Aachen:
            Ed. Herodot Rader Verlag.

Taylor, J. Garth
1976   The Inuit middleman in the Labrador baleen trade. Paper presented at the 75th
            Annual Meeting of the American Anthropological Association, Washington D.C.

Unglik, Henry
1993   Metallurgical study of an iron bloom and associated finds from Kodlunarn Island. In *Archeology of the Frobisher Voyages*, ed. W. Fitzhugh and J. Olin, 181-212. Washington: Smithsonian Institution Press.

Wayman, M.L. and R.M. Ehrenreich
1993   Metallurgical study of small iron finds. In *Archeology of the Frobisher Voyages*, ed. W. Fitzhugh and J. Olin, 213-20. Washington: Smithsonian Institution Press.

Acculturation in the Arctic:
The Inuit Meet Martin Frobisher

Robert M. Ehrenreich
National Materials Advisory Board
National Research Council

Michael L. Wayman
Department of Mining, Metallurgical, and Petroleum Engineering
University of Alberta

RÉSUMÉ

Les expéditions de Martin Frobisher à l'île de Baffin entre 1576 et 1578 constituent le premier contact connu que les Inuit ont eu avec les Européens. Bien que les documents historiques témoignent que les échanges ont surtout été marqués par le vandalisme et les prises d'otages, les conséquences qui en ont découlé sur les deux cultures en contact ont laissé des traces dans le folklore local et les journaux occidentaux. On a trouvé, au cours de fouilles récentes, du métal venu d'Europe au centre de cercles de tentes indigènes qui dateraient du XVIe siècle, ce qui confirme que les Inuit avaient obtenu des objets de fonte soit en dévalisant les Européens, soit en faisant du troc avec des membres des expéditions. L'article étudie l'ampleur réelle des interactions entre les cultures concernées, se fondant sur l'examen des pièces métalliques archéologiques pour interpréter les légendes inuit et les documents historiques.

ABSTRACT

Frobisher's expeditions to Baffin Island between 1576 and 1578 mark the Inuit's first known encounter with Europeans. Although historical records state that interaction was predominantly confined to scavenging and hostage-taking, the effect on both cultures is evident in local folklore and western journals. The discovery, during recent excavations, of European-derived iron within apparently sixteenth century indigenous tent rings confirms that Inuit were obtaining smelted metal either by ransacking European sites or trading with the expeditions. This paper explores the actual extent of interaction between these cultures, using the examination of archaeological ironwork to elucidate Inuit legend and historical record.

Introduction

The expeditions of Martin Frobisher to Baffin Island between 1576 and 1578 mark the earliest encounters between Inuit and European. Although the annals of history report little interaction between the cultures - and, when there was contact, it was punctuated by severe mistrust - the effects are clearly evident in the folklore of the Inuit and the journals of the explorers. Among the Inuit, tales of the Europeans and place-names like Kodlunarn Island - Kodlunat being the Inuktitut term for Europeans and Americans [Rowley 1993] - have been passed down from generation to generation. For the Europeans, the impact of the encounters is evident in the voyagers' journals, the English artwork of the period, and the fact that actual Inuit were taken to England by the explorers.

Until recently, a methodology was not available for studying the types of interaction that actually took place between the cultures. However, the survey of the region by a joint American-Canadian archaeological team over the past two years has resulted in the discovery of apparently European-derived materials, including iron, in early Inuit tent-rings, confirming that the Inuit obtained artifacts from the Frobisher expeditions and that some interaction occurred. This article will explore the types of interaction that took place between these cultures, using the historical evidence as a base and the preliminary analysis of the few pieces of archaeological ironwork discovered to help elucidate the evidence of Inuit legends and explorers' journals.

Historical Evidence

The historical evidence encompasses two main sources: the explorers' own accounts, the most complete of which was written by George Best, Frobisher's lieutenant on the first two voyages and captain of the *Anne Frances* on the third; and Inuit traditional lore, which was first recorded by Charles Francis Hall [1865] during his stay in the region between 1860 and 1862.

The Explorers' Journals

Although the mariners described many aspects of the voyages in great detail, only cursory accounts were given of contact with the Inuit. Interaction appears to have been mostly limited to gift-giving and hostage-taking. Only for the first voyage does Best mention trade: "[H]e had sundry conferences with them, and they came aboard his ship and brought him salmon and raw flesh and fish .... They exchanged coats of seal and bearskins and such like with our men and received bells, looking glasses, and other toys in recompense thereof again" [Stefansson and McCaskill 1938, 1:49]. Most direct contact ceased, however, when, as Best states: "After great courtesy, and many meetings, our mariners, contrary to their Captain's direction, began more easily to trust them, and five of our men going ashore, were by them intercepted with their boat, and were never since heard of to this day again" [Stefansson and McCaskill 1938, 1:49]. During the final two voyages, face-to-face contact with the Inuit was limited to battles and ploys for obtaining hostages. Best states that gifts of "points" and trinkets were still given to try to coerce the Inuit to return the men [Stefansson and McCaskill 1938, 1:67], but the gifts were now left in the deserted Inuit settlements after the inhabitants had been driven away. Although Best does not describe these "points" in any detail, they are of relevance in conjunction with an arrowhead recovered from Kodlunarn Island which will be discussed later.

Inuit scavenging of Frobisher sites is also alluded to in the journals. Frobisher's lieutenant-general, Edward Fenton, captain of the ship the *Judith*, reported on the third Frobisher voyage that: "upon that island we found certain osmonds of iron carried thither by the people of the country" [Harbottle et al. 1993]. Scavenging was neither exhaustive nor comprehensive, however, and similar objects were untouched on other occasions: "we went to the countess island...wherein our judgments all things remained as we left them in so much as we found diverse osmonds which we left uncovered lying in this place untouched by the people" [Harbottle et al. 1993]. Thus, artifacts such as iron blooms, referred to here as osmonds, were only periodically found and taken by the Inuit. It should also be noted that periodic scavenging continued long after the voyages as well. Hall found that Inuit women were still using Frobisher bricks for polishing brass ornaments in the nineteenth century [Hall 1865, 277].

Inuit Folklore

Inuit folklore is unfortunately not as complete as the English journals, and Hall's record of it is biased by his main objective, which was to show that the fate of survivors of lost Arctic explorations could still be learned long after their demise. The method by which the tales were passed down the generations was eloquently described by one Inuit as: "When our baby boy gets old enough, we tell him all about you, and about all those kodlunas who brought brick, iron, and coal to where you have been, and of the kodlunas who built a ship on Kodlunarn Island...when boy gets to be an old Inuit he tell it to other Inuit, and so all Inuit will know what we now know" [Hall 1865, 445].

The tale of greatest concern to Hall dealt with the fate of the five captured crewmen. Inuit lore states that they wintered on Kodlunarn Island and then, the following spring, three of the men built a ship in a trench on Kodlunarn while the other two watched, according to one Inuit, "all same as captains" [Hall 1865, 473]. The Inuit supposedly did not assist in the building of the ship, but did help put it to sea. The masts were erected at a cliff near Kodlunarn Island, which is still called by the Inuktitut term for "place where a mast is put up" [Rowley 1993]. Before the kodlunat departed, the Inuit sang a song wishing them quick passage and much joy. Unfortunately, the five men attempted to depart too early in the season and were forced back by storms and frozen hands. Lore states that the Inuit built them igloos and brought them food, but they all perished.

The second tale of interest to Hall concerned the "heavy stone" brought by the explorers. The Inuit spoke of two types: a smaller, rougher variety and a larger, smoother one which even the strongest Inuit could lift but to the knees. The smaller type was identified as the iron blooms described in Fenton's journal. The larger type, used by younger Inuit as a test of strength and many others as a seat, was an anvil [Hall 1865, 452]. It transpired that the Inuit had later tumbled the anvil into the sea, believing that it was adversely affecting their hunting.

Other tales recorded in less detail concerned: the kodlunat's first arrival in two boats, then three boats, then many boats, which is accurate, with roughly thirteen ships having arrived in the last year; the five Inuit killed in a battle with the explorers; and the four Inuit taken by the explorers back to England and never returned. Although these tales are corroborated by western accounts, Hall's limited interest in them restricted the data accumulated.

It can be seen in both the historical records and the Inuit folklore that interaction between the cultures was limited and uneasy. There was deep mistrust on both sides, and for reason. Yet some contact did occur, even if only gift-giving and scavenging. Thus, the archaeological record requires further examination to clarify what occurred and to help us learn more about the process of acculturation. However, before these interactions can be discussed, the previous indigenous metals system of the region must first be defined.

Metalworking in the Arctic

Although not smelters of metal, the Arctic people coldworked iron and copper as early as 800 BC. In fact, the quantity of metals used was such that McGhee [1984, 15] has stated that Thule society of A.D. 1000-1600 was "with little exaggeration, an Iron Age culture". McCartney [1992] portrays the Arctic inhabitants as having an epi-metallurgical, socio-political, societal structure, meaning that it had all the aspects of a metal-based society - such as a reliance on metals, a well-established exchange system, and an associated status to the material - even though they did not produce the metal from raw ores.

Iron entered the Arctic exchange network from three primary sources. The first source was meteoritic iron [Wayman 1988]. Meteoritic iron artifacts have been found in archaeological site contexts throughout the Eastern Arctic, from Greenland to Hudson Bay. Small flakes of iron, suitable for use in blades, were created and detached from the surface of meteorites by laboriously pounding with hammerstones. The main source of meteoritic iron was the Cape York region of northwest Greenland, which provided at least 58 tons, but smaller falls may have provided additional material for use throughout the Arctic.

The second source of iron was native, or telluric, iron associated with the basalt outcrops of the west coast of Greenland [Wayman 1988]. The Arctic inhabitants crushed the basalt, removed the coin-sized flakes of iron contained, and coldworked the metal into appropriate artifacts. Buchwald and Mosdal [1985] catalogued at least ten knives and one harpoon point dating from before A.D. 1650 that were made from native iron.

The final form of iron used was smelted wrought iron, which entered the Arctic exchange network via indirect contact [Wayman 1988]. Fragments of iron entered the region in driftwood at least as early as the coming of the Norse to Greenland in A.D. 985; it may also have been traded from Siberian sources, via Alaska, at about the same time. Although rare, wrought iron artifacts have been discovered in site contexts dating from the past one thousand years as far south as northwestern Hudson Bay and as far north as Cornwallis and Ellesmere Islands.

Results of Metallurgical Analysis of Recovered Ironwork

The survey of Countess of Warwick Sound in August 1990 by the joint American-Canadian archaeological team yielded the first ironwork *from Inuit contexts* thought to be contact artifacts from the Frobisher expeditions. Previously, four iron blooms had been discovered, but these were from Frobisher contexts [Unglik 1993]. The iron artifacts found during the 1990 field season were recovered from Inuit tent rings and comprised an arrowhead, a bloom, a wedge, and a flake. The arrowhead was a surface find discovered in the remains of an Inuit tent ring on the west side of Kodlunarn. The bloom and flake were recovered from a tent ring on Lookout Island in Cyrus Field Bay, fifteen miles north of Kodlunarn. The bloom appears to have been cold hammered in a futile attempt to work it and the flake was detached from the bloom during this process.

The wedge was a surface find in a tent ring on Tikkoon Point; also found at that site were pieces of Frobisher tile, chert flakes, a cut iron nail, and a percussion cap. The rest of this structure has not yet been excavated.

The Prince of Wales Northern Heritage Centre in Yellowknife permitted the arrowhead and wedge to be metallurgically examined to assist in the determination of whether the artifacts were actually Frobisher contact materials and whether they were fabricated by European blacksmiths or local Inuit. Identification of the fabricators is useful, since it may shed some light on whether the artifacts were made from scavenged materials or were trade items. If the microstructure of the artifacts showed that they were heavily coldworked, then they were more probably fabricated by the Inuit and produced from items scavenged from Frobisher sites. Whereas if the microstructure of the artifacts showed that they were hotworked or cast, then they were definitely fabricated by Europeans and most probably traded or given as gifts by the explorers. This is especially important for the arrowhead discovered on Kodlunarn, since this could have been one of the "points" mentioned by Best and alluded to earlier in this article.

Unfortunately, the metallurgical evidence cannot categorically determine the sources and dates of the ironwork [Wayman and Ehrenreich 1993]. The arrowhead was made of wrought iron typical of that produced over three millennia in many parts of the world; thus, it is not possible to speculate on when the iron was smelted or the artifact forged. The wedge was a grey cast iron and, again, is consistent with Elizabethan cast iron as well as more recent cast irons. Thus, there is nothing in the microstructure of the material that could unambiguously associate it with, or dissociate it from, the Elizabethan period and England, although our analysis does categorically show that it was not made by the Inuit.

Minor element concentrations of the artifacts do tenuously link these artifacts with Frobisher blooms, however. The arrowhead and wedge have high phosphorus contents similar to the iron blooms previously recovered from Frobisher contexts [Unglik 1993]. Various, but not all, iron ores contain phosphorus contents sufficient to produce such artifacts, and England has two major sources of this ore type. Thus, their high phosphorus contents and similarity to the blooms are not inconsistent with the suggestion that the arrowhead and wedge might have originated in England and were transported to Kodlunarn by the Frobisher expeditions.

The artifacts' microstructures provided more convincing evidence of the fabricators of the objects [Wayman and Ehrenreich 1993]. The wedge was in the as-cast condition and, as such, could not have been made, or even mechanically worked, by the Inuit. The arrowhead is in the hotworked condition, with little or no coldworking having been done in the final shaping. The arrowhead does have a slight curvature, which might suggest that it was produced from a previous object; but the fact that the microstructure shows it to be in the hotworked condition is not consonant with the possibility that the arrowhead was made by the Inuit. The Inuit are not believed to have used hotworking technology, and most of their artifacts have grain structures that are heavily coldworked. Thus, it seems probable that the arrowhead was made by European blacksmiths.

To summarize the results of the metallurgical examination: the arrowhead and wedge have compositions and microstructures that neither definitely ascribe them to, nor unequivocally exclude them from, the Elizabethan period. The grain structures imply that neither were manufactured by the Inuit, however, and that both were most likely imported. The high phosphorus contents may intimate that the artifacts were English in origin, but the evidence is far from conclusive [Wayman and Ehrenreich 1993].

Conclusions

This preliminary study presents three issues. First, it stresses most emphatically that more research is required. Excavation of blacksmithing sites on Kodlunarn Island, further surveys of Inuit settlement sites and Frobisher mines on outlying islands, and more analyses of ironwork and ironworking residues are required to identify the metals and metalworking techniques used by the Frobisher expeditions; the object being to be able to identify Elizabethan materials when found on Inuit sites, and to determine the extent of Inuit reworking and scavenging of iron. Only in this manner can we clarify the types of contact that occurred between European and Inuit, and advance our understanding of both the effects of these contacts and the method of acculturation of foreign materials by the Inuit.

Second, this preliminary study corroborates the explorers' written records concerning the giving of gifts. Although only tenuously linked to the Frobisher voyages, the arrowhead discovered on Kodlunarn Island supports Best's statements in his log that "points" were given to the Inuit. Although the true typology of these "points" is actually unknown, the evidence supporting the hypothesis that they were arrowheads is: 1) the microstructure of the recovered arrowhead suggests that it was not produced by the Inuit, and therefore was imported; 2) the location of the arrowhead in a tent ring implies that it belonged to the local population, although the date of the tent ring is uncertain, since no associated artifacts were discovered by which to date it; and 3) the "point", as referred to by Best, was a particular artifact type which was not a knife, since Best also mentions knives in his journal [Stefansson and McCaskill 1938, 1:116]. It would also seem reasonable for an artifact like an arrowhead, or "point", to be commonly traded by Europeans because it was small and simple to produce, but still of real value to the Inuit. Thus, the correlation of the arrowhead with the "point" mentioned in the explorers' journals strongly supports the explorers' assertions that finished artifacts were being obtained by the Inuit via direct contact.

Third, the preliminary data presented here shows that iron was not always acquired by the Inuit simply as a source of new stock. The history of the blooms and the anvil shows that iron obtained from the Frobisher voyages could be deemed worthless or socially significant depending on the artifact. The blooms were thought to be "heavy stones", which were not consistently collected and were apparently not exploited as a source of iron. This may have been because they were not recognized as containing iron, or because the Inuit did not have the capability to complete the processing necessary to produce useful iron objects from the raw material. The raw product of the direct smelting of iron is an amorphous lump of slag and metal which must be repeatedly heated and hammered to expel the slag and form a coherent piece of iron. The blooms brought by the explorers were not finished and thus the iron was hidden in a mass of slag [Ehrenreich 1993]. The one bloom that was found to have been cold hammered on Lookout Island shows that some Inuit were curious about the "heavy stone", but that they could not make use of the iron contained within it.

The anvil demonstrates that iron could also gain social significance. The anvil could have been an invaluable resource. The same techniques used to produce the small blades of meteoritic iron described earlier could have been used to detach iron flakes from the anvil as well. However, the anvil was left intact and remained within the Inuit culture as an integral part of the tales about the kodlunat, a vehicle for the display of physical prowess, and a seat for important Inuit, until roughly two hundred and fifty years after the expeditions, when it was finally tumbled into the sea because of a belief that it was adversely affecting hunting--an ultimate demonstration of its profound impact on, and perceived importance to, the society. Thus, ironwork could acquire significant social value within Inuit society as well as just being a source of material.

References

Buchwald, V.F., and G. Mosdal
  1985   Meteoritic iron, telluric iron and wrought iron in Greenland. *Meddelelser om Gronland, Man and Society*, no. 9.

Ehrenreich, R.M.
  1993   An evaluation of the Frobisher iron blooms. In *Archeology of the Frobisher Voyages*, ed. W. Fitzhugh and J. Olin, 221-30. Washington: Smithsonian Institution Press.

Hall, C.F.
  1865   *Arctic Researches and Life Among the Esquimaux*. New York: Harper and
           Brothers.

Harbottle, G., Cresswell, R., and R.W. Stoenner
  1993   Carbon-14 dating of the Kodlunarn Island iron blooms.   In *Archeology of the
           Frobisher Voyages*, ed. W. Fitzhugh and J. Olin, 173-80. Washington: Smithsonian
           Institution Press.

McCartney, A.P.
  1992   Canadian Arctic trade metal: reflections of prehistoric to historic social networks.
           In *Metals in Society: Theory Beyond Analysis*, ed. R.M. Ehrenreich. Philadelphia:
           MASCA.

McGhee, R.
  1984   Contact between Native North Americans and the medieval Norse: a review of the
           evidence. *American Antiquity* 49:4-26.

Rowley, S.
  1993   Frobisher *miksanut*: Inuit accounts of the Frobisher voyages. In *Archeology of the
           Frobisher Voyages*, ed. W. Fitzhugh and J. Olin, 27-40. Washington: Smithsonian
           Institution Press.

Stefansson, V., and E. McCaskill, eds.
  1938   *The Three Voyages of Martin Frobisher: in Search of a Passage to Cathay and India
           by the North-west, A.D. 1576-8*. 2 vols. London: Argonaut Press.

Unglik, H.
  1993   Metallurgical study of an iron bloom and associated finds from Kodlunarn Island.
           In *Archeology of the Frobisher Voyages* ed. W. Fitzhugh and J. Olin, 181-212.
           Washington: Smithsonian Institution Press.

Wayman, M.L.
  1988   The early use of iron in Arctic North America. *Journal of Metals* 40 (September):
           44-45.

Wayman, M.L., and R.M. Ehrenreich
  1993   Metallurgical study of small iron finds. In *Archeology of the Frobisher Voyages*,
           ed. W. Fitzhugh and J. Olin, 213-20. Washington: Smithsonian Institution Press.

Martin Frobisher's Mines and Ores

Donald D. Hogarth
Department of Geology, University of Ottawa

David T. Moore
(formerly) Department of Mineralogy
The Natural History Museum

Peter W. Boreham
Dartford Borough Museum

RÉSUMÉ

Les carrières de Frobisher, au sud-est de l'Île de Baffin, sont les premières mines de l'Amérique au nord du Mexique. Selon les chiffres officiels, les exportations de minerai vers l'Angleterre étaient, en 1577, de 158 tonnes; en 1578, de 1 136 tonnes. Nous pouvons aujourd'hui situer trois mines avec certitude : les mines *Countess of Warwick*, *Countess of Sussex* et *Winter's Furnace*, toutes trois dans le détroit de Countess of Warwick ou près de cet endroit. Un emplacement possible est aussi connu pour la mine de *Denham's Mount* (baie de Victoria). Trois autres mines ne peuvent être situées qu'approximativement : *Best's Blessing* (île Resolution), *Sussex Island* (détroit de Beare), et *Fenton's Fortune* (détroit de Sabine). Toutes ces mines sont à ciel ouvert, peu profondes, que des ouvriers ont creusé, difficilement, sans l'aide d'explosifs.

Le minerai noir (*black ore*) d'âge protérozoïque se retrouve en minces lambeaux intercalés dans du gneiss à biotite et de l'amphibolite : les uns sont minces, les autres prennent la forme de «boudins», certains sont coupés par des dykes de granite, d'autres enfin sont faillés. À la mine *Countess of Warwick*, le minerai noir en amas dans le noyau des boudins est entouré d'une croûte fissile de matériel micacé.

Le minerai noir de cent échantillons se divise, selon la nomenclature minéralogique, d'une part en dix-sept types basiques et ultrabasiques caractérisés par de la hornblende en gros cristaux abondants, et d'autre part en deux autres types ultrabasiques où, signe particulier, prédominent de gros cristaux de diopside. Le minerai noir des mines *Countess of Warwick* et *Countess of Sussex* recèlent des minéraux spécifiques, aux textures peu communes, qui permettent, avec une certaine assurance, d'établir des liens entre ces derniers et des échantillons provenant d'un dépôt de minerai, à Dartford (Angleterre), et du site d'échouement d'un navire venu de Frobisher, à Smerwick Harbour (Irlande). Par rapport aux roches de la croûte continentale, le minerai noir, qui est riche en chrome et en nickel, pourrait provenir d'un matériel fondu situé à la base de la croûte terrestre, ou encore du manteau, à la fois plastique et de température élevée, qui a été éjecté vers la surface puis contaminé par l'eau lors de son ascension. Suite à leur migration, il y a environ 1 800 millions d'années, les roches se sont érodées pour être ensuite exposées à la surface. Quant au minerai rouge (*red ore*) fourni par un indice de la mine *Jonas Mount*, il ne peut être localisé pour l'instant. Il est possible cependant qu'il s'agisse d'un chapeau de fer aurifère, c.-à-d. qu'il viendrait d'une zone superficielle de sulfures altérés.

Les analyses originales du minerai noir, qui ont révélé une teneur en or de l'ordre de dizaines d'onces par tonne, ont été de toute évidence largement faussées. D'autres vérifications effectuées peu après, qui indiquaient une ou deux onces par tonne, montrent une teneur en or encore incroyablement élevée, ces nouvelles analyses multipliant de 2 000 à 20 000 fois cet or que des essais modernes ont permis de déceler dans 37 échantillons, et de 200 à 400 fois l'or récemment trouvé dans deux autres échantillons. L'explication la plus probable de ces divergences repose dans l'incompétence ou la malhonnêteté des essayeurs de Frobisher, bien que l'on ne puisse éliminer avec certitude l'hypothèse selon laquelle un additif en or ait été accidentellement ajouté aux creusets.

ABSTRACT

Frobisher's trenches in southeastern Baffin Island were the first mines in the Americas north of Mexico. The official total of ore landed in England was 158 tons in 1577 and 1136 tons in 1578. At present, the location of three mines is definitely known: Countess of Warwick, Countess of Sussex, and Winter's Furnace (all in or near Countess of Warwick Sound). A possible location is known for Denham's Mount mine (Victoria Bay). Three other mines, Best's Blessing (Resolution Island), Sussex Island (Beare Sound), and Fenton's Fortune (Sabine Bay), can be located approximately. All mines were shallow open pits, worked arduously, without the benefit of blasting powder.

Proterozoic (1,800 million year-old) "black ores" occur as narrow interlayers in biotite gneiss and amphibolite, some attenuated, some disrupted into "boudins", some cut by granite dykes, and some offset by faults. At Countess of Warwick Mine, massive "black ore" in the core of "boudins" is bordered by a fissile rind of micaceous material.

The "black ores" (of one hundred samples) can be divided into seventeen basic and ultrabasic types, according to mineralogy, characterized by abundant coarse-grained hornblende and two other ultrabasic types, characterized by predominant coarse-grained diopside. "Black ores" at Countess of Warwick and Countess of Sussex Mines contain distinctive suites of minerals with unusual textures and can be matched, with some confidence, with samples from Dartford, England (an ore-storage depot), and Smerwick Harbour, Ireland (site of a beached Frobisher vessel). Compared to crustal rocks, "black ores" are rich in chromium and nickel, and may have been derived from molten material at the base of the earth's crust, or possibly from the mantle, squeezed upward in a hot plastic state, and contaminated with water in its upward journey. After this migration ceased, the rocks were deeply eroded and exposed to plain view. "Red ore" from a spot occurrence at Jonas Mount cannot be located today, but it may represent an auriferous weathered sulphide capping (a "gossan").

Most early analyses of "black ores" (with tens of ounces gold per ton) are obviously exaggerated, and later ones (with one or two ounces gold per ton) are still unbelievably rich, the latter reporting 2,000-20,000 times the gold observed in thirty-seven samples assayed by modern methods, and 200-400 times the gold recently analyzed in two other samples. The most likely explanation for the discrepancy is incompetency or dishonesty of Frobisher's assayers but we cannot eliminate with certainty accidental introduction to the crucible charge of a gold-bearing additive.

This paper is taken, with minor additions and changes, from a chapter in the book *Martin Frobisher's Northwest Venture, 1576-1581: Mines, Minerals and Metallurgy*, by D.D. Hogarth, P.W. Boreham and D.T. Moore, presently being prepared for publication.

Introduction

Gold was the object of Martin Frobisher's second and third voyages to Baffin Island. After ore, reportedly of spectacular grade, was discovered in the first voyage (1576), the second (1577), and third (1578) voyages were sent out to fetch it. The rock was quarried, without the benefit of explosives, from shallow trenches in exceedingly hard rock. In the meantime, small assay furnaces were set up in the Baffin Island area, with Jonas Shutz, a German metallurgist, in charge of assaying in the second expedition, and Robert Denham, a London goldsmith, in charge of assaying in the third. Official weights of ore landed in England were 158 tons from the second expedition, and 1136 tons from the third [MS 1, 327-28].

Most of the ore was the hard, glittering black variety, "black ore", discovered in a number of localities near the mouth of Frobisher Bay. No record of the on-site assays survives but, on return of the third voyage, Robert Denham claimed the average lading could be expected to grade "almost an onse gold in c [1 cwt] of ewer [ore]" or twenty ounces (Troy) per long ton [MS 2].

In this paper we will discuss the mines and nature of Frobisher's ores. Besides samples from Baffin, we will describe some from Dartford (England) - ore storage depot after the third voyage, and Smerwick Harbour (Ireland) - site of the beaching of a wrecked Frobisher vessel in 1578. Finally, we will outline a geological model for the origin of an unusual rock, *viz.* Frobisher's "black ore".

Rediscovery of "black ore" on Kodlunarn and Baffin Islands, 1861-1985

As a by-product of the search for Franklin relics, Charles Francis Hall discovered Frobisher's landfalls and located the site of a mining operation on Kodlunarn Island (Countess of Warwick Mine), near the mouth of Frobisher Bay. He identified an inland trench, the Reservoir Trench, as a possible mine site and discovered coal heaps that had been left on Kodlunarn and nearby islands [Hall 1864, 2:150-56]. A trench on the north shore of Kodlunarn Island, the Ship's Trench, was described as an excavation used to repair and build ships - i.e. it served as a makeshift drydock.

The next scientific investigation was by Sharat Roy, geologist with the Rawson-MacMillan expedition of 1927. Roy [1937] noted a stockpile of black rock near the Ship's Trench but, as he was unable to locate similar rock *in situ* nearby, concluded the fragments were "apparently foreign to Kodlunarn" and had been placed "on the edge of the island, where they could be readily loaded into the ships' holds". He collected and described a specimen of black "amphibolite" from this storage heap and dark green "pyroxenite" from "an outcrop about two hundred yards" from Kodlunarn Island. Roy believed that Frobisher mined various types of dark igneous and metamorphic rock and that it was a bronzy biotite (rather than pyrite) that attracted the attention of miners and assayers.

As part of a program of reconnaissance mapping (1:500,000) of the Arctic islands by the Geological Survey of Canada, R.G. Blackadar visited Kodlunarn Island in 1964 and 1965. He found bedrock on the northeast side of Frobisher Bay to be a light-coloured gneiss [Blackadar 1967a] but, in a description of Kodlunarn Island, Blackadar [1967b] stated that the trenches penetrated layers of amphibolite containing small flakes of biotite. He noted that the two trenches were aligned, suggesting that Frobisher mined amphibolite from a single horizon in both trenches.

In 1974, Kodlunarn was visited by W.A. Kenyon and associates, representing the Royal Ontario Museum. The investigations were mainly archaeological, but Kenyon returned with 50 kg of rock. He also illustrated the tell-tale chisel scars left by Elizabethan miners and described coal deposits at Victoria Bay, Baffin Island, previously noted by Hall [Kenyon 1975a]. In addition, he pinpointed several possible Frobisher quarries on mainland Baffin.

Visits to Kodlunarn Island were also made by Hogarth and Gibbins for the Department of Indian Affairs and Northern Development of Canada in 1975, 1983, and 1985. The following publications have resulted from this research: geology of Kodlunarn Island [Hogarth and Gibbins 1984; Hogarth et al. 1985], preliminary classification of Frobisher ores [Hogarth 1985], precious metals in the ores [Hogarth and Loop 1986], and mining and metallurgy in the Frobisher voyages [Hogarth 1993]. The most important conclusions were:

1. Frobisher mined both trenches at Kodlunarn Island, but the Ship's Trench was essentially finished in 1577; in 1578 mining was mainly centred on the Reservoir Trench.

2. Stockpiles of ore near the Reservoir Trench had a local derivation, whereas the derivation of pieces of ore near the Ship's Trench was both local and from other mines.

3. Fenton's Fortune of Kenyon [1975b, 175] is not Fenton's Fortune of Frobisher, which was on the opposite side of Countess of Warwick Sound. The former is a doubtful mine and probably represents a sea cave.

4. Frobisher tested "black ore" at Kodlunarn Island and Little Hall's Island by oxidizing fine-grained greenish mica to a golden mineral by ignition in air at red heat. The rock was initially roasted in the ship's furnace.

5. Frobisher's largest mine, the Countess of Sussex Mine, was tentatively pinpointed on Baffin Island, 9 km west-northwest of Kodlunarn Island.

6. Except for a very few early proofs, the Elizabethan assays of Frobisher's ore suggest silver, not gold mines (both in metal content and in contemporary sterling value). The Elizabethan valuation of precious-metal content was grossly inflated, probably due, at least in the later assays, to inadvertent addition of contaminant to the furnace charge. The high values reported in the early assays may have been due to faulty analytical procedures.

Figure 1: The western wall of the former Dartford Priory, Kent, showing large blocks of Frobisher's "black ore" used in its reconstruction.

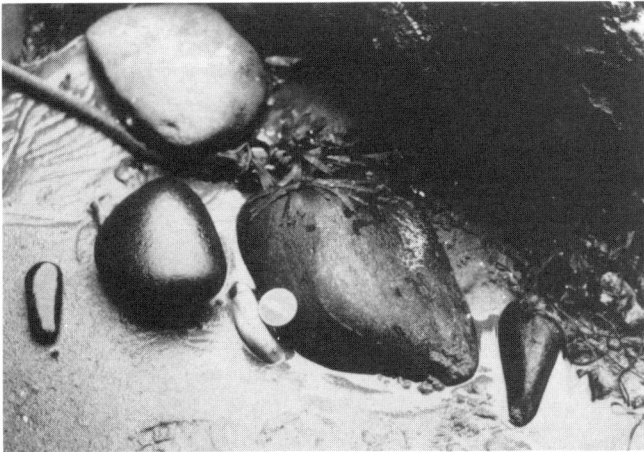

Figure 2: Dark-coloured cobbles on the beach below Fort Dún-an-Óir, Smerwick Harbour, Ireland, representing water-worn pieces of "black ore" brought from Baffin Island in 1578 by the *Emanuel* of Bridgwater. Lens cap of camera indicates scale.

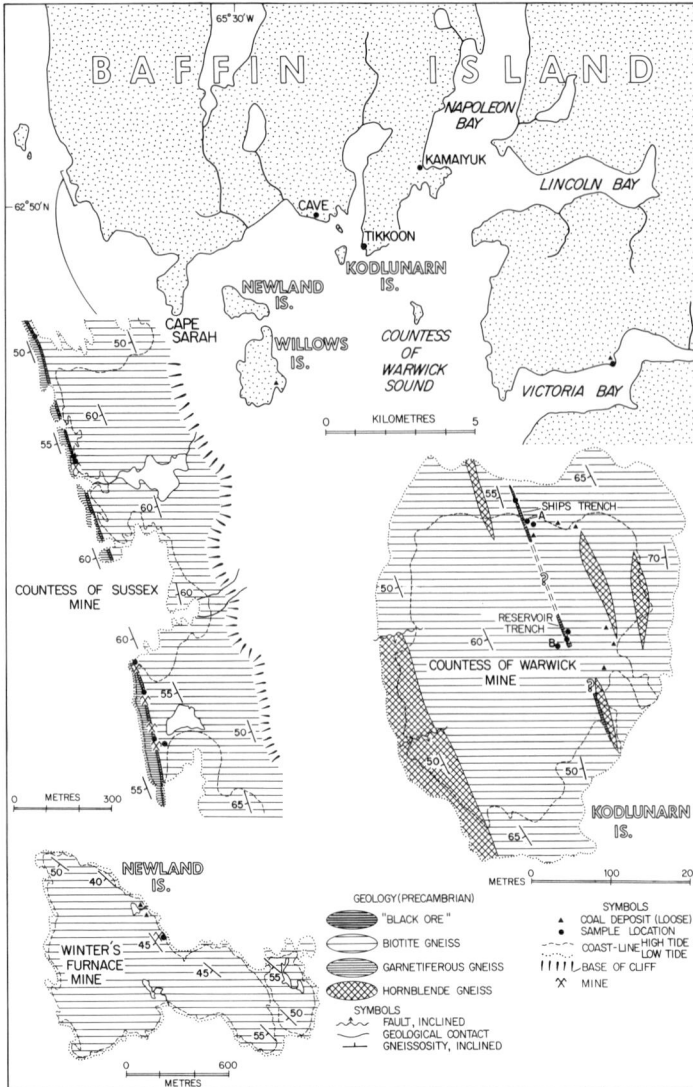

Figure 3: Frobisher mines and sample sites, Countess of Warwick Sound and vicinity, southeast Baffin Island. Geographic names are those of present usage.

"Black ore" at Dartford

The Frobisher rock at Dartford has been known for many years. In 1921, during the making of a cable trench from the pattern shop of Hall's Engineering works on Priory Road, the foundations of the old wall of the manor house were breached, exposing large blocks of black, hornblende-rich rock. Samples were sent to Cambridge and examined by Professor V.C. Illing, who reported augite, olivine, plagioclase and biotite associated with hornblende [unpublished notes in the Dartford Borough Museum]. Further specimens were recovered from a drainage ditch near the Thames estuary and sent to Cambridge, where Dr. R.E. Priestley identified them as "micaceous amphibolite" [Stefansson and McCaskill 1938, 2:249]. A large black specimen, acquired later, was examined by Dr. C.E. Tilley and found to be micaceous "hornblende pyroxenite" [Roy 1937, 34]. Two thin sections, now in the Harker collection at Cambridge, perhaps from specimens collected about the same time, are also hornblende pyroxenite. Dr. C. Ritchie [1964] published a photograph showing a block of "peridotite" in the old wall surrounding the Dartford manor house. Obviously the Dartford rock comprises an assortment of rock types.

A surprisingly large quantity of the "black ore" has been preserved in the borough. Some is incorporated in a 120 m section of Tudor boundary wall fronting Priory Road. This boundary wall was constructed some time after the spring of 1579 to reinforce the western perimeter of what was formerly King Henry VIII's manor house. Other sections of wall around the site are medieval or nineteenth and twentieth century. Only a small fragment of the manor house survives today, representing part of the western gatehouse.

More than 530 pieces of "black ore" are visible on the exterior face of the wall fronting Priory Road. Blocks of ore in excess of 30 cm by 30 cm are not uncommon (*Fig. 1*). A small quantity of "black ore" was also used for patching in some of the nineteenth and twentieth century rebuilding of the wall.

In 1976-77 and again in 1982, the Dartford District Archaeological Group uncovered specimens of "black ore" in excavations at the site of the manor house. Those found during the 1976-77 excavations were not associated with any specific context or feature. Samples of ore found in 1982 were retrieved from a pit which also contained Tudor floor tiles.

"Black ore" has been excavated from other localities in Dartford, most notably on the site of the former Bull and George Inn, Dartford High Street. Here specimens of ore were retrieved from primary fill in a sixteenth century cess pit. A small quantity of "black ore" was also retrieved in 1988 from a site at Home Orchard, Bullace Lane, close to Dartford High Street. Additional blocks of "black ore" were discovered in 1984 during excavations in a private garden in King Edward Avenue, Dartford, approximately 250 m north of the Dartford Road. The distribution of "black ore" in Dartford supports the theory that the rock became available for general building purposes after smelting operations ceased.

Yet another site was described by R.E. Priestley [in Stefansson and McCaskill 1938, 2:249]. Samples were collected about 1930 during excavations "in the course of drainage works", from a site originally in Dartford Harbour but "now lying some distance inland". Stefansson and McCaskill [1938] believed the rock was dumped into the harbour after it proved worthless.

"Black ore" at Smerwick, southwest Ireland

The solid or native rock at Fort Dún-an-Óir, Smerwick Harbour, comprises a succession of sandstone, conglomerate, and tuff [Horne 1974, 1976; Todd et al. 1988], with strata separated by fault and unconformity, and ranging in age from Devonian (*ca.* 400 million years) to Silurian (*ca.* 450 million years). Cradled between cliffs of these Palaeozoic rocks are coves with sandy beaches, exposed at low-to-medium tide and fringed by cobble strands. The cobbles are mainly derived from the local rock, but a few are quite distinct and bear no resemblance to the *in situ* exposures (*Fig. 2*). Those collected in 1987 [Hogarth and Roddick 1989] were of two types: *A*, hornblende with diopside and ilmenite (distinctive trace quantities of vanadium, little chromium), and *B*, hornblende and forsterite (distinctive trace quantities of chromium, little vanadium). Type *B* was also found on Baffin Island and at Dartford. These rocks contrasted with type *C*, hornblende with plagioclase from Kodlunarn Island (distinctive trace quantities of nickel but little chromium and vanadium). It was here at Smerwick that the *Emanuel* of Bridgwater, loaded with Baffin "black ore", was beached as a wreck in 1578 [Hogarth and Roddick 1989]. However, the *Emanuel* did not load at Kodlunarn, which explains the absence of *C* ore at Smerwick. Types *A* and *B* do not belong to Ireland.

Occurrences in the Baffin Island area

Three of Frobisher's mines of "black ore" can now (February 1992) be identified (*viz.* Countess of Warwick, Countess of Sussex, and Winter's Furnace) as can possibly one other (Denham's Mount). Information concerning the original discovery and operation of these and other Frobisher mines is summarized in Table 1. Similar "black ore" is most obvious at other occurrences in the region (e.g. Tikkoon Point and

Kamaiyuk) and must have been known and tested by Frobisher's men in 1578. The "black ore" stands out in marked contrast to the light coloured Precambrian biotite gneiss. Occurrences are located in *Figure 3*. All mines were worked by sledge, wedge, crowbar, pick, and shovel. Blasting powder was not employed by Europeans until the following century [Moray 1665; Hoover and Hoover 1950, 119n].

Countess of Warwick Mine, Kodlunarn Island:

The Countess of Warwick Mine on Kodlunarn Island (Frobisher's Countess of Warwick Island) was discovered July 29, 1577; it produced 158 tons of "black ore" that year. The first mine seems to have been the Ship's Trench, at the north end of the island. This trench was essentially finished in 1577, for its outline today corresponds closely to that described by Count Mendoza after the second voyage [Hume 1894, 567-69]. Mining during the third voyage, therefore, was probably confined to the interior, or Reservoir Trench; but this opening was abandoned in favour of other mines, after a week's arduous work. It had produced 65 tons, from tough unyielding rock, which were loaded into three barks [tonnage estimate of E. Sellman in Stefansson and McCaskill 1938, 2:69-70]. The island then became the centre of administration and assaying for the duration of this expedition in Baffin, after which it was lost to Europeans for nearly three hundred years.

On Kodlunarn, "black ore" can be traced across the eastern part of the island for 300 m (*Fig. 3*). It crops out on the extremities of the island and appears to have once been exposed in a trench in the middle (the Reservoir Trench, *Fig. 4*). The payzone, a black interlayer in a rather monotonous grey gneiss, is extremely hard. This feature reportedly caused the demise of the mine, which "fayled being so hard stone to breke" [E. Sellman in Stefansson and McCaskill 1938, 2:70]. Add to this the inconsistent and narrow widths of the payzone, which pinches and swells and, in places, is disconnected into isolated lenses or "boudins". In the intertidal zone, just below the Ship's Trench (*Fig. 5*), a boudin of "black ore" attains a maximum width of 35 cm; at another locality (below the Reservoir Trench) it has narrowed to 25 cm. This mine had real problems, regardless of the grade of ore.

The ore itself is composed largely of pitch-black, glittering hornblende, a "blacke stone, much lyke to a seacole in coloure, whiche by the waight seemed to be some kinde of Mettal or mynerall" [G. Best in Stefansson and McCaskill 1938, 1:51]. The periphery of the ore lenses is micaceous, but the black mica gives way to a black pyroxene in the interior of the lenses, and both minerals are readily transformed to a golden yellow after roasting at red heat. This chameleon-like property appears to have attracted the voyagers to this island in 1577.

Figure 4: The Reservoir Trench (Kodlunarn Island), 25 m long, excavated in 1578 and supplier of about sixty-five tons of "black ore" for the Dartford works. Ore was mainly type *C1*, with lesser amounts of types *A6*, *C2*, and *C3* (Table 2).

Figure 5: "Black ore" layers, below the Ship's Trench (Kodlunarn Island), that have been stretched and separated into isolated lenses or "boudins". The ore (dark) is type *C1* in the centre, separated by a rind of type *C2* from the surrounding biotite gneiss (light). Chisel, 15 cm long, indicates scale.

Figure 6: Exposure of ore (1.5 m diameter) in a Frobisher excavation, on the south peninsula of Countess of Sussex Mine (Baffin Island), worked by Fenton's and Frobisher's companies under Gilbert Yorke, August 1578. This remnant of "black ore" (type *A1*) may have been abandoned because too tough to break. The ridge behind, composed of "barren" amphibolite, separates two shallow pits.

Figure 7: Spoil heaps (off ridge, 90 m long, in background) on the south peninsula of Countess of Sussex Mine (Baffin Island). Trails of spilled "black ore" suggest that transportation was by man, cart, or wheelbarrow, southward (to the left in this photograph) along the flats (below the ridge) to tidewater.

Table 1 *Frobisher's mines, listed in order of discovery*

Mine	Approximate location	Discovered	Worked	Type of ore	Remarks
Little Hall's I.	N side, mouth of Frobisher Bay	By R. Garrand Aug. 10 1576		"Black"	Initial discovery of loose specimen, July 1577 attempts to locate ore *in situ* proved a failure.
Jonas Mount	15 km NNE of Kodlunarn I.	By G. Bona & J. Shutz 1577		"Yellow" & "red"	High Au assays. Sand and small pieces only. July, August 1578 attempts to locate more ore unsuccessful.
Leicester I.	Beare Sound	July 26 1577	July 26 1577	"Black"	20 tons mined and stockpiled 1577, ready for loading 1578.
Countess of Warwick	Kodlunarn I.	July 29 1577	July 29 - Aug. 21 1577; Aug. 1-9 1578	"Black"	Headquarters of mining operations 1578. Rock difficult to mine. Assay furnace site 1578.
Winter's Furnace	4 km SSW of Kodlunarn I.	By E. Fenton July 21 1578	July 21-*ca.* 25 1578	"Black"	Rock difficult to mine. First assay furnace of 1578.
Fenton's Fortune	15 km SSE of Kodlunarn I.	By E. Fenton July 29 1578	Aug. 9 - 15 1578	"Black" some "white"	R. Philpott in charge. Ore lean and difficult to transport to ships. Small tonnage available.
Sussex I.	Beare Sound	Aug. 7 1578	Aug. 9 - Sept. 1 1578	"Black"	Principal mine in Beare Sound.
Best's Blessing	S-side, mouth of Frobisher Bay	By G. Best Aug. 9 1578	Aug. 10 - 25 1578	"Black"	Large tonnage available but ore thought to be low grade.
Countess of Sussex	9 km WNW of Kodlunarn I.	By T. Morris & R. Davis	Aug. 11- 25 1578	"Black", "red" & mixed	G. Yorke in charge. Ore considered high grade.
Denham's Mount	9 km ESE of Kodlunarn I.	By A. Diar *ca.* Aug 15 1578	Aug. 19 - 29 1578	4 types	Ore considered high grade. Furnaces installed nearby.

Table 2 *Classification of "black ores"*

Group, type and mineral association	loc*	no#
A. Pyroxene hornblendite		
A1. Hornblende + diopside + ilmenite	I,E,B	11
A2. Hornblende + diopside + enstatite	E,B	3
A3. Hornblende + diopside + biotite	B	1
A4. Hornblende + diopside + biotite + scapolite	B	1
A5. Hornblende + enstatite + ilmenite	B	2
A6. Hornblende + diopside + enstatite + spinel	B	1
B. Olivine hornblendite		
B1. Hornblende + forsterite + diopside	I,E,B	13
B2. Hornblende + forsterite + enstatite + magnetite	I,E,B	5
B3. Hornblende + forsterite + spinel	B	1
C. Amphibolite		
C1. Hornblende + enstatite + plagioclase	E,B	21
C2. Hornblende + biotite + plagioclase	B,I,E	15
C3. Hornblende + plagioclase + spinel	B,E	3
C4. Hornblende + diopside + plagioclase	B	6
C5. Hornblende + diopside + biotite + plagioclase	E,B	6
C6. Hornblende + diopside + enstatite + plagioclase	E,B	3
C7. Hornblende + diopside + plagioclase + garnet	B	1
C8. Hornblende + plagioclase + garnet	B	2
D. Pyroxenite		
D1. Diopside + forsterite + spinel	E	1
D2. Diopside + enstatite + spinel	B	4

* locality: B - Baffin Island area; E - Dartford (England); I - Smerwick (Ireland)
# Number of specimens

Countess of Sussex Mine, Baffin Island:

The Countess of Sussex Mine, 9 km (5.5 miles) west-northwest of Kodlunarn Island and "adjoininge to the Maine", was discovered by Thomas Morris (master of the *Francis* of Foy) and Robert Davis (master of the *Ayde*) on August 10, 1578. From August 12 to August 27 it was worked continuously by about 100 men and, during this two-week interval, 455 tons of ore (estimate of Edward Sellman) were loaded into six small ships and the galliass *Ayde*. It was Frobisher's largest mine. However, pertinent assays were not made here, but on Kodlunarn Island.

The most northerly occurrence was rediscovered by Gibbins and Hogarth during a reconnaissance helicopter survey in 1985. The southern occurrences were rediscovered by Hogarth in 1990 and all occurrences were examined in detail by Ala and Hogarth in 1991. They lie on two adjacent peninsulas (*Fig. 3*), in the approximate positions given by Sellman [Stefansson and McCaskill 1938, 2:65] and Fenton [Kenyon 1981, 65].

The geology of this area is rather simple. A layer of crumbly black amphibolite, a well defined marker 6 to 8 m thick, is sandwiched between tan-to-grey biotite gneiss on the east, and pale tan garnetiferous gneiss on the west. The assemblage dips steeply to the west. We have traced the amphibolite across the two peninsulas for a total of 1450 m but this includes a 300-metre length covered by waters of the bay between them.

Layers of "black ore" (hornblendite) up to 1.5 m thick (*Fig. 6*) were restricted to the amphibolite but were found along its entire length. Compared to Countess of Warwick mine, the occurrences were more easily worked. The "black ore" was thicker, more persistent, and more easily freed from the fissile wallrocks. However, the continuity was interrupted by minor faults and a number of dykes of coarse-grained granite, which now stand up like walls above the mined ore.

On the north peninsula, the marker horizon was traced for 700 m. In one place a large hole in amphibolite extends to tidewater and its outline suggests an old mine. At the back are several hornblendite layers. The hole fronts deep water, even at low tide, and is well protected from the elements. It would have made an ideal loading site. However, elsewhere on this peninsula the amphibolite is in the intertidal zone, a setting that Frobisher's party seemed to avoid.

Better evidence of mineral exploitation was seen on the south peninsula. Here mining was confined to a length of 220 m, with two small trenches in the extreme north of the peninsula and a number of shallow scrapings and five spoil heaps southward (*Fig. 7*). The greatest elevation in this interval was 7 m above high tide. Ore, mainly "black", was seen in pieces along the whole length of the peninsula, but contemporary accounts also noted "red" (possibly garnetiferous or weathered hornblendite) and "mixed" (possibly feldspathic hornblendite). Banded "black ore" almost identical to the Smerwick cobbles was very common here.

Trails of hornblendite suggest ore was loaded from both north and south peninsulas. Ore was carried in specially woven baskets, but wheelbarrows were also available. In August 1578, the flats to the east of the ridge of hornblendite must have been a veritable highway. It is interesting to note that the *Emanuel*, which had taken thirty tons from the mine, was debited for a "druge" - a narrow, man-driven cart - possibly used to transport ore on the north peninsula, where the ship loaded [MS 3, 9v; MS 4, 82].

Winter's Furnace Mine, Newland Island:

A partially filled trench on Newland Island was discovered in 1990. It was 18 m long and 2 m wide and was thought to represent Frobisher's tiny Winter's Furnace Mine. Here 5 tons of "black ore" were mined in 1578, loaded into the *Armonell*, and shipped to England. Remains of a small heap of "black ore" lie just east of the trench. Two loose coal deposits 100 m northwest were rediscovered by Hall in 1861 [Hall 1864, 2:76-80] and possibly mark the location of an assay furnace operated in 1578.

Denham's Mount Mine, Victoria Bay:

This mine can be located only approximately. Here a deposit of loose coal about 25 m long was rediscovered by Hall in 1861 [Hall 1864, 2:156-58], visited by Kenyon [1975b], and the Smithsonian expeditions of 1990 and 1991; it probably marks the site of furnaces set up at Frobisher's "Dyer's Passage". The nearby mine, from which 260 tons were shipped in 1578, is probably covered by scree from a post-Frobisher landslide (talus is omnipresent here). However, at tidewater intermittent exposures of coarse amphibolite, 200 m north of the coal, may represent Frobisher's "mixed ore".

Classification of "black ores"

One hundred samples of "black ore" have been studied. They have been classified mainly according to their mineralogical composition (Table 2). There are four rock groups (pyroxene hornblendite, olivine hornblendite, amphibolite and pyroxenite) and 19 types of dominant mineral association. Three of the mineral associations are similar to those of certain "black ores" but were probably not themselves loaded into Frobisher's ships, *viz.* *A3* (Tikkoon), *A4* (Tikkoon) and *C6* (cave on Baffin Island). With the exception of *D1*, (Dartford), all rock types representing specimens collected at Dartford and Smerwick have known counterparts in Baffin. The three most important types will be described below. Typical appearance under the microscope is shown in *Figure 8*.

Chromium (Cr) and nickel (Ni) are characteristically high in "black ores". For example, Kodlunarn Island - ten samples of various types of ore averaged 310 ppm Cr, 420 ppm Ni; Smerwick Harbour - ten cobbles of *B1* averaged 1300 ppm Cr, 750 ppm Ni; Dartford - one specimen of *B1* gave 1975 ppm Cr, 700 ppm Ni; Countess of Sussex Mine - one specimen of *B1* gave 1535 ppm Cr, 630 ppm Ni. These values (all unpublished) are well above the crustal average of 110 ppm Cr and 89 ppm Ni [Li and Yio 1966] and within the range of compositions of ultramafic rocks analyzed in recent years.

Type *A1*: diopside hornblendite

This rock [type *A* of Hogarth and Roddick 1989] is composed mainly of coarse-grained, glittering black hornblende, which appears green under the microscope. Diopside, a subordinate mineral, is present in smaller grains. Some calcite is seen as small white lenses. The rock is characterized by light green layers of diopside, alternating with black layers of hornblende. As distinct from other types, it contains significant trace quantities of vanadium. We have found it at Smerwick Harbour (four specimens), Countess of Sussex Mine and Tikkoon Point (three specimens each), and Dartford (one specimen). It has not been found in the payzone at Countess of Warwick Mine and seems to be lacking, *in situ*, on Kodlunarn Island, but large boulders near the Reservoir Trench (*Fig. 9*) are thought to be glacial erratics, derived from Tikkoon Point 800 m to the east.

Type *B1*: olivine, pyroxene hornblendite

This rock (type *B* of Hogarth and Roddick 1989) comprises ten of our seventeen "black ore" cobbles from Smerwick Harbour, but it has also been found at Countess of Sussex Mine (North Peninsula, one locality only, two specimens) and Dartford (one specimen). In hand specimen, most of the cobbles resemble those of type *A1*: they are layered due to alternating bands rich in diopside and hornblende (*Fig. 10*). Under the microscope, the hornblende has a distinctive tan colour. Microscopic olivine (forsterite) is interspersed in the hornblende layers. In addition, a special suite of minor minerals and significant quantities of chromium set this type apart from all others. In fact, the Dartford and Smerwick specimens were probably derived from a very restricted area at Countess of Sussex Mine.

Type *C1*: enstatite amphibolite

This rock characterizes our Dartford suite, accounting for eleven of the twenty-two specimens. It was also found in seven specimens from Kodlunarn Island (representing both Ship's Trench and Reservoir Trench). The rock is homogeneous, with a faint layering detectable microscopically. The main mass is coarse-grained black hornblende (average diameter 1.2 mm), which is green in thin section. Feldspar lenses (only detectable under the microscope) and minerals within the feldspar (enstatite and the remainder of the hornblende) have an average grain size one-quarter that of the surrounding hornblende. The feldspar is a plagioclase, extremely rich in calcium. Another notable feature of the rock is an almost complete lack of opaque minerals. Pyrite and magnetite, together, rarely exceed one or two tiny grains per microscope slide. Chemically it is distinguished by significant trace quantities of nickel, and nickel is in greater abundance than chromium. The other three specimens, tentatively placed with *C1*, are from Winter's Furnace and Victoria Bay. They are similar but differ somewhat in chemical composition, mineralogy and texture.

Application of the classification scheme

Pigeon-holing the various types has led to the identities of rocks that were preferentially mined and exported by Frobisher, as well as to locating his loading sites in Baffin. Thus type *C1*, which characterizes half of our Dartford suite, was probably derived from Countess of Warwick Mine and not from the seven other localities examined. The fact that piles of ore at certain Dartford sites were almost exclusively *C1* (e.g. all ten specimens from a single trench), suggests that ore of the second voyage was kept separate from ore of the third. Furthermore, the distinctive *B1* ore, found at Dartford, Baffin, and Smerwick, shows that the *Emanuel* was loaded at the north peninsula, Countess of Sussex Mine. Conversely, the identity of *B1* ore was used as evidence to establish the final resting place of the *Emanuel* at Smerwick.

That calcite-rich *A1* ore appears to have been neither mined from large boulders on Kodlunarn nor *in situ* at Tikkoon suggests that this type of rock was bypassed purposely. Possibly it was examined in 1577 and failed the roasting test.

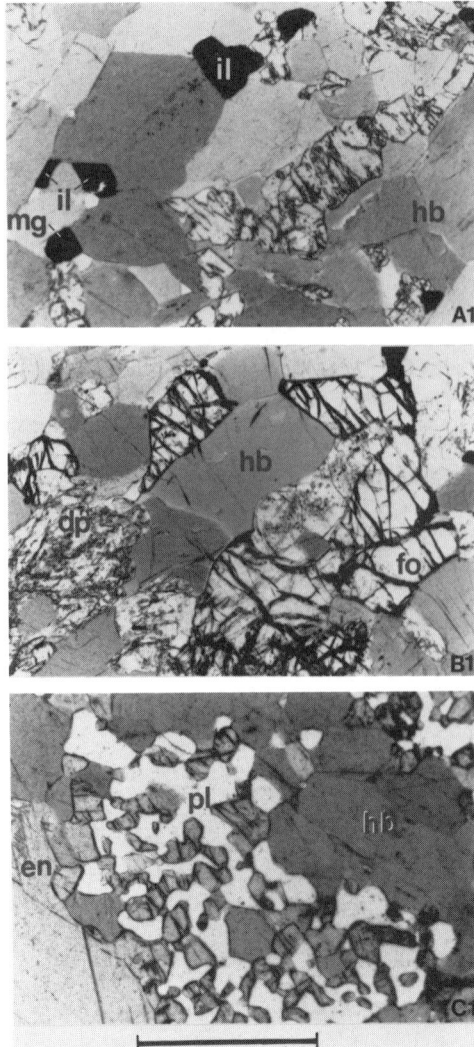

Figure 8: Typical "black ores" viewed under the microscope. Bar scale is 1 mm long. Mineral constituents: dp diopside, en enstatite, fo forsterite, hb hornblende, il ilmenite, mg magnetite, pl plagioclase. Sample localities: *A1* - Coosgorrib (Fort Dún-an-Óir, Ireland); *B1* - North peninsula of Countess of Sussex Mine (Baffin Island); *C1* - Priory Road (Dartford, England).

Figure 9: Glacially transported blocks or "erratics" (1 m long) of type *A1* "black ore", Kodlunarn Island, possibly derived from Tikkoon Point, 800 m to the east.

Figure 10: Typical appearance of highly contorted type *B1* "black ore" from the north peninsula, Countess of Sussex Mine, Baffin Island.

Table 3 *Bulk assays in London and vicinity and pilot-plant tests near Dartford*

No.	Date completed	Wt (cwt)	Location	Assayer	Voy	Assay (oz/T) Au	Ag
1	Nov. 1, 1577	1	Tower Hill	J. Shutz	2	13.3	
2	Dec. 6, 1577	1	Tower Hill	J. Shutz	2	13.3	
3	Jan. 23, 1577	1	Agnello's house	J-B. Agnello	2		
4	Jan. 30, 1578	2	Cripplegate	J. Broad	2		
5	Feb. 21, 1578	1	Kranich's house	B. Kranich	2	13.5	51
6	Mar. 6, 1578	2	Tower Hill	J. Shutz *et al.*	2	2.6	64
7	Nov. 13, 1578	40	Dartford	J. Shutz	2		
8	Nov. 13, 1578	40	Dartford	J. Shutz	2		
9	Dec. 29, 1578	20	Dartford	J. Shutz	2		
10	Jan. 20, 1579	10	Dartford	J. Shutz	3		
11	Feb. 17, 1579	10	Dartford	J. Shutz	3	1.2	35
12	Mar. 24, 1579	2	Tower Hill	J. Shutz	2	1.7	49
13	July 28, 1583	1	Tower of London	W. Williams	2(?)	nil	0.04
14	July 28, 1583	1	Tower of London	W. Williams	2(?)	nil	0.1

(table 3, cont.)

| No. | Other data and remarks | PRO | References | | |
			SM (page)	BL (folio)	H&L (page)
1	"First great proof"	SP 12/122/62	124	4R	260(1)
2	"Second great proof"	SP 12/122/62	125	4R	
3	"yt succeeded not well"	SP 12/122/62	126		
4	"It did succead well"	SP 12/122/62	126		
5	Silver parted with stibnite	SP 12/122/67	127-9	5V	260(2)
6	"Third great proof"	SP 12/123/5	131-2	4V	260(4)
7	The result proved "verye evill"			10R	
8	Results were "somewhat reasonable"			10R	
9	Work "succeeded but evill"			12V	
10	Assay gave £10/T				
11	35 oz/T silver remained in slag	SP 12/129/43	149-50		
12	28 oz/T silver remained in slag	SP 12/130/15	150-1	13R	260(6)
13	Values obtained from bead diameter	SP 12/161/41			261
14		SP 12/161/41			261

Abbreviations:
BL   British Library, Lansdowne MS 100/1 [*ca.* 1581]
H&L   Hogarth and Loop (1986), pp. 260 (with number of assay) and 261
PRO   Public Record Office
SM   Stefansson and McCaskill (1938), vol. 2
Voy   Voyage represented

Gold and silver

Precious metals were analyzed by modern methods: atomic absorption spectroscopy/graphite furnace for silver (Ag); neutron activation analysis/NiS extraction for gold (Au) and platinum (Pt). They were low in thirty-nine analyzed specimens. Amphibolite from the sea cave on Baffin Island had the lowest values (2 ppb Au, <50 ppb Ag, 3 ppb Pt), amphibolite and hornblendite from Kodlunarn Island somewhat higher (6 ppb Au, 70 ppb Ag, 5 ppb Pt). Gold in amphibolite and hornblendite from Dartford (21 ± 3 ppb) was consistently above that in the Baffin and Kodlunarn Island specimens.

Two specimens from Dartford showed significant gold: E23/2 (180 ppb Au) and E44/19 (125 ppb Au). The former was the only olivine pyroxenite (type *D1*) in our suite and the only specimen in which the arsenides gersdorffite and niccolite were observed. Presumably the gold was present as native metal inclusions in the arsenides. Specimen E44/19, an amphibolite (type *C1*), contained a small amount of pyrite (with 5.4% Ni) through which gold was distributed inhomogeneously. Although gold, *per se*, was not observed, it was probably present as tiny grains of native metal that were beyond the resolution of our imagery.

The low content of precious metals in our suite may be linked to the dearth of sulphides and arsenides into which these elements would partition at high temperature. "Red ore" from Jonas Mount was not available for our research. It had been in short supply, even during the voyages. It may have represented an iron-rich capping over weathered sulphides, a gossan, in which case the high assay obtained by Burchard Kranich of 40 oz Au/T or 1200 ppm [B. Kranich in Stefansson and McCaskill 1938, 2:139] was possibly correct. Gold and silver are known to concentrate during weathering, in some instances resulting in rich soils and gossans, even in northern Canada [Boyle 1979, 431-45]. "Red ore" from Jonas Mount, a loose sand, is different from "red ore" from Countess of Sussex Mine, solid rock.

Let us now consider the early gold proofs of "black ore" (Table 3) and pose the question: where did the Elizabethan assayers go wrong? The highest values certainly belong to the earliest assays [Hogarth and Loop 1986], but it is not clear whether the gold was completely "parted" (or separated) from silver, nor are we given details of analytical procedure. After assay No. 5, tests in England were made before a delegation of commissioners and the gold content of the ore dropped immediately from 13½ to 2½ ounces per ton. One may suspect mischief in the early assays, but the later, supervised, tests are also difficult to explain. The latter report a gold content of about 1½ ounces per ton - 2,000-20,000 times the content of thirty-seven of our samples, and 200-300 times the non-conformist "black ores" E23/2 and E44/19. In the Elizabethan assays at Dartford, galena (elsewhere associated with appreciable gold) was a major component of the crucible charge [MS 6, 183-85], but it is hard to believe that Shutz, reputedly acquainted with metallurgical technology of the day, would not have tested his additive for precious metal and made allowance for it. The inescapable conclusion is that either the analysts were incompetent or that Jonas Shutz, Robert Denham, and perhaps others, added gold-bearing material to the charge deliberately. However, what sustaining advantage the assayers hoped to gain in fraud is difficult to imagine.

Origin of the "black ores"

Mineralogy and bulk-rock chemistry of "black ores" suggest metamorphic derivation from the deep crust or upper mantle. For example, the occurrence of olivine, chrome spinel, enstatite and diopside, and a small but significant nickel-chromium abundance in the bulk-rock composition, point to a deep source. There is nothing in the present data to suggest these rocks were not initially magmatic. However, only five of our specimens (pyroxenite) have mineral compositions characteristic of magmatic rocks. Hornblende, the principal constituent of the other "black ores", is a typical metamorphic mineral. Therefore, if we assume an igneous origin, the rocks have undergone considerable changes since crystallization. The lack of migration of elements from the "black ore" into the wall rock, the fractured but otherwise unchanged biotite gneiss at the contact, and the very coarse-grained and pristine nature of the hornblende, suggest the "black ores" were injected as cooled solids into the wall rock and that metamorphic transformations had taken place previously at depth.

As material rich in magnesium, iron, and silicon migrated upwards, it slowly cooled and assimilated constituents (including water) from the wall rocks. This would explain the generation of hornblende, a hydrous mineral. Migration was along the avenue of easiest access: the natural grain or "foliation" of the rock. As upward migration and cooling continued, chemical reactions and ion exchanges become more sluggish, and at about 650°C, atomic interchange between neighboring minerals virtually ceased [Hogarth and Roddick 1989]. Finally, upward migration came to a halt altogether and the rocks were trapped several tens of kilometers below what was then the surface of the earth. The time was early Proterozoic, 1,800 million years ago. It remained for deep erosion to expose these narrow layers of rock or "sills" to plain view.

ACKNOWLEDGEMENTS: The investigation of "black ores" from Dartford was facilitated through the loan of specimens by Mr. C. Baker (Dartford District Archaeological Group) and Dr. A.M. Clark (The Natural History Museum). Two thin sections of Dartford "black ore" in the Harker Collection were examined through the kindness of Dr. G.A. Chinner (Cambridge University). Four specimens of "black ore" from Baffin Island area were provided from the Kenyon collection at the Department of New World Archaeology, Royal Ontario Museum.

We would like to thank: Messrs. R. Hartree and J. Loop (University of Ottawa) for X-ray spectrographic, atomic absorption, and direct-current plasma analyses of samples; Dr. C.T. Williams (Natural History Museum) for instrumental neutron activation analyses; Mr. E.W. Hearn (University of Ottawa) for line drawings and photography; and Ms. S. Downing (University of Ottawa), Ms. J. Hayes (University of Ottawa) and Ms. M. Low (Natural History Museum) for typing. Early drafts of the manuscript were read by Dr. R.W. Boyle (Geological Survey of Canada) and by Drs. R. Hutchison, C.J. Stanley and R.F. Symes (Natural History Museum).

One of us (D.D.H.) would like to acknowledge the Natural History Museum for facilities and assistance during sabbatical leave, 1988-89. He is particularly indebted to the former Keeper of Mineralogy, Dr. A.C. Bishop, without whose encouragement this research would not have taken place. Transportation in Frobisher Bay, Baffin Island, was via the longliner *Pitsiulak* and D.D.H. is grateful to Dr. W.W. Fitzhugh (Smithsonian Institution) for accommodation with his field parties in 1990 and 1991. Davin Ala (undergraduate student, University of Ottawa) was his field assistant in 1991. The abstract was translated into French by Drs. A.E. Lalonde and K. Benn (University of Ottawa).

References

A. Publications

Blackadar, R.G.
    1967a   Geological reconnaissance, southern Baffin Island, District of Franklin. *Geological Survey of Canada Paper* 66-47.

    1967b   Kodlunarn Island and Frobisher's "gold". *The Arctic Circular* 17(1): 1-12.

Boyle, R.W.
    1979   The geochemistry of gold and its deposits (together with a chapter on geochemical prospecting for the element). *Geological Survey of Canada Bulletin* 280.

Hall, C.F.
1864   *Life with the Esquimaux.* 2 vols. London: Sampson Low, Son, and Marston.

Hogarth, D.D.
1985   Petrology of Martin Frobisher's "black ore" from Frobisher Bay, N.W.T. *GAC-MAC Annual Meeting*, Program with Abstracts 10: A 28.

1993   Mining and metallurgy of the Frobisher ores. In *Archeology of the Frobisher Voyages*, ed. W. Fitzhugh and J. Olin, 137-46. Washington: Smithsonian Institution Press.

Hogarth, D.D., and W.A. Gibbins.
1984   Martin Frobisher's "gold mines" on Kodlunarn Island and adjacent Baffin Island, Frobisher Bay, NWT. *Contributions to the Geology of the Northwest Territories* 1:69-78.

Hogarth, D.D., and J. Loop.
1986   Precious metals in Martin Frobisher's "black ores" from Frobisher Bay, Northwest Territories. *Canadian Mineralogist* 24:259-63.

Hogarth, D.D., J. Loop, and W.A. Gibbins.
1985   Frobisher's gold on Kodlunarn Island - fact or fable? *CIM Bulletin* 78:75-9.

Hogarth, D.D., and J.C. Roddick
1989   Discovery of Martin Frobisher's Baffin Island "ore" in Ireland. *Canadian Journal of Earth Science* 26:1053-60.

Hoover, H.C. and L.H. Hoover, eds. and trans.
1950   *De Re Metallica.* New York: Dover Publications.

Horne, R.R.
1974   The lithostratigraphy of the late-Silurian to early Carboniferous of the Dingle Peninsula, Co. Kerry. *Geological Survey of Ireland Bulletin* 1:395-428.

1976   Geological guide to the Dingle Peninsula. *Geological Survey of Ireland Guide*, series 1.

Hume, M.A.S., ed.
1894   *Letters and State Papers Relating to English Affairs, Preserved in the Archives of Simancas.* Vol. 2 (Elizabeth I, 1568-1579). London: British National Archives.

Kenyon, W.A.
1975a   "All is not golde that shineth". *The Beaver*, Summer, 40-46.

1975b   *Tokens of Possession: the Northern Voyages of Martin Frobisher.* Toronto: Royal Ontario Museum.

1981   The Canadian Arctic journal of Capt. Edward Fenton 1578. *Archivaria* 11:171-203.

Li, T., and C. Yio.
1966   The abundance of chemical elements in the earth's crust and its major tectonic units. *Scientia Sinica* 15:258-72.

Moray, R.
1665   A way to break easily and speedily the hardest rocks, communicated by the same person, as he received it from Monsieur Du Son, the inventor. *Philosophical Transactions* 1:82-85.

Ritchie, C.I.A.
1964   Dartford's doubtful Eldorado. *Kent Life*, October, 64-5.

Roy, S.K.
1937   The history and petrography of Frobisher's "gold ore". *Field Museum of Natural History. Geological Series* 7:21-38.

Stefansson, V., and E. McCaskill, eds.
1938   *The Three Voyages of Martin Frobisher in Search of a Passage to Cathay and India by the North-west, A.D. 1576-8.* 2 vols. London: Argonaut Press.

Todd, S.P., B.P.J. Williams, and P.L. Hancock.
1988   Lithostratigraphy and structure of the Old Red Sandstone of the northern Dingle Peninsula, Co. Kerry, Southwest Ireland. *Geological Journal* 23:107-20.

B. Manuscripts

MS 1.   Lok, M. [1581]. Summary accounts, 1576-1581. Public Record Office, E 164/36, ff. 317-329.

MS 2.   Lok, M. to Lord Burghley 1578. Hatfield MS. 161/71.

MS 3.   Lok, M. 1578. Accounts, third voyage. Huntington Library, HM 713.

MS 4.   Sellman, E. 1578. Accounts, third voyage. Public Record Office, E 164/36, ff. 45-164.

MS 5.   Fitzhugh, W.W. 1991. Archeology of the Frobisher voyages and European Inuit contact. Field and research report for 1991. Smithsonian Institution.

MS 6.   Lok, M. [1579]. Accounts, buildings and works at Dartford. Public Record Office, E 164/36, ff. 167-187.

Preliminary Report on Excavations at Kuyait (KfDf-2) and Kamaiyuk (KfDe-5), Frobisher Bay, Baffin Island, N.W.T.

Lynda Gullason
Department of Anthropology, McGill University

William Fitzhugh
Arctic Studies Center, Smithsonian Institution

Anne Henshaw
Department of Anthropology, Harvard University

RÉSUMÉ

L'article décrit les résultats préliminaires des fouilles archéologiques menées en 1991 dans deux sites historiques inuit de grandes dimensions, Kuyait et Kamaiyuk. Il semblerait que Kuyait aurait été occupé entre le milieu du XIXe siècle jusqu'au début du XXe siècle, alors que Kamaiyuk était actif au cours les expéditions de Frobisher (1576-1578) et quelque temps après. Des artefacts récupérés dans ces sites, dont des ossements et un outillage lithique, de même que des objets d'origine européenne modifiés mais semblables à des artefacts inuit traditionnels, fournissent des renseignements détaillés quant à l'introduction d'objets européens dans les sites inuit et à leur influence sur les comportements des habitants. La gamme des constructions va des habitations au plan bien établi, à structure polylobée et à demi souterraines, appartenant à la première autant qu'à la dernière période historique, d'une part, à un *qarmak* datant de la fin du XIXe siècle. Suite à ces fouilles, commence d'apparaître une idée précise du type d'objets élizabéthains qui se trouvaient dans les maisons inuit de la première période historique, et des conditions de leur utilisation et de leur mise au rancart.

ABSTRACT

This paper describes the preliminary findings of archaeological investigations conducted in 1991 at two large historic Inuit sites, Kuyait and Kamaiyuk. Kuyait appears to have been occupied from mid-nineteenth to early twentieth century, while Kamaiyuk was likely inhabited during and shortly after the Frobisher expeditions (1576-1578). Artifactual data recovered from these sites, including Inuit bone and lithic tools as well as modified European goods resembling traditional Inuit artifacts, provide extensive information on the incorporation of European material into Inuit sites and behavioural systems. The structures ranged from well-defined, multi-lobed, semi-subterranean dwellings from both the early and later historic periods, to a qarmaq dating to the late nineteenth century. From these excavations a definite pattern has emerged indicating kinds of Elizabethan material present in early historic Inuit houses, and later conditions of their use and discard.

Introduction

One of the principal goals of the Meta Incognita Project involves archaeological investigation of Inuit culture change from the sixteenth to early twentieth century - particularly change associated with the Frobisher voyages - in order to understand the nature of cultural relations between the Inuit of Frobisher Bay and different European groups with whom they came in contact. The Inuit-European contact experience was not universal. Europeans' motives varied widely depending on the goals of their enterprises, which included exploring, mining, whaling, trapping, trading, and missionizing. The Inuit who received them had varying agendas as well. Some sought the social and economic changes contact brought; other groups ignored or actively avoided the newcomers [Ross 1977, 1979; Stevenson, 1984]. The contact process was also influenced by matters of proximity and access of Inuit to European vessels or shore stations, seasonality of Inuit and European activity, and other factors. Even within a given population, opportunities for and responses to contact differed; for example, between European-hired whaleboat captains and traditional hunters, or between men and women.

This paper describes the preliminary findings of one component of the Meta Incognita Project: investigations conducted in 1991 at two historic Inuit sites - Kuyait (KfDf-2) and Kamaiyuk (KfDe-5) - located near Frobisher's Kodlunarn Island base camp (*Fig. 1*). Historic Inuit occupations at Kuyait date to the nineteenth/twentieth centuries, while Kamaiyuk seems to have been inhabited during and shortly after the Frobisher expeditions (1576-78). The structures excavated at these sites include semi-subterranean sod-house dwellings, qarmat (plural of qarmaq), and middens dating to both early and later periods of European contact. Artifacts recovered from these sites - including traditional Inuit items, Inuit tools made from European materials, and European goods - provide information on the incorporation of European material into Inuit cultural and behavioural systems. The excavations reveal patterns in the types of European materials utilized by Inuit people as well as changes in these patterns through time. Also evident are changes in patterns of usage, modification, and discard as these items passed from active use into the archaeological record.

The Kamaiyuk site is of particular importance because it was visited in 1577 by Frobisher's lieutenant, George Best, who provided the first English language description of an aboriginal site in the New World, as well as the first detailed European account of an Inuit site in the Arctic.

A number of archaeological studies of Inuit-European interaction have concluded that northern native peoples were not passive recipients of change, but instead adapted creatively to changing circumstances and took advantage of opportunities that reinforced traditional modes of adaptation [Fitzhugh 1985; Gullov 1985; Hickey 1984; Jordan 1978; Jordan and Kaplan 1980; Kaplan 1983, 1985; Mathiassen 1931; Sabo 1979; Savelle 1985; Taylor 1976]. The Frobisher Bay region represents an unusual opportunity to investigate Inuit-European interaction because two typologically and chronologically distinct contact episodes occurred: the sixteenth century voyages of Martin Frobisher, and the nineteenth/twentieth century commercial marine mammal hunting and trapping eras.

Each of these contact phases left a unique signature in the Inuit archaeological record. In addition to the impact of such contacts in the area of material culture, such as adoption of European artifacts or use of European materials to improve traditional forms, research has shown that Inuit culture underwent changes in other aspects as well. Earlier settlement patterns were modified to take advantage of new opportunities to trade with, or be employed by, Europeans; new house forms were adopted in response to changes in Inuit social and economic activities; and new religious patterns emerged following such activities of wage employment and missionization [Kaplan 1983, 1985; Ross 1979]. With the establishment of a permanent European settlement in Frobisher Bay in the twentieth century, Inuit culture was transformed into modern Inuit society and in the process traditional culture forms took on new shapes. While coping with the realities of a modern urban settlement, Inuit have also sought to revitalize their cultural identity through political action, the media, and tourist industries.

Throughout this period, Inuit culture was affected by the processes of retention, adoption of new technology, and creative adaptivity exhibited by other traditional societies in their encounters with Western society [Broom et al. 1954]. But the studies explored here are not directed only at culture contact; they also explore the internal dynamics of Inuit cultural change, document Inuit cultural history, and explore the possible effects of environmental factors on Inuit demography and resource utilization through the historic period [Molloy, Henshaw, and Marino, in press].

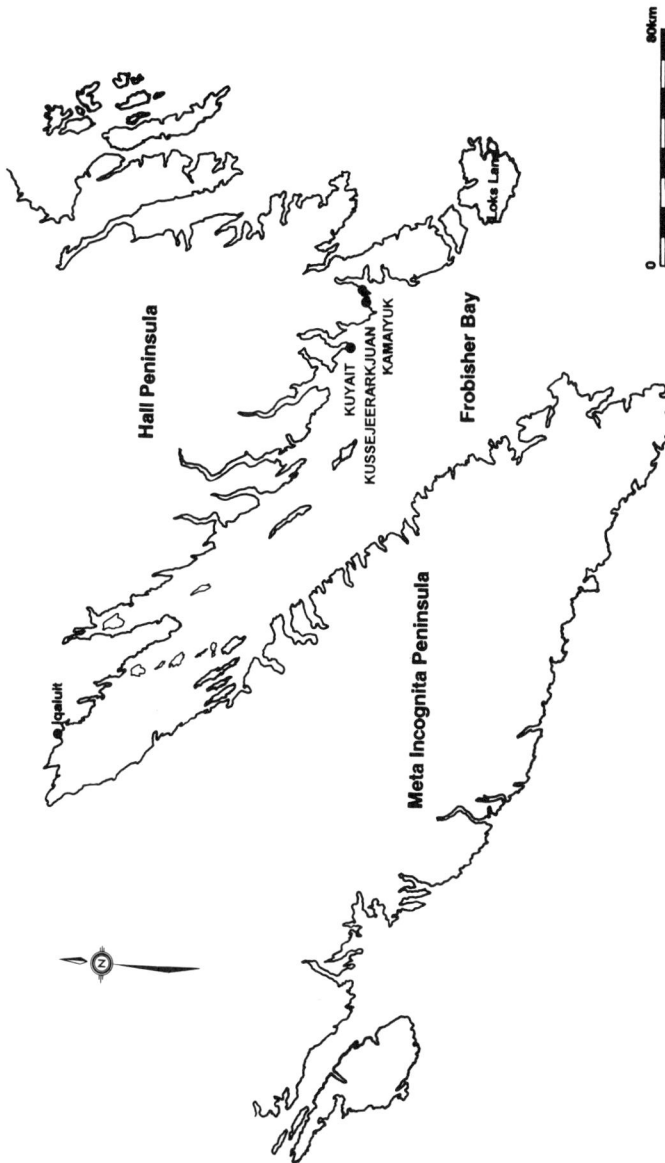

Figure 1: Map of Frobisher Bay

Ethnographic Profile

The Inuit (*Nugumiut*) who lived in Frobisher Bay have been described by Hall [1970, originally 1864] and Boas [1964, originally 1888]. Hall, a journalist and explorer, lived among these people for more than a year in 1861-62, while Boas never visited Frobisher Bay and obtained his information from Inuit informants in Cumberland Sound, some of whom were Frobisher Bay people or had ties with them. Unfortunately, neither observer provides a detailed view of *Nugumiut* culture. According to Hall and Boas, various *Nugumiut* groups occupied most of the Frobisher Bay region, ranging from interior caribou-hunting territories around Lake Amadjuak to the mouth of Frobisher Bay. Their summer sites consisted of sealskin tent camps located at char fishing areas, especially near Iqaluit. During the fall people lived in qarmat (heavily constructed skin-covered tents with low sod and rock walls) at seal and caribou hunting locations on the central bay islands and coasts. In winter people gathered in large snowhouse villages on the sea-ice or seaward locations near the outer coast in areas where walrus, seals, polar bears, and caribou could be hunted. Winter villages were most common around Waddell Bay, Beecher Peninsula, Countess of Warwick Sound, and in Cyrus Field Bay and Grinnell Bay to the north [Boas 1964, 14]. As in other Inuit societies, the *Nugumiut* were in frequent contact with groups in neighbouring regions, especially those of Cumberland Sound and south Baffin Island.

This late nineteenth century settlement pattern had changed from earlier times when Thule and early historic Inuit lived in large sod-house villages during the winter season. In the Classic and early Developed Thule period (*ca.* eleventh to fourteenth centuries), these villages were mostly located near the head of Frobisher Bay; but during the later Developed Thule period (*ca.* A.D. 1400), Inuit winter sod-house settlements also began to be established in outer bay locations, it has been suggested, and a winter subsistence economy focusing on ring seal replaced the mixed terrestrial-marine hunting strategy practised in the earlier periods [Jacobs and Stenton 1985; Stenton 1987]. (Faunal analysis carried out on the outer bay Inuit sites will shed light on this issue). The amount of whalebone and baleen retrieved from occupations dating to this period decreased substantially in relation to the Classic Thule period, suggesting a decline in whale hunting [Sabo and Jacobs 1980, 499]. Sometime prior to Hall's and Boas' visits, Inuit abandoned use of sod-house villages in favour of more mobile snowhouse settlements (although Sabo and Jacobs [1980, 501] suggest that onshore winter dwellings continued as a seasonal option and were occasionally used as qarmat). Residence at outer bay sites also facilitated access to European whalers whose activities centered in these regions after 1850. An interesting problem that has not been considered in the past, and needs investigation, concerns the importance of European contacts in this settlement and economic change [Stenton 1987, 40-41].

Field goals and methods

The goals of our field work were to identify and test Inuit sites dating from the period of the Frobisher voyages to the present, with emphasis on sixteenth to nineteenth century sites. Our 1990 survey had located two large winter sites in the vicinity of Countess of Warwick Sound with historic period sod-house foundations containing artifacts dating to the Frobisher period and later. The 1991 strategy was aimed at sampling and excavating several structures in each site to determine their sequence of occupation, which we expected from previous tests should represent pre-contact Thule, Frobisher, and post-Frobisher periods.

Excavations at Kuyait began on 10 July with a crew of ten. During the month of July we excavated three structures in addition to mapping and testing other habitations and features. On 31 July, with a crew of six, we moved to Kamaiyuk (KfDe-5) and spent the remainder of the season at that location, returning to Iqaluit on 29 August.

Excavation grids of 2 m by 2 m units were established for each house and were tied into site survey baselines and datum stokes. Excavation followed natural stratigraphic and cultural levels which were subdivided into 10 cm arbitrary levels when necessary. Three-dimensional provenience was taken on all artifacts. Soil matrix was screened through quarter-inch mesh (sixteenth-inch mesh was used for concentrations of seed beads, etc.). Faunal remains were lot-bagged by feature and natural layer within individual quadrants of the 2 m by 2 m units. Because large whalebone house structure elements were poorly represented and consisted mainly of rib fragments, these remains were mapped and photographed but were not collected. One to two kilogram soil samples were collected from each natural layer and from major cultural features, such as hearth deposits, for laboratory and entomological studies. Wet sieving was attempted in the field but the high percentage of organics, composed of woody, herbaceous, and rooty materials, prevented effective screening. Archaeological testing was conducted outside houses in order to identify associated activity areas and middens. After house excavations were completed a planview of each structure was drafted using the unit level record forms and on-site measurements in the house. Contour profile maps were drawn of the major structural features within the houses and a detailed map was made of each site by transit.

Results

Kuyait (KfDf-2)

This large site, located at the southwestern entrance of Wiswell Inlet, consists of twelve recognizable structures (both semi-subterranean house mounds and qarmat) as well as tent rings and caches. Full excavations were made at three structures: Houses 8, 12, and 3 (*Fig. 2*). Each produced a wealth of faunal remains and varying amounts of artifact material representing different phases of European contact. Test excavations conducted outside the houses to identify associated activity areas produced Dorset midden material, but no evidence of deeply-stratified Neoeskimo middens. Instead, most of the Inuit midden material was located within the wall parameters of each structure or in external surface scatters.

HOUSE 12   House 12 can be described as a structure type known ethnographically as a qarmaq, or "winterized tent". However, interpretations vary as to specific construction features and season of occupation, due to differing ethnographic descriptions [Park 1988]. This structure had been placed in a sloping grassy declivity sheltered to the west and north by high ledges. The site's outcropping ledges served as foundations for the structure's walls, while the natural slope of the ground surface created a three-sided, raised, lateral and rear sleeping area, once the occupants had excavated (to a depth of 15-20 cm) a small 1 m by 1.5 m area, which served as an extension of the passageway floor entry to the tent. Test excavations outside the qarmaq yielded no contemporaneous activity areas or middens, only a surface sheet scatter of refuse. House 12 produced a rich deposit of more than six hundred artifacts recovered from two stratigraphic components: a qarmaq occupation dating to the late nineteenth/early twentieth centuries overlying a Paleoeskimo midden containing Dorset and traces of Pre-Dorset material. The latter existed only under the southern half of the structure.

The artifact assemblage from the later historic contact period occupation reveals evidence of a complex culture transfer process which included: retention of items of basic Inuit technology; manufacture of traditional Inuit forms with new materials of European origin; and wholesale introduction of new artifact types and forms. Traditional Inuit items such as bone awls and slate ulus were found together with such items as an ulu made from brass sheet metal, glass scrapers, a ceramic bowl used as an oil lamp, and cartridge cases. Even children's toys displayed a rich admixture of cultures: a small stone kudlik, a lead soldier, and a glass marble.

Because qarmat are not well documented archaeologically, House 12 will provide useful baseline data for studies of these poorly known structures as well as for culture contact research generally.

HOUSE 8   House 8, also excavated completely, was a large, bilobate, semi-subterranean habitation dating to the historic period. This structure is similar to other bilobate structures investigated in southeastern Baffin Island dating to the Developed Thule/Inuit period [Collins 1950;   Jacobs and Stenton 1985;   Schledermann 1975; Stenton 1987]. Its plan reveals two raised sleeping platforms built as separate rooms, each with its own hearth (a pile of fire-burned and fat-encrusted slabs), separated by a hugh boulder and surmounting rocks used as a central roof support. Between the two rooms was a paved common room floor with access to the outside through a sunken paved passage. A small storage alcove was found beneath the front of the sleeping platform in the north room.

Both cultural and natural site formation processes complicate understanding of the occupation sequence of this structure. The last occupation, represented by the structure described above, had been constructed by remodelling earlier Thule and Dorset structures here, and both Thule and Dorset remains were found in the House 8 walls. In addition, the existence of several phases of Inuit occupation were evident in multiple floor paving episodes. Further modification was noted in the movement of hearth positions, and the blocking and filling (perhaps even walling off) of the east platform.

Despite the large size and elaborate construction of this structure, very few artifacts were found. They included traditional items such as trace buckles and slate endblades and ulus. In addition, a 1990 test pit produced an iron harpoon endblade from the living floor pavement. A number of relatively undiagnostic European artifacts were recovered including seed beads, tubular beads, fragments of iron barrel-hoops, an iron spike, a handwrought nail, and a piece of bottle glass. Datable artifacts are mostly from the nineteenth century and include a metal food label, beads, ceramic fragments (dating 1825-50), and a child's leather shoe. The shoe was found just below the sod and may post-date the house occupation. A few Elizabethan artifacts were found on the house floors and sleeping platforms, including: unglazed roof tile fragments; a piece of green-glazed, red-pasted stove tile; and fragments of English flint. In addition to the low density of artifacts in House 8, there was an absence of slate working, an absence of iron from the latest living floor, and a relative scarcity of iron throughout the deposit. These features probably indicate a relatively early period of European contact, geographic marginality to European influence, a short period of occupation, or a combination of all three. The artifact assemblage generally indicates a mid-nineteenth century occupation, perhaps predating Structure 12 by fifty to one hundred years, but there is a distinct paucity of material culture of either origin (traditional Inuit or European).

Dating the final occupation of House 8 presents some difficulties. With the nearby whaling activities at Cape Haven [Eber 1989; Fraser and Rannie 1972; Stevenson 1984; Wakeham 1898], Cape True [Hall 1970], and farther away at Cumberland Sound [Goldring 1986; Stevenson 1984], much more European material culture should have been available to Frobisher Bay Inuit after 1840. If, on the other hand, the assemblage pre-dates 1800, with the more recent items representing post-occupational disturbance, as the stratigraphic context of some artifacts suggests, a question has to be asked as to why there is so little lithic material present in this large and carefully constructed house? A suggested solution may be that iron may have been present in sufficient quantity to replace slate technology, but, with careful use and curation, did not find its way into the archaeological deposit. Such behaviour is characteristic of technological transition periods, the Bronze Age/Iron Age horizon, for example [Ehrenreich 1990]. Alternatively, small amounts of iron may have been present but did not survive the acidic soil conditions of pH 4.5; however, their corrosion products, iron oxides, would remain to stain the soil. It is hard to explain the lack of European material when Structure 12 had such a comparatively rich artifact assemblage. If House 8 indeed represents a later contact period, it will provide an interesting comparison to House 12 which clearly post-dates it. Furthermore, a single radiocarbon sample on cranberry twigs yielding a date of 110 ± 50 B.P. (A.D. 1660-1955, calibrated age with 2 sigma range) does not resolve the issue.

HOUSE 3   House 3 was a small, semi-subterranean, single-room structure containing three components: evidence of an early twentieth century "boil-up" or hunting bivouac in the sod level, and two clay-sealed, pre-contact, Thule components. In contrast to the clearly-defined architecture of House 8, House 3 was an architectural "disaster". This structure was difficult to interpret because solifluction had destroyed most of the house except for the entrance passage area. After removing what appeared to be "frost boil" (deposits consisting of a grey/tan clay overburden from the lowest stratigraphic level located in the house centre), a small remnant Thule component was isolated in the living floor area. Artifacts recovered here include a ground slate endblade, a drilled ground slate ulu, a slate preform, a possible boot creaser, a ground slate bowdrill, and an antler toggling harpoon head [possibly Type 4; McGhee 1984, 47, plate 3]. Wood associated with the harpoon head was radiocarbon dated to 240 ± 80 B.P. (A.D. 1460-1955, calibrated age with 2 sigma range). Dorset materials were found in the sods but were mainly concentrated in buried peat deposits situated directly above bedrock in the south end of the entrance passage and adjacent to the passageway along the southeast perimeter. The only diagnostic artifacts from post-Thule context in this structure came from the sod level: a clay pipebowl fragment, a 40-44 gun shell, several twelve-gauge shotgun primer bases, rifle cartridges, and several scraps of iron, all dating to the nineteenth/twentieth centuries.

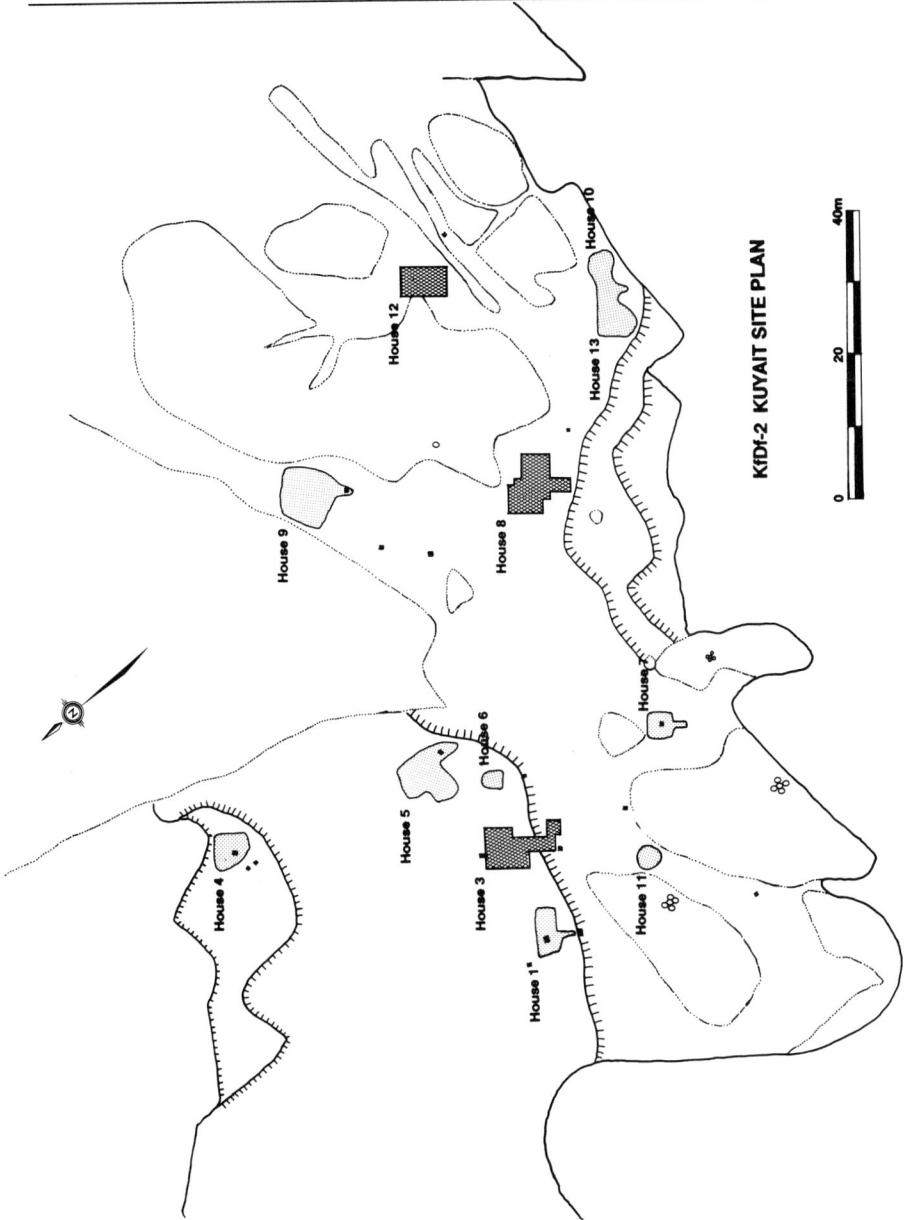

Figure 2: Kuyait site plan

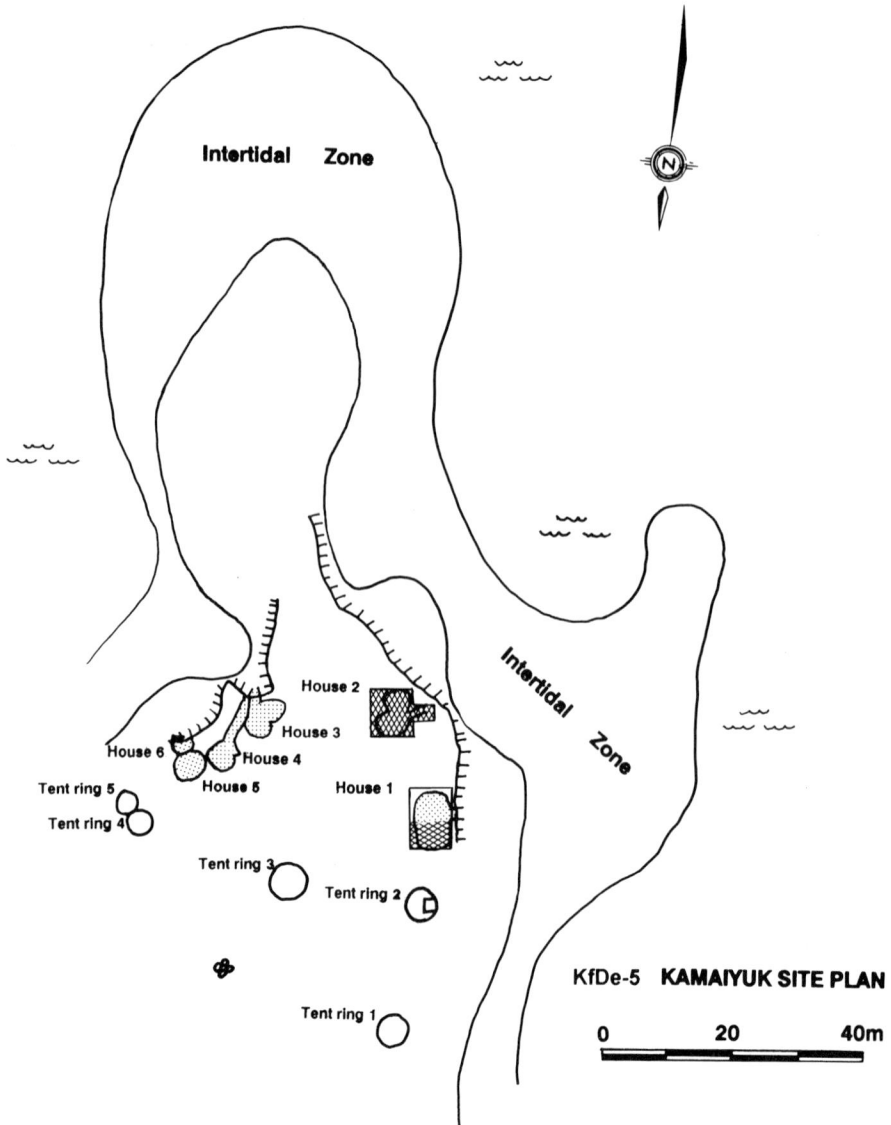

Figure 3: Kamaiyuk site plan

House 3 appears to have been occupied at least twice in Classic Thule times, with two stratigraphic layers. The frost boil that burst through the sleeping platform and pushed the remains of the house forward onto the living floor capped this pre-contact component and thoroughly jumbled the pre-existing structure. An unusual feature of this house was the absence of floor pavements in the entrance passage. Two courses of flagging appear to form a small step above a boulder-filled passageway. In both the passage and the living area cobbles and boulders appear to have been brought in and covered in turf to form the floor, instead of the usual flagging stones. Because House 3 was destroyed by post-depositional processes, it is of limited use for further study.

Kamaiyuk (KfDe-5)

The second month of the field season was spent at Kamaiyuk, a village site located on the southern tip of a small peninsula on the west side of Napoleon Bay, 3 km northeast of Kodlunarn Island (*Fig. 1*). The site is located on a rocky point mantled by grass-covered middens and contains sod-house foundations littered with seal, walrus, and whale bones. The site consists of four large and two small semi-subterranean structures together with caches, tent rings, and other features (*Fig. 3*). The sod structures are of obvious Neoeskimo origins, having prominent rock-reinforced sod walls, entrance tunnels, and single or double sleeping platforms/rooms. Evidence of earlier periods of occupation, however, is found along the entire seaward edge of the site where shoreline erosion has exposed Thule and Dorset period middens. Eroded remnants of these middens extend across a low swale, underwater at high tide, to a rocky point extending south of the site. Erosion has destroyed the entrance passages and parts of the front walls of all six Neoeskimo houses, and monthly high tides enter the interior of House 2. It was evident that storm-driven ice and waves regularly cause severe destruction, especially during the fall when the site lacks a protective ice barrier. Human disturbance in the form of amateur excavations and dismantling of wall and interior stone features, as well as scavenging for whale and walrus bone, was noted in several houses.

Kamaiyuk is the only large Inuit sod-house village site in Countess of Warwick Sound and is almost certainly the village described by Frobisher's captain, George Best, in 1577 [Stefansson and McCaskill 1938, 1:64-65, spelling altered slightly for comparison]:

> Upon the maine land over against the Countesses Iland we discovered, and behelde to our great marvell, the poore caves and houses of those countrie people, which serve them (as it shoulde seeme) for their winter dwellings, & are made two fadome under grounde, in compasse rounde, lyke to an Oven, being joyned fast one by another having houles like to a Foxe or Conny berrie ....
> They undertrench these places with gutters so, that the water falling from the

hills above them, may slide awaye without their anoiaunce & are seated
commonly in the foot of a hil, to shelter them from the colde winds, having their
dore and entrance ever open towards the South .... From the ground upward they
builde with whale bones, for lacke of timber, which bending one over another,
are handsomly compacted in the toppe togither, & are covered over with Seales
skinnes, which in stead of tiles, fenceth them from the rayne. In eache house
they have only one roome, having the one halfe of the floure raysed with broad
stones a fote higher than [the] other, whereon strawing Mosse, they make their
nests to sleepe in.

Our work at Kamaiyuk consisted of mapping and testing houses and features,
sampling external middens, and excavating two of the site's largest dwellings. Midden
samples currently under analysis indicate lengthy Dorset and Thule occupations. Dorset,
Thule, and Frobisher period artifacts were also recovered from the walls of Houses 1 and
2, suggesting that these structures post-dated the Frobisher period. It is difficult to
evaluate the existence of midden deposits associated with specific structures (because of
severe marine erosion) but some remnants were evident along the fronts of the houses.
However, judging from the vast quantity of bone recovered from inside the structures'
walls, much discard appears to have taken place within habitations; perhaps abandoned
structures were used as dumping grounds.

HOUSE 2   Similar in construction to House 8 at Kuyait, this house is a bilobate sod-
walled structure with a paved floor, bench risers, and partially paved sleeping platforms.
A large pile of stones surmounted by a stone pillar had been erected at the intersection
of the two rooms to support the roof. Fat-encrusted hearth piles were present adjacent
to each platform. Two structural phases are indicated. Originally the house had two
lobes with a common living floor, but eventually the south lobe was walled off and was
used as a faunal refuse area.

Analytically, this house is difficult to interpret due to a sequence of construction
phases, but at least three major components are represented. Dorset materials were
found in the walls, the floor pavement, and in abundance in the lower levels of the east
sleeping platform. Neoeskimo materials include ground slate ulus and soapstone vessel
fragments, a bone knife handle, and a harpoon with a metal endblade resembling
Matthiassen's [1927, 148, plate 40.4] Type 5 specimens from the living floor.
Elizabethan materials were found both in wall deposits and in floor pavements presumed
to represent the latest occupation. Among these are fragments of roof and stove tiles and
three or four different ceramic types of probably Elizabethan origin (*Fig. 4*). Excavation
of Kodlunarn Island deposits is needed to determine this suggested association. This
house also yielded non-ceramic artifacts of early European origin, including a small
(pewter?) sheet fashioned into an ulu blade and a "pistol-grip" style hardwood tool or
knife handle. It would appear that the latest occupation of this structure, dating the final
architectural phase, was shortly after the Frobisher voyages and that the Frobisher

Figure 4a: Examples of stove tile fragments recovered from Kuyait and Kamaiyuk

Figure 4b: Examples of ceramic vessel fragments recovered from Lincoln Bay (KfDf-1), Kuyait, and Kamaiyuk

artifacts resulted from scavenging from Kodlunarn Island rather than from direct contact or trade. Radiocarbon dates from *in situ* heather and crowberry plants provide a basis for site chronology. A sample of heather from the living floor dated 390±70 B.P. (A.D. 1410-1650, calibrated with 2 sigma range); a spruce sample from the east lobe dated 230±60 B.P. (A.D. 1500-1955, calibrated with 2 sigma range); and a birch sample from an upper pavement, possibly from an earlier structure, dated 450±60 B.P. (A.D. 1400-1624, calibrated with 2 sigma range).

HOUSE 1   This structure was selected for excavation because its form resembled a type of large, rectangular, multi-platform structure known in seventeenth century Labrador and Greenland as a communal house [Jordan 1977; Jordan and Kaplan 1980; Kaplan 1983, 1985; Taylor 1976]. It was hoped that the house would contain material culture of a post-Frobisher, pre-whaling contact occupation. Material exposed along the erosion edge included late Dorset artifacts and Frobisher tile fragments.

Time permitted completion of only seven of twelve excavation units in this house, resulting in clearing of the entire north half of the house and the living floor. The north end of the house was built into a 1.5 m high bedrock ledge which served as the house wall. The living floor was flagged and a raised sleeping platform stretched along the long east side of the house. The front portion of the east end of the platform had been partially flagged and a large hearth pile was located in the northwest corner of the house. The east end of the entrance passage nearest the living floor was well-defined, but most of the outer portion of the passage and parts of the front wall had been destroyed by marine erosion.

Upon excavation, House 1 lost its communal house appearance, as there began to emerge the existence of a stone pile with a roof support pillar and a wall foundation separating the north and south ends of the sleeping platform. It now appears that this structure is an elongated form of the common east Baffin Inuit bilobate house type.

The house contained both Dorset and historic Inuit artifacts. Historic material was restricted to a few stove tile fragments and corroded metal fragments. Slate endblades and three slate ulus were recovered in association with the latest occupation floor, which also contained Elizabethan tile fragments. However, because these tiles continued to be scavenged by Inuit from Kodlunarn Island in Hall's day, and because tile materials were also found in wall sods, it is probable that this house, like House 2, also post-dates the Frobisher period. The artifact assemblage from House 1 resembled that of House 2 and probably dates to a similar early European contact period rather than the later, more intense contact phase that Inuit experienced with the Euro-American whalers of the nineteenth century. The single radiocarbon sample produced a date of 380±80 B.P. (A.D. 1410-1660, calibrated with 2 sigma range). As in the case of Kuyait House 8, the absence of iron and paucity of slate working is probably due to limited access and careful curation of metal. On the other hand, a number of small slate tools were found here, including miniature ulus and knife blades that seem to indicate continued use of slate for children's or women's implements. Whether these represent an as yet undefined pre-contact Thule horizon or persistence of slate technology in gender- or age-specific contexts needs further analysis. The presence of Dorset material in wall deposits suggests House 1 also was built into a former Dorset structure at this location.

Preliminary Conclusions

Six cultural phases are represented in our finds from Kuyait and Kamaiyuk: Pre-Dorset, Dorset, and four stages of Neoeskimo culture history. Pre-Dorset culture is known only from the presence of a few tools found in redeposited context at Kuyait House 12 and in the Kamaiyuk middens. No *in situ* Pre-Dorset components were isolated and no dating samples were recovered. Without more data little can be said about this early period of settlement except that its unground burins indicate a 3400-4000 B.P. date. Both of these sites also have Dorset sod-house middens whose shore-side deposits are eroding into the sea. Dorset artifacts occurred in the sod walls and sub-floor deposits in each of the Neoeskimo houses excavated. It appears that Thule and later Neoeskimo groups utilized Dorset sod-house sites both as a source of sod and as foundations for their own dwellings. The Dorset occupations here are primarily from middle and late Dorset periods, based on the presence of unifacially-flaked, asymmetrical, side-notched knives and scrapers, and broad concave-based endblades [Maxwell 1985].

The four stages of Neoeskimo culture begin with a pre-contact phase of Thule culture represented in a thin Thule horizon in the frost-heaved remains of Kuyait House 3. Thule materials were also found frequently in secondary context in wall and sub-floor deposits in later Neoeskimo houses built into, or with sods from, Thule period structures. These Thule remains resemble those from other Thule sites in the Eastern Arctic and included only lithic materials. No Thule bone or wood artifacts were identified.

A second Neoeskimo (Inuit) component is represented by an early (sixteenth to seventeenth century) contact phase at Kamaiyuk. Two of the six houses present at this site were excavated in 1991. These houses usually have two partially-paved sleeping platforms, each with its own hearth, sharing a paved common room and entrance passage. Kamaiyuk was in active use as a winter site by Inuit at the time it was visited and described by George Best in 1577. However, our excavations indicate that Houses 1 and 2 date after the Frobisher period but earlier than Kuyait House 8. This chronology is suggested by the larger amounts of Frobisher material in the walls and absence of late trade beads, strap iron, and other materials found at Kuyait House 8. The question remains as to whether the Kamaiyuk houses shortly post-date the Frobisher voyages or represent an occupation whose members scavenged from Kodlunarn for a couple of hundred years prior to nineteenth century whaling. The absence of much post-Frobisher European material at Kamaiyuk provides some indication of isolation of Frobisher Inuit from European contact during the seventeenth and eighteenth centuries. If contact was made with the Dutch, who were whaling and trading along the east coast of Davis Strait in the early seventeenth century [de Jong 1978], or with Hudson Bay Company vessels active in Hudson Strait and south Baffin then or later [Cooke and Holland 1978], we should be able to define an archaeological signature for this period based on ceramic types, clay smoking pipes, or compositional analysis of metal. If there were no documented seventeenth and eighteenth century contact episodes, then we still have the problem of distinguishing immediate post-Frobisher contact from seventeenth and eighteenth century scavenging behaviour at Kodlunarn Island.

The third component, witnessed at Kuyait House 8, appears to represent a later contact phase dating to the mid-nineteenth century. This house is extremely large and, like the Kamaiyuk houses, has two sleeping platforms isolated as separate rooms attached to a common central floor space. The relative lack of Inuit material and absence of an external midden suggests that this house was occupied relatively briefly by Inuit who had limited access to European goods. European material culture, like traditional Inuit artifacts, was scarce. As at Kamaiyuk, Elizabethan materials, including small pieces of coal, flint, and tile from Kodlunarn Island, were found, together with a few diagnostic early and later contact period beads and mid-nineteenth century ceramics. This house collection suggests a period of extremely limited contact with Europeans, with only marginal use of scavenged Kodlunarn Island collections.

A final phase is seen in the later nineteenth/twentieth century occupation in the Kuyait House 12 qarmaq with its extensive evidence of Inuit contact with European commercial whalers and traders. The impact of this late phase of European contact is also noted in the abandonment of the large two-family winter dwellings and introduction of smaller single-family houses. This phase also occurs as a major component of the large Kussejeerarkjuan qarmat site (KeDe-7) on the mainland north of Kodlunarn Island. Kussejeerarkjuan, first located in 1981 [Fitzhugh and Olin 1993] and tested in 1990 [Fitzhugh 1990], contains a large number of late nineteenth to early twentieth century fall and early winter dwellings and was to be a research target of the 1992 field season.

The following remarks summarize our preliminary findings from these Neoeskimo occupation phases. Judging from present evidence, pre-contact Thule sites formerly existed at both the Kuyait and Kamaiyuk sites, but structures dating to this period seem to have been so extensively remodelled for use by later occupants as to be unrecognizable. At present it appears that the pre-contact Thule occupation in outer Frobisher Bay was relatively light and probably began after A.D. 1400. No large Thule winter sites have been found, and Thule middens appear small in such sites as Kuyait and

Kamaiyuk. It is perhaps more significant, since these sites have in most cases been reoccupied and modified beyond recognition by later Inuit, that few pre-contact Thule summer or fall camps have been found. These sites are usually notable because they contain highly conspicuous large stone architecture.

At Kuyait, a period of intensive adaptation to European whaling, trapping, and trading is evident from the remains of the House 12 qarmat, while the large two-family House 8 structure, dating only *ca.* 50-100 years earlier, suggests a period of extremely limited contact with Europeans and only marginal utilization of scavenged Elizabethan material.

Although these sites have not yielded intact "Frobisher period" house floors or features, a definite pattern has emerged as to kinds of Elizabethan material present in early historic Inuit houses and conditions of their use and discard. Early contact sites contain Frobisher roof and stove tile in fair quantities, as well as (more rarely) crucibles and Frobisher ceramic vessel fragments. Softer tile ceramics were often used to burnish Inuit metal ornaments, a function identified by Inuit to Hall. Elizabethan coal and flint are also found in post-Frobisher Inuit sites, both in sod dwellings and in summer tent rings, as are occasional trade beads and metal - sometimes fashioned into harpoon endblades, knives, and ulus or, more commonly, appearing as amorphous metal lumps. These same materials are found at early historic Thule sites located at the head of the bay, 180 km away, in comparable quantities. The assemblage from Kamaiyuk is characterized by a relative lack of ground slate tools and may thus represent a technological transition in which the new materials were highly curated.

Finally, future research on historic period Inuit culture requires an adequate data base of documented archaeological material from Kodlunarn Island. Kodlunarn represents the totality of Elizabethan culture as it was available to the Frobisher Bay Inuit. The Inuit who met Frobisher and his men were exposed to only a small segment of Elizabethan culture: that pertaining to mining, metallurgy, and exploration. The Kodlunarn site represents the universe of new goods, materials, and ideas from which the Inuit selected; it is therefore vital for properly identifying and dating Elizabethan remains from Inuit sites and for distinguishing them from European materials of post-Elizabethan periods.

Current Research

The preliminary results reported here are being amplified by results from excavations at Kuyait and Kamaiyuk continued in 1992. Work at Kamaiyuk was especially important as this site is significant historically as the first aboriginal site visited and described by English explorers in the New World. Best's account indicates that the site was being used as a winter village at the time of the Frobisher voyages; therefore it may be expected to contain the largest quantity of Elizabethan materials that Inuit obtained by trade, salvage, or scavenging from Kodlunarn Island and other Frobisher sites. Excavation of the site's structure and midden deposits were given high priority due to the rapid rate of destruction presently underway from natural causes and, to a lesser extent, from human disturbance. Even though the existing Kamaiyuk houses appear to post-date the Frobisher period, important information can be obtained from Frobisher artifacts and evidence of their use and modification by Inuit even from secondary context. The 1992 field work has provided information from Houses 3-6 which further confirm the chronological placement of this site and will facilitate comparisons with other sites.

Currently, research is in progress to identify and date archaeological data from the 1991 and 1992 seasons. Analysis of wood and charcoal from 1991 has been completed, and radiocarbon samples have been run [see Laeyendecker, this volume]. Archival studies and oral history, European material culture identification, and analysis of subsistence and environmental data are underway. We expect the results of 1992 excavations at Kuyait and Kamaiyuk to provide new information on early contact phases. Work was also initiated (in 1992) at the large late nineteenth century whaling contact qarmat site at Kussejeerarkjuan, in Countess of Warwick Sound, to further define this later phase of Inuit contact history.

The aim of our work has been to address a period in Inuit culture history that has not been studied archaeologically and for which little written material is available. In addition to documenting the development of Inuit culture from Thule times into the twentieth century, our work is exploring environmental relationships and processes of culture contact and exchange. This research will be coordinated with excavations and analysis of materials from Kodlunarn Island and with archival studies related to the Frobisher voyages and later European contacts.

Community participation has been a strong part of our research plans. Local Inuit took part in the 1990-92 field work. It is our hope that the information and training obtained by Inuit participating in this part of the Meta Incognita Project will be useful to the Iqaluit community in expanding knowledge of their own cultural heritage.

ACKNOWLEDGEMENTS: This field work was funded in part by the Smithsonian Institution, the Canadian Museum of Civilization, the Polar Continental Shelf programme, the Wenner Gren Foundation, the Canadian Graduate Student Fellowship of the Canadian Embassy, the Northern Scientific Training programme, the Challenge 1991 programme, and Harvard University summer field funds. We greatly appreciated help from our hard-working field crew, including Michael Bradford, Kim Gardener, Dosia Laeyendecker, Dan Odess, Patrick Saltonstall, Ned Searles, and Jeannette Smith. Thanks are also due to the *Pitsiulak* crew including Captain Perry Colbourne, Sophie Morse, Paloosie Pishuktie, Ooleetua Pishuktie, and Juta Ipelee. We are also indebted to Bob Longworth and Lynn Cousins of the Science Institute of the Northwest Territories and Bill McKenzie and Mary Ellen Thomas for logistic support and field assistance.

References

Boas, Franz
1964   *The Central Eskimo.* Reprint. Lincoln: University of Nebraska Press. (Originally published 1888)

Broom, Leonard, B.J. Siegal, E.Z. Vogt, and J.B. Watson
1954   Acculturation: an exploratory formulation. *American Anthropologist* 56:973-1002.

Collins, Henry B.
1950   Excavations at Frobisher Bay, Baffin Island, N.W.T. In *Annual Report of the National Museum for the Fiscal Year 1948-1949.* National Museum of Canada Bulletin 118:18-43.

Cooke, Alan, and Clive Holland
1978   *The Exploration of Northern Canada, 500-1920: a Chronology.* Toronto: Arctic History Press.

de Jong, C.
1978   A short history of old Dutch whaling. In *Geschiedenis van de Oude Nederlandse Walvisvaart*, ed. C. de Jong, vol.3, 289-325. Pretoria: University of South Africa.

Eber, Dorothy Harley
1989   *When the Whalers Were up North: Inuit Memories from the Eastern Arctic.* Boston: David R. Goine.

Ehrenreich, Robert
1990   Considering the impetus for the bronze-to-iron transition in prehistoric Britain. *Journal of Metals* 42:36-38.

Fitzhugh, William W., ed.
1985   *Cultures in Contact: the Impact of European Contacts on Native American Cultural Institutions, A.D. 1000-1800.* Washington: Smithsonian Institution Press.

1990   Archeology of the Frobisher voyages: field report for 1990. Arctic Studies
                Center, Smithsonian Institution.

Fitzhugh, William and Jacqueline Olin, eds.
1993   *Archeology of the Frobisher Voyages*. Washington: Smithsonian Institution
                Press.

Fraser, Robert, and William Rannie
1972   *Arctic Adventurer: Grant and the Seduisante*. Lincoln (Ont.): W.R. Rannie

Goldring, Philip
1986   Inuit economic responses to Euro-American contacts: Southeast Baffin Island
                1824-1940. *Canadian Historical Association, Historical Papers*, 146-72.

Gullov, Hans Christian
1985   Whales, whalers and Eskimos: the impact of European whaling on the
                demography and economy of Eskimo society in West Greenland. In *Cultures in
                Contact*, ed. W. Fitzhugh, 71-96. Washington: Smithsonian Institution Press.

Hall, Charles Francis
1970   *Life with the Esquimaux: a Narrative of Arctic Experience in Search of Survivors
                of Sir John Franklin's Expedition*. Edmonton: Hurtig. (Originally published
                1864)

Hickey, Clifford G.
1984   An examination of processes in cultural change among nineteenth century Copper
                Inuit. *Etudes/Inuit/Studies* 8(1): 13-36.

Jacobs, John, and Douglas Stenton
1985   Environment, resources, and prehistoric settlement in upper Frobisher Bay,
                Baffin Island. *Arctic Anthropology* 22(2): 59-76.

Jordan, Richard
1977   Inuit occupation of the Central Labrador coast since 1600 A.D. In *Our
                Footprints are Everywhere*, ed. C. Brice-Bennett, 43-48. Nain (Lab.): Labrador
                Inuit Association.

1978   Archaeological investigations of the Hamilton Inlet Labrador Eskimo: social and
                economic responses to European contact. *Arctic Anthropology* 15(2): 175-85.

Jordan, Richard, and Susan Kaplan
1980   An archaeological view of the Inuit/European contact period in Central Labrador.
                Etudes/Inuit/Studies 4(1-2): 35-45.

Kaplan, Susan
  1983   Economic and social change in Labrador Neo-Eskimo culture. Ph.D. diss.,
           Department of Anthropology, Bryn Mawr College.

  1985   European goods and socio-economic change in early Labrador Inuit society. In
           Cultures in Contact, ed. W. Fitzhugh, 45-69. Washington: Smithsonian
           Institution Press.

Mathiassen, Therkel
  1927   *Archaeology of the Central Eskimo*. Copenhagen: Gyldendolske Boghandel,
           Nordisk Forlag.

  1931   Inugsuk, A Mediaeval Eskimo Settlement in the Upernavik District, West
           Greenland. *Meddelelser Om Gronland* 77(4): 147-340.

Maxwell, Moreau
  1985   *Prehistory of the Eastern Arctic*. Orlando: Academic Press.

McGhee, Robert
  1984   *The Thule Village at Brooman Point, High Arctic Canada*. National Museum of
           Man, Mercury Series, Archaeological Survey of Canada Paper 125.

Molloy, Paula, Anne Henshaw, and Bruno Marino
  in press Culture-environment interaction in the North Atlantic: controlling the climate
           variable. *Proceedings of the 24th Annual Chacmool Conference*. Calgary:
           University of Calgary Archaeology Association.

Park, Robert
  1988   "Winter houses" and qarmat in Thule and Historic Inuit settlement patterns: some
           implications for Thule studies. *Canadian Journal of Archaeology* 12:163-75.

Ross, W. Gillies
  1977   Whaling and the decline of Arctic populations. *Arctic Anthropology* 14:1-8.

  1979   Commercial whaling and Eskimos in the Eastern Canadian Arctic 1819-1920.
           In *Thule Eskimo Culture: An Anthropological Retrospective*, ed. A. McCartney,
           242-66, National Museum of Man, Mercury Series, Archaeological Survey of
           Canada Paper 88.

Sabo, George
  1979   Development of the Thule culture in the historic period: patterns of material
           culture change on the Davis Strait coast of Baffin Island. In *Thule Eskimo
           Culture: An Anthropological Retrospective*, ed. A. McCartney, 212-41, National
           Museum of Man, Mercury Series, Archaeological Survey of Canada Paper 88.

Sabo, George, and John Jacobs
    1980   Aspects of Thule culture adaptations in southern Baffin Island. *Arctic* 33(3):
                487-504.

Savelle, James
    1985   Effects of nineteenth century European exploration on the development of the
                Netsilik Inuit culture. In *The Franklin Era in Canadian Arctic History 1845-
                1859*, ed P. Sutherland, 192-214. National Museum of Man, Mercury Series,
                Archaeological Survey of Canada Paper 131.

Schledermann, Peter
    1975   *Thule Eskimo Prehistory of Cumberland Sound, Baffin Island, Canada*. National
                Museum of Man, Mercury Series, Archaeological Survey of Canada Paper 38.

Stefansson, Vilhjalmur, and Eloise McCaskill, eds.
    1938   *The Three Voyages of Martin Frobisher in Search of a Passage to Cathay and
                India by the North-west, A.D. 1576-8*. 2 vols. London: Argonaut Press.

Stenton, Douglas
    1987   Recent archaeological investigations in Frobisher Bay, Baffin Island, N.W.T.
                Canadian Journal of Archaeology 11:13-48.

Stevenson, Marc
    1984   Kekerton: preliminary archaeology of an Arctic whaling station. On file at
                Prince of Wales Northern Heritage Centre, Government of the Northwest
                Territories, Yellowknife.

Taylor, J. Garth
    1976   The Inuit middleman in the Labrador baleen trade. Paper presented at the 75th
                Annual Meeting of the American Anthropological Association, Washington.

Wakeham, William
    1898   *Report of the Expedition to Hudson Bay and Cumberland Gulf in the ship
                "Diana" under the command of William Wakeham*. Ottawa: S.E. Dawson.

Analysis of Wood and Charcoal Samples From Inuit Sites in Frobisher Bay

Dosia Laeyendecker
Arctic Studies Center
Smithsonian Institution

RÉSUMÉ

Les fouilles réalisées dans les deux villages historiques que les Inuit utilisaient durant l'hiver, Kuyait et Kamaiyuk, à l'extérieur de la baie de Frobisher, ont livré de nombreux artefacts, ainsi que des échantillons organiques appartenant soit à la période historique, dont des restes d'origine européenne, soit à des ensembles plus anciens d'origine thuléenne et dorsétienne. L'article décrit les résultats préliminaires obtenus après analyse des échantillons de bois et de charbon recueillis lors des fouilles de deux habitations à Kuyait, et d'une autre habitation et d'une partie d'une seconde à Kamaiyuk. L'aire botanique en question se situe dans la région sud de la toundra arctique. Les ressources en bois se limitent à des arbrisseaux tels que le saule, le boulot et la bruyère. La plus grande partie des matériaux trouvés dans les échantillons dérivait du bois flotté de l'Arctique, dont l'épinette, le mélèze et le pin. Quant à l'occurrence du chêne, du hêtre et, à l'occasion, d'autres bois «exotiques», elle ferait suite à leur introduction par les premiers voyageurs européens (Frobisher, par exemple); mais on a retrouvé récemment ces mêmes essences dans le bois flotté de certaines grèves éloignées de la baie de Frobisher.

ABSTRACT

Excavations at two Historic Inuit winter village sites, Kuyait and Kamaiyuk, in outer Frobisher Bay yielded many artifacts as well as organic samples from the historic period, including remains of European origin, and from older Thule and Dorset components. This paper describes preliminary results from the analysis of wood and charcoal samples from the excavation of two houses at Kuyait and from one house and part of a second at Kamaiyuk. Botanically the area is located within the southern region of the Arctic tundra. Local wood sources are restricted to small dwarf shrubs, such as willow, birch, and heath plants. Most of the material found in the samples was derived from Arctic driftwood, including spruce, larch, and pine. Occurrences of oak, beech, and occasional other "exotic" woods may be due to their introduction by early European voyagers (Frobisher, for instance), but these woods are also found among recent driftwood on some beaches in outer Frobisher Bay.

Introduction

In the summer of 1981 surveys and test pit excavations were carried out by scientists from the Smithsonian and other institutions on Kodlunarn Island, the site of Martin Frobisher's summer camp in southeastern Baffin Island, in what is now known as Frobisher Bay. Although Frobisher did not overwinter there, he established a camp consisting of several stone and wooden structures and also a kind of dry dock where ships could be repaired. Wood and charcoal samples were collected from test pits in these structures and analyzed. The woodsamples were mostly very decayed, which made it difficult to identify them, but the numerous charcoal fragments were well preserved and could be identified [Laeyendecker 1992]. It was found that almost all of this charcoal could be traced to English trees; that information, together with data from the accounts of the Frobisher voyages [Stefansson and McCaskill 1938], made it clear that this charcoal (and the wood) had been brought to Kodlunarn Island by the Frobisher expeditions.

The next focus of investigation was the Historic Inuit sites on the mainland in the vicinity of Kodlunarn Island; there contact between Frobisher's men and the local southeast Baffin Inuit population could be studied. These sites were found during the summer of 1990 by a joint American-Canadian archaeological expedition coordinated by William Fitzhugh. Excavation began in the summer of 1991. Radiocarbon dates on samples from these sites fall mostly within the time period of the Frobisher voyages. Two more years of fieldwork are planned, but enough has been accomplished so far to justify a preliminary report.

The analysis of wood and charcoal samples from two Historic Inuit winter village sites will be presented in this paper. Kuyait 1 (KfDf-2), located on the south tip of the Wiswell Inlet Peninsula, contains many sod house foundations, tent rings, and other structures. Dorset remains also are eroding along the shore of this large site. So far samples have been analyzed from two of the three excavated structures at Kuyait: House 3, a frost-damaged historic period sod house with a Thule component and early Dorset material in a midden; and House 8, a large, probably early Historic, bilobed, sod-walled winterhouse. The other site that was excavated in 1991, Kamaiyuk 1 (KfDe-5), located 3 km northeast of Kodlunarn Island, was described in the accounts of the Frobisher voyages [Stefansson and McCaskill 1938, 64]. This large site contains several Historic

Inuit sod house structures that apparently were built inside older Thule and Dorset remains. All structures have been damaged by marine erosion and some by visitors. Samples have been analyzed from House 1 (only partly excavated), House 2 (a bilobed structure), and from a test pit in House 3. Radiocarbon dates are already available from each of these structures (Table 2).

Southern Baffin Island is located beyond the polar treeline at a latitude of 62°. The landscape is formed by the crystalline rocks of the Precambrian Shield and is hilly rather than mountainous, but rugged. On the south side of Frobisher Bay, glacier ice covers the Meta Incognita peninsula. On the north side of Frobisher Bay, ice and snow usually disappear during the summer months. The average July temperature is below 10° C. (50° F). Spring arrives about mid-June and the winter sets in by the end of September. Midwinter is very cold and continuously dark. Southeastern Baffin Island gets a lot of snow, up to 600 cm per year [In-Cho Chung 1989, 9]. The tundra is wetter than any other landscape on earth. Permanently frozen ground underlies a thin layer of soil which thaws during the summer and freezes in the winter. Lakes and ponds are formed as a consequence of melting permafrost and subterranean ice. Bogs and mires, polygons, water-filled cracks, and peaty hummocks form characteristic features in this landscape, caused by cryogenic processes. The high degree of moisture is a direct result of low evaporation because of insufficient heat. The temperature is not high enough to evaporate the yearly amount of precipitation [Chernov 1985, 15]. This region, the low Arctic tundra zone, is mostly covered with a continuous vegetation of mosses and heath plants, miniature herbs and grasses with dwarf shrubs (mostly willows). Colorful lichen cover the rocks. The flowering tundra in the month of July is a spectacular sight.

Usually wood remains from archaeological sites reflect local vegetation and plant use. In the Historic Inuit houses from Kuyait and Kamaiyuk we find small twigs of crowberry (*Empetrum nigrum*) and willow (*Salix sp.*) on floor pavements or sleeping platforms. These twigs, usually of the same size (3-5 cm long), were probably used for flooring, and for insulation or bedding. This material, if found in large enough quantity, is ideal for radiocarbon dating. However, most of the wood and charcoal samples identify to wood species not derived from the local vegetation. These woods - among others, spruce and larch from northern boreal forests, and also temperate hardwoods like oak and beech - must have been obtained either from driftwood sources, or through trade or other findings. Some of these woods may have been scavenged from Frobisher's camp on Kodlunarn Island.

Driftwood occurs in various amounts in the waters and along the beaches of the Arctic. Native people have always collected and still use driftwood for fuel and tool making. This wood originates in the boreal and subboreal forest regions of Scandinavia, northern Russia, Alaska, and Canada, floats down in the drainage of large rivers, and is transported in the pack-ice following the direction of the currents in the Arctic Ocean, before it is deposited on beaches that can be reached by open water. Driftwood is not abundant all over the Arctic; in some areas it is generally scarce, while in the Western Canadian Arctic and Alaska, for instance, no shortage of driftwood has ever been felt [Giddings 1941]. The presence or absence of driftwood is dependent on many factors, among them fluctuating climatic conditions, summer temperatures, ocean currents, and beach morphology. The drier and less vegetated the area is, the longer the wood can be preserved; here older logs are found [Bartholin and Hjort 1987]. In emergent coastal areas of the Canadian Arctic raised beach terraces are found often to have driftwood even on the highest levels [Blake 1972]. The oldest dated driftwood find from the Canadian Arctic dates to about 8500 B.P. [Dyke and Morris 1990, 7]. In central regions of Frobisher Bay driftwood generally seems to be scarce. However, during the survey of 1991 two beaches with much driftwood were found along Chapell Inlet and Lefferts Island in the southeast end of Frobisher Bay. This wood had been washed up onto the current storm line by the tides. In this area the land is sinking and the beaches are eroding away, so no beach terraces have been formed and there is no spatial or elevational differentiation between older and younger driftwood. Instead driftwood remains from across the centuries are found in a single horizon: what seem to be older worm-eaten logs occur together with quite recent industrial and shipborne waste. This makes it difficult to determine what driftwood was available at the time of the Frobisher period, in order to distinguish between wood that would have been found locally and wood that was definitely introduced by the Frobisher expedition (or later by others).

A collection was made of thirty-nine driftwood samples from eight locations in southeast Frobisher Bay, Kuyait Inlet, Sumner Island, Sharko Peninsula, Chapell Inlet, and Lefferts Island, and in middle Frobisher Bay at Minguktu 1.

Method

In the field great care was given to proper excavation and conservation of organic artifacts and samples. Dwelling structures were excavated in 2 m by 2 m squares, by arbitrary 10 cm levels as well as by stratigraphic levels; most of the soil was screened using quarter-inch mesh. Charcoal, wood, and other organic samples were excavated by hand. In addition soil samples of two to three litres each were collected from features and baulks within the structures. Flotation in the field was attempted, but was found to be impractical, because of time restrictions and the cold. Flotation in the lab does not seem to work, because of the stickiness of the soil. It might work if a flocculating agent were added, but so far it does not seem to serve the purpose of retrieving wood and charcoal fragments. After these soil samples were picked through by hand for wood and charcoal fragments, they were sent away for further macrobiological investigation. Field conservation of organic artifacts focused on immediate, short-term stabilization of the objects, and packing them with as little damage as possible. A conservation manual [Cross, Hett, and Bertulli, 1989] from the Canadian Northwest Territories was used as a guide. As a general rule, wet and damp objects, which comprised the bulk of the material, were kept in that condition, often bagged with wet sphagnum moss, while dry items were packed dry. Fragile pieces were reinforced and handled as carefully as possible. By and large, wood and charcoal samples may be best preserved by collecting them in plastic bags. Even after several months we found the wood still wet, with little further decomposition.

About ninety wooden artifacts were excavated during the 1991 field season. The majority were probably *wick-trimmers*, which are wooden sticks, 10-20 cm long, about 1-2 cm in diameter and usually burned at one end. These sticks were used to handle the moss wick in a soapstone oil lamp and are known from Dorset sites as well as Thule and Inuit sites. Also found were a number of *float plugs*, *game pieces*, *tool handle parts*, and a *bow end*. One of the tool handles seems to be of European design. This is the only wooden artifact that has been identified to species. All artifacts are deposited at the Canadian Museum of Civilization and, to date, have not been identified to species or to possible origins of wood sources.

Compared to finds from sites in Labrador, charcoal samples were few and in most cases not from well-defined hearth features. Because oil was used as fuel by the Historic Inuit in southeast Baffin Island, the hearth features in the houses consisted of blackened flat stone slabs layered with a residue of feathers, hide and bone, all conserved in a hard fat-congealed crust. The charcoal that was found usually occurred in the upper sod layer and was probably used in more recent fires. Test pits from Dorset components were found to have larger charcoal samples; in one instance a charcoal sample contained local willow twigs (*Salix sp.*), which was convenient for dating purposes.

Wood fragments, consisting of cut wood and debitage, were excavated in great numbers. The wood was reasonably well preserved because of the frozen conditions in the soil of the Arctic tundra. However very few pieces of cut wood - which must have been parts of toolhandles, shafts, stakes, etc. - were found in recognizable forms; therefore relatively few wooden artifacts were recovered. No bowl fragments were identified. It is possible that freezing under a heavy load of soil results in flattening and otherwise transforming of the pieces. More research should be done in this direction.

In the laboratory at the Smithsonian Institution the organic samples were sorted; charcoal samples were dried, but the wood fragments were kept in wet condition in their plastic bags. Two methods of microscopy were used: reflected light for the examination of charcoal, and transmitted light to study wood slides. The wood slides were made by hand with a one-edged razor blade. The wood was deteriorated but identification at least to genus was usually possible. Sometimes the wood was rotten and very soft as a result.

In that case it was very difficult to section. On other occasions the wood was firm enough to make the slide, but the wood structure was so deteriorated that identification was still impossible. Textbooks on wood identification [among others: Panshin and de Zeeuw 1970; Schweingruber 1978] were used to aid the analysis.

Five driftwood samples were sent to the University of Lund in Sweden for dendrochronological analysis, to add specimens to an ongoing study of tree ring patterns in Arctic driftwood. As a result one of our samples, from Minguktu 1 in the mid-Frobisher Bay area, was dated to 1924 on the outer tree ring (no bark remained on this sample), and the source of the wood was traced to the Yukon river valley in Alaska. The tree therefore had drifted down the Yukon river into the Bering Sea, through Bering Strait, into the Arctic Ocean, and "down" east or west of Greenland to Frobisher Bay [Eggertsson, pers. com. 1992].

Results

Preliminary results of analyses of wood and charcoal from two excavated houses at **Kuyait 1** and from one fully excavated and one partly excavated house at **Kamaiyuk 1** are discussed below. An overview is given in Table 1, and a list of radiocarbon dates in Table 2.

Kuyait 1 (KfDf-2), House 3:

House 3 was a single room, rectangular structure with an entrance passage and midden of uncertain association, located at the western side of the site near and facing the beach. Dorset lithic tools and flakes were found in this eroding beach terrace and also in a lower level in the midden between the entrance passage of House 3 and the beach. The interior of the house was destroyed by solifluction and could not be reconstructed. A Thule component was found in the disturbed floor pavement, with a few ground slate tools and a toggling harpoon head, while the remains in the entrance passage were mostly nineteenth or twentieth century. Very few Frobisher period artifacts were recovered. Among the Historic Inuit artifacts found were a single bone tool and a few worked ivory pieces. The lower level of the midden and entrance passage yielded early Dorset stone tools. Few wooden artifacts were excavated. Seven wick-trimmers (most of them found in the midden outside the house), a cut wood fragment with a drilled hole, and two more unidentified cut wood fragments were found in the entrance and in the midden. In the north wall area of the house was found a round grooved object (3.5 cm diameter and 0.8 cm thick) which may be a game (checker) piece, or part of a top. This artifact resembles the picture of a whalebone disk mounted on a wooden stem, described from the Inugsuk period in Greenland [Jordan 1984, 544]. As noted before, the wooden artifacts are being preserved at CMC and have not been identified to wood species yet. The wood samples, probably mostly pieces of debitage, have been described and identified (Table 1). In House 3 remains of local vegetation (willow twigs) were found only in the lowest level of the midden, associated with Dorset tools. Wood and charcoal fragments excavated from features inside the house were all derived from driftwood: spruce, larch, pine, oak, beech, and sweetgum. The largest variety of wood species was found in the entrance passage in connection with eggshells and twentieth century artifacts. Thus it is supposed that the wood fragments originated as recent driftwood finds, even though pieces of oak and beech may have been available in the area since Frobisher's time.

Kuyait 1 (KfDf-2), House 8:

House 8 was a bilobed structure with floor pavement, two sleeping platforms, sod walls, and a long entrance passage. Storage space was found under the western sleeping platform, and two hearth places were situated on the east and the west side of the central floor. These hearths were built of stacked flat slabs that were very crusty and covered with layers of congealed fat, bone, feathers, hide, and baleen. Frobisher-period artifacts such as tile fragments were found, as well as Thule ground slate tools, Dorset stone tools, Historic Inuit bone and ivory implements, soapstone pot fragments, and nineteenth/twentieth century remains - among them beads, a few pieces of ceramic, glass, and pieces of iron. Wooden artifacts include: unidentified cut wood pieces; wick-trimmers; a socketed handle and some other possible parts of handles and shafts; sticks or pins (drills?); a few drilled, flat slat fragments; and a knobbed fragment that may have been part of a toggle.

This large house yielded relatively more charcoal samples and a lot of wood debitage. The charcoal was mostly found in the upper level of the excavation; it was probably the remains of recent activity, dating after the latest occupation of the house. One charcoal sample, found under a surface boulder in the east lobe of the house, consisted of tiny twigs, seeds, and even an intact flower from the composite family. This very delicate charred material must have been instantly converted to carbon by being covered with hot ashes, in the way the discarded weeds from gardens of Pompeii were preserved. The charred flower is a unique occurrence and also indicates a summer event. However, we believe that this sample is also post-house occupation. A few large charcoal samples were collected from the pavement floor in the middle of the house. These samples were found to contain only spruce and thus were derived from driftwood. Wood samples were plentiful, especially in the lower levels of the entrance passage. The

Table 1 *Occurrences of wood and charcoal samples at the different sites, and wood identifications in these samples*

Site name House #	# charcoal samples identifications	# wood samples identifications
Kuyait 1 (KfDf-2) House 3	7 spruce, larch, crowberry, sweetgum(?)	20 spruce, larch, pine, oak, beech, willow, sweetgum(?)
Kuyait 1 (KfDf-2) House 8	17 spruce, larch, willow	29 spruce, larch, pine (*P. strobus* type and *P. silvestris* type), willow, oak
Kamaiyuk 1 (KfDe-5) House 1	4 spruce, larch, willow	6 spruce, larch, willow, birch
Kamaiyuk 1 (KfDe-5) House 2	5 spruce, heather, (beech, oak)	42 spruce, larch, pine (*P.strobus* type), crowberry, willow, birch, oak

Table 2 *Radiocarbon dates*

site House #	C-14 age years B.P. sample content	calibrated age, two sigma statistics
Kuyait 1 (KfDf-2) House 3		
Kuyait 1 (KfDf-2) House 8, floor	110 +/- 50 B.P. wood, crowberry	
Kamaiyuk 1 (KfDe-5) House 1, floor	380 +/- 80 B.P. charcoal, spruce	A.D. 1410-1660
Kamaiyuk 1 (KfDe-5) House 2, floor south lobe upper pavement	390 +/- 70 B.P. wood, crowberry 230 +/- 60 B.P. wood, spruce 450 +/- 60 B.P. wood, birch	A.D. 1410-1650 A.D. 1500-1954 A.D. 1400-1624

wood fragments were identified to species of spruce, larch, pine, oak, and willow. Most were derived from driftwood, but oak fragments may be of Frobisher origin. Willow fragments occurred in the samples in the form of twigs; as such, they were considered to be from local vegetation and contemporaneous with the house occupation. However, in some samples the willow fragments seemed to be derived from a different, larger wood source; because willow was found in the Frobisher samples from Kodlunarn Island, this possibility must be kept in mind. In the sleeping platform, and also on the pavement floor, small twigs of crowberry (*Empetrum nigrum*) were found; they might have been used as bedding and flooring material. These samples were taken for radiocarbon dating and resulted in a modern date for the house, 110 +/- 50 B.P. (Table 2). From Thule sites along northwestern Hudson Bay, arctic heather (*Cassiope tetragona*) was described as platform covering, in accordance with findings by Boas [McCartney 1977, 14, 182].

Kamaiyuk 1 (KfDe-5), House 1:

The excavation of House 1 was to be continued in the 1992 field season. The architecture of the house was unclear, partly because of damage from marine erosion, which had destroyed most of the entrance passage. The house was built against a rock formation on the north side, where a raised paved platform was found as well as a hearth area. Floor pavement was recovered in the centre of the house. Historic Inuit artifacts, Frobisher-period tile fragments, and Thule and Dorset tools were found in the different features. Very few wooden artifacts were recovered: wick-trimmers, a possible handle, stakes, and some unidentified cut wood pieces. Two large charcoal samples, containing spruce and larch fragments that must have been derived from driftwood, were collected from the living floor pavement. One of these samples was radiocarbon dated to 380 +/- 80 B.P. (Table 2). In the wood samples we did not find much from local vegetation. Some willow twigs were recovered, but not enough for dating purposes. One small twig of birch with bark was found in the hearth area. The other samples consisted of spruce and larch. No oak or other exotic hardwoods were found in this house.

Kamaiyuk 1 (KfDe-5), House 2:

House 2 was a bilobed, sod-walled structure with a paved central living floor, two sleeping platforms, hearth areas, and a partly destroyed entrance passage. The house had been reoccupied and in the process the architecture changed; this caused some problems with interpretation. Many Dorset stone tools were found in the lower levels of the east platform and in what remained of the east wall. Thule materials occurred sparingly in the floor and walls, a few Historic Inuit bone artifacts were found in the upper levels, and European artifacts were recovered from the walls and the floor. Among the latter was found a wooden tool handle, identified as maple (possibly root wood from the European maple: *Acer campestre*). Other wooden artifacts were mostly wick-trimmers and unidentified cut wood fragments. We also recovered a socketed handle part, a bow end, two possible box fragments, and several wooden plugs. One flat rectangular piece with three round blackened depressions was probably a fire board, which is also described as a fire hearth or base [Friedman 1975, 96]. Round sticks, sometimes with burned ends, may have been used as fire drills. Most of the wood samples were identified to driftwood: spruce, larch, and pine (Table 1). Two small fragments of oak were found in the north wall, and in the south wall one large fragment of beech charcoal, which may have found its way here from a Frobisher structure on Kodlunarn Island. On the living platform a sample of crowberry (*Empetrum nigrum*) twigs was collected for radiocarbon dating. The result was 390 +/- 70 B.P. A driftwood sample from the south lobe dated to 230 +/- 80 B.P. (Table 2). This room seems to have been walled off from the rest of the house during a later occupation. The oldest date from the house, 450 +/- 60 B.P. (Table 2), resulted from a sample of birch twigs with the bark intact, from the upper layer in the east sleeping platform. Here a remnant of pavement was found with spots of crusty soil that included some organic material containing baleen, leather, feathers, and scattered bits of charcoal. Bone artifacts were also recovered from this possibly older cultural layer, which was modified by the reoccupation of the house.

Conclusions

Birch twigs were found only at Kamaiyuk, in House 1 as well as House 2, in the upper layers associated with crusty soils, containing organic material. This is interesting, because birch is restricted to favourable habitats in the inner and middle parts of northern Frobisher Bay [Andrews et al. 1980). It seems not to occur very often near Kamaiyuk; therefore it is noteworthy that it was found in both houses and probably in the same features.

For flooring crowberry (*Empetrum nigrum*) was used both in Kuyait House 8, Kamaiyuk House 2, and Kamaiyuk House 3 (not discussed here). Apparently this was used centuries ago as well as in more modern times, because the dates range on this material from 390 +/- 70 B.P. (Kamaiyuk, House 2) to 110 +/- 50 B.P. (Kuyait, House 8). Willow twigs seem to have been used at Dorset sites, but so far the sample is too small to state this with any certainty.

The houses excavated at Kamaiyuk were older than the houses at Kuyait. At Kuyait, in the more recent houses, a larger variety of wood species was recovered due to a combination of environmental and cultural factors. The future direction of research includes a refinement of the species identification, in order to identify different species of oak for dendrochronological analysis, which will help to date the more recent Inuit structures. The oak samples should be targeted for dendrochronology, both because the European oak chronology is well established and because oak was found in samples from the Frobisher structures on Kodlunarn Island, in Historic Inuit houses and as driftwood on the beaches.

References

Andrews, J.T., W.N. Mode, P.J. Webber, G.H. Miller, and J.D. Jacobs
  1980   Report on the distribution of dwarf birches and present pollen rain, Baffin Island, N.W.T., Canada. *Arctic* 33(1): 50-58.

Bartholin, T.S., and C. Hjort
  1987   Dendrochronological studies of recent driftwood on Svalbard. In *Methods of Dendrochronology*, ed. L. Kairukstis, Z. Bednarz and E. Feliksik, vol. 1, 207-19. Polish Academy of Sciences Systems Research Institute.

Blake, W.
  1972   Climatic implications of radiocarbon dated driftwood in the Queen Elizabeth Islands. *Arctic Canada Universitas Ouluensis* 3(1): 77-101

Chernov, Y.I.
  1985   *The Living Tundra*. Cambridge: University Press.

Chung, In-Cho
  1989   *Eastern North America as Seen by a Botanist: Pictorial*. Vol. 1, *The Arctic Region*. Seoul: Samhwa Printing Co.

Cross, S., C. Hett, and M. Bertulli
  1989   *Conservation Manual for Northern Archaeologists*. Prince of Wales Northern Heritage Centre Archaeology Report No. 6.

Dyke, A., and T.F. Morris
  1990   *Postglacial History of the Bowhead Whale and of Driftwood Penetration; Implications for Paleoclimate, Central Canadian Arctic*. Geological Survey of Canada Paper 89-24.

Friedman, J.P.
  1975   The prehistoric uses of wood at the Ozette archaeological site. Diss., Department of Anthropology, Washington State University.

Giddings, J.L.
    1941   Dendrochronology in northern Alaska. *University of Arizona Bulletin*, 12(4),
                Laboratory of Tree Ring Research Bulletin 1.

Jordan, R.H.
    1984   Neo-Eskimo prehistory of Greenland. In *Handbook of North American Indians*,
                ed. W. Sturtevant. Vol. 5, *Arctic*, 544-548. Washington, Smithsonian
                Institution.

Laeyendecker, D.M.
    1993   Wood and charcoal remains from Kodlunarn Island. In *Archeology of the
                Frobisher Voyages*, ed. W. Fitzhugh and J. Olin, 155-72. Washington:
                Smithsonian Press.

McCartney, A.P.
    1977   *Thule Eskimo Prehistory along Northwestern Hudson Bay*. National Museum of
                Man, Mercury Series, Archaeological Survey of Canada Paper 70.

Panshin, A.J., and C. de Zeeuw
    1970   *Textbook of Wood Technology*. Vol. 1. New York: McGraw-Hill.

Schweingruber, F.H.
    1978   *Microscopic wood anatomy*. Birmensdorf (Switz.): Swiss Federal Institute for
                Forestry Research.

Stefansson, V., and E. McCaskill, eds.
    1938   *The Three Voyages of Martin Frobisher in Search of a Passage to Cathay and
                India by the North-west, A.D. 1576-8*. London: Argonaut Press.

Inuit Oral History:
The Voyages of Sir Martin Frobisher, 1576-78

Susan Rowley

RÉSUMÉ

L'histoire des expéditions de Frobisher est bien connue grâce aux relations de voyages rédigées à l'époque. Mais de tels documents, écrits par des Européens, ne fournissent qu'une seule version des faits. Les traditions orales inuit rapportent une autre interprétation. L'article examine deux sources de l'histoire orale des Inuit. Il s'agit, d'une part, de témoignages recueillis par Charles Francis Hall dans les années 1860 et, d'autre part, de l'histoire telle qu'elle a été racontée, au cours de l'hiver de 1991, par un groupe d'aînés d'Iqaluit.

ABSTRACT

The history of the Frobisher voyages is well known from documents written at the time of these expeditions. These documents written by Europeans contain only one side of the story. Inuit interpretations of these visits are contained in their oral history. In this paper two sources of Inuit oral history are examined. These are the testimony collected by Charles Francis Hall in the 1860s, and oral history shared by the elders of Iqaluit in the winter of 1991.

Introduction

History is the interpretation and understanding of past events. Generally, it is based upon documents written at the time of the events. For the history of many parts of the world, and of the "New World" in particular, only the European colonialists kept written documents. Therefore the history of these regions tends to be extremely biased, recorded as it is from only one viewpoint. Usually it is possible only to speculate on the feelings of the indigenous peoples as they met Europeans for the first time. As a result, native peoples are frequently treated by historians as passive actors in a play written, directed, and staged by Europeans. However, in some cases this history need not be so one-sided. Oral traditions describing encounters with Europeans were recounted and transmitted across generations by native peoples. These accounts, where they exist, offer a new dimension to our interpretation of culture contact history. The voyages of Sir Martin Frobisher are one example of such an occurrence. Through their oral history the Inuit of Frobisher Bay maintained and passed on their memories of these voyages from generation to generation.[1]

The Oral Traditions

The first non-Inuk to hear, collect, and try to interpret the oral history surrounding the voyages of Sir Martin Frobisher was the American, Charles Francis Hall.[2] Hall visited Frobisher Bay from 1860 to 1862. A journalist by trade, he was driven by his belief that members of the lost Franklin expedition were still alive in the Arctic. They had been adopted by Inuit families and were living in the vicinity of King William Island. It was Hall's mission to locate these men and return them to their real families. He therefore arranged transport to the north on the whaling ship *George Henry*. When the ship arrived in Beare Sound, between Frobisher Bay and Cumberland Sound, it was too late in the year for the Inuit to consider embarking on the lengthy and dangerous voyage to the west coast of Hudson Bay and onwards to King William Island. Hall had to content himself with practising his mapping skills and learning to travel with the Inuit.

On one of his voyages with the Inuit, Koojese, a local boat leader for the whalers, pointed out a location where *qallunaat* (non-Inuit) had lived and built a boat. Hall, surveying the treeless barren ground, decided that this story was not credible. As a result, he noted in his journal, it was not until several interviews later that he connected this tradition with the voyages of Sir Martin Frobisher [Hall 1864, 221].

The only written source Hall had available on board ship that covered the Frobisher voyages was Barrow's *A Chronological History of Voyages in the Arctic Regions* (1818). From this source Hall learned that five men had been captured by the Inuit on the first voyage. Despite enquiries on later voyages, nothing had been learned of their fate. However, Frobisher and his men suspected the worst, and the discovery of some of the missing men's clothes (on the second voyage) seemed to confirm their worst suspicions.

Once Hall had determined, to the best of his ability, that the Inuit still remembered the voyages of Frobisher, he became impassioned by the history of the lost men. Through interviews with elders he discovered that the lost men had not been killed by the Inuit. Instead the Inuit had looked after them throughout the cold winter. Then, in the spring, the Englishmen had built a boat and attempted to leave the north. Unfortunately it was still too early in the season and they soon froze, and eventually died.[3]

Despite the importance of his research and recording of oral history testimony as fact, much of what Hall could have discovered was lost. Hall asked questions and interpreted the answers in the way that made the most sense for his own aims and objectives. Hall's greatest desire in life was to prove that the missing Franklin survivors would have been looked after by the Inuit and therefore could still be alive. His discovery, therefore, that the Inuit had fed, clothed, and housed the lost Frobisher men - in his mind at least - must have added extra weight to his cause. He must have seen this as positive publicity for future fundraising for his next expedition to the Arctic [contra Rowley 1993[4]].

What does this probable bias of Hall's mean for current interpretations of his oral history data? The most drastic solution would be to discard his information as useless. This would be extremely unfortunate. Hall's data, while undoubtedly skewed in its interpretation, is nonetheless the content of interviews he conducted with the Inuit. There is no evidence that Hall actually fabricated people's replies to his queries. Rather, his flaws were the lesser of placing his own interpretation on their replies and of not investigating other avenues of questioning. Undoubtedly, had Hall had access to a more complete account of the Frobisher voyages, his questions would have delved more deeply into the chronology of the expeditions and the events the Inuit were describing. Therefore, while the testimony Hall gathered remains an invaluable resource, care must be paid to its interpretation. Re-interpretation of this material is currently underway, working with the unpublished accounts of interviews recorded by Hall in his private journals.[5]

Today

Much has changed in Frobisher Bay since Sir Martin's voyages. Today the majority of the local Inuit population live in the community of Iqaluit, located at the head of Frobisher Bay. Iqaluit was established as a military weather station and possible staging route to Europe during World War II. Since the Inuit migrated into the community, their hunting lifestyle has mostly been replaced by a mixed economy based on government, service industries, tourism, government assistance, and some hunting. In addition, young people attend government-operated educational facilities and learn from a curriculum developed and instructed primarily by southern educators. In the face of this contemporary situation it is valid to pose the following question: is there anything left of the oral history surrounding the Frobisher voyages?

There are many reasons to argue that the oral record has been irreparably disrupted and that no evidence surrounding the Frobisher voyages could be recoverable. The most commonly voiced opinion is that too much time and too many contact events have occurred in the interim. Inuit lifestyles and the transmission of traditional knowledge have been dramatically altered. Therefore, no material surrounding the Frobisher voyages would have survived. After all, it is over 416 years since the first Frobisher voyage took place. Hall's testimony was collected in the 1860s and its survival is credible because there was little Inuit-European contact following Frobisher's voyages and preceding Hall's arrival with American whalers.

After Hall, contact with Europeans and Americans was constant, if not consistent, in its intensity. This contact led to a profusion of diseases which wiped out large numbers of people. In particular, tuberculosis and measles were responsible for practically depopulating Frobisher Bay between the late 1800s and the mid-1900s. Given the increased susceptibility of the extremely aged sector of the population to death through disease, it is likely that many of the elders would have passed away during these epidemics. With their death the transmission of oral history from one generation to the next would have been interrupted. This argument is substantiated by Hall's biographer, who wrote in a footnote:

> Since the great influx of outsiders during World War II and after, the Frobisher Bay Eskimos have lost their oral tradition, and they no longer tell stories about Frobisher - or about Hall. Nowadays there is nothing remarkable or memorable about kadloonas [qallunaat] coming to their land. [Loomis 1971, 133-34]

Another possible argument against the survival of oral history concerning the Frobisher voyages is that these traditions are relatively unimportant. In the face of the stress Inuit society has undergone in the post-World War II years, it would seem unlikely that these relatively minor traditions would have survived.

While all these arguments contain merit, they are based on a line of reasoning that suggests there to be nothing left and that therefore it would be a waste of time to interview elders concerning these traditions. Contra these arguments run the arguments for why some of the oral traditions might have survived. These are outlined below.

Traditions surrounding first contact with strangers survive longer than traditions about later contact. This is not surprising. Once the strangers have established themselves and are a known quantity, the local people will still be interested in when these outsiders first arrived and what they were like. Later stories, unless they are of extremely unusual events, are less likely to be remembered since the events they describe have become commonplace and are therefore unexceptional. Traditions surrounding Sir Martin Frobisher and his men (the Vikings notwithstanding) would fall into this category of first contact.

Next, the change in lifestyle, portrayed as so damaging to Inuit traditions, is very recent. The elders of Iqaluit grew up on the land. While their economy was a mixed hunting and trapping one their lifestyle was not so different from that of their ancestors who encountered Frobisher. Some of the elders grew up in the Countess of Warwick Sound and camped at many of the places visited by Frobisher and his men.

In conjunction with this, traditions that are tied to a landscape have a greater chance of surviving than do others. We know that at least two places in Countess of Warwick Sound were named as a result of Frobisher's visits. These are Kodlunarn Island (*Qallunaat*) and Nepouetiesupbing (*Naparutsiturvik*).[6] There may be others. When young Inuit were learning the local geography, so necessary to successful survival, the history of the place-names was also relayed. Therefore, while some traditions may have lost their importance and been lost, those attached to place-names maintained their prominence.

Finally, despite introduced diseases and population shifts through time that have led to dramatic changes in the Frobisher Bay population, there are still many residents whose families have lived in the Frobisher Bay region since at least the time of Charles Francis Hall. Hall kept detailed records of the people he met, recording their names and familial relationships. Many of the names he recovered are specific to southern Baffin Island. These names are still found among today's population, indicating direct ancestral links. The people Hall talked with were descendants of Inuit who lived in the region when Frobisher visited the Bay. Therefore their contemporary relatives are also direct descendants of the Inuit who encountered Frobisher and his men.

The facts presented argue that there is an equally strong case that some of the oral traditions concerning the voyages of Sir Martin Frobisher might still exist. However, why bother if Hall recorded this oral history? As we have seen, this was not the case. Hall's questions were directed solely at understanding the history of the lost men. As a result, he never discussed Inuit interactions with the Frobisher people, location of mines, etc. Although the information Hall gathered is extremely important, it is unlikely that it is the entire history remembered by the people.

Thus there are two conflicting arguments: 1) that the oral history has been lost; and 2) that the oral history may still persist to this day. It is important to ascertain which is correct, for several reasons. One of these is to investigate the extent to which the transmission of oral testimony has been disrupted by the recent potentially "overwhelming" changes in Inuit society. Another is to record those traditions that still remain. While the case can be made that many of today's elders were raised in an environment where the traditions were still being transmitted, the same cannot be argued for today's youth. Although innovative teaching methods and oral history are being introduced into the school programme, the overwhelming focus of young people's attention is on southern lifestyles. Many of the traditions are now at the point of being lost. Therefore it is important that remaining traditions be recorded for the Inuit of the future. Also, collecting remaining history concerning Frobisher will allow us to compare the testimony of today with that gathered by Hall. This presents a unique opportunity to document the changes that have occurred in an oral narrative over the space of 130 years.

Research

To ascertain if any oral history about Inuit-Frobisher contact still exists, research on the Frobisher voyages has been integrated into a larger research project. This project is concerned with culture contact in the Frobisher Bay region through time. It is concerned primarily with re-integrating the Inuit into their history, thereby providing them with the opportunity to express their opinions and beliefs about contact with Europeans and North Americans. In this way their role in their own history will change from that of passive actor to active participant. This project was proposed to the Iqaluit elders in late 1990 and the first field work took place in 1991.

Many of the Iqaluit elders belong to the Iqaluit Elder's Society. This group holds weekly meetings in its own building. These meetings are generally informal gatherings which anyone can attend. It was at one of these meetings that my interpreter and I made our initial contact with the elders and arranged several interviews. These interviews were preliminary in nature. Our aim was to begin to get to know the elders and to learn from them the topics they felt comfortable discussing. Historic Inuit society is often regarded as egalitarian in nature; however, this does not mean that everyone was a generalist. In Inuit society, as in all societies, certain individuals were renowned for the skills they had.   Today's elders prefer to discuss topics about which they feel knowledgable and will recommend visiting others to talk about other topics. Through these meetings and discussions we have begun to build up information on the different elders and their areas of expertise.

Frobisher Contacts

The voyages of Sir Martin Frobisher were not the primary focus of the interviews with Iqaluit elders. Therefore, during these informal interviews, questions focusing on the voyages were raised only when relevant and where a subjective decision was made by both the interviewer and interpreter that such a question would not cause offense.

Four elders were asked whether they had heard any stories about Kodlunarn Island. All elders replied in the affirmative and stated that *qallunaat* had built a ship there a long time ago. One elder referred to a spot where the same ship was wrecked prior to its refurbishment and two referred by name to the locale where the mast had been stepped in. In one interview this latter information was recounted in a manner identical to how it had been told to Hall 130 years earlier.

These preliminary interviews, therefore, confirmed beyond any doubt that the elders of Iqaluit are still familiar with the oral history surrounding the first contact their ancestors had with *qallunaat*. However, these interviews also confirmed that these oral traditions are fast disappearing. The elders we spoke with sometimes expressed reluctance to discuss the traditions about Kodlunarn Island. They considered that they did not know the traditions well enough to pass them on accurately. One collaborator informed us that she was never told the history directly. It was information she overheard during adult conversations. As children were not supposed to listen to adult conversations she felt it was not proper behaviour for her to pass this information on to others.

Further Research

Preliminary discussions in Iqaluit have shown the critical nature of continuing the contemporary oral history research. Therefore this research will continue with the co-operation and collaboration of the Iqaluit elders, in order to illuminate the history of this first contact encounter.

This research will not only shed new light on the Frobisher voyages but will also accomplish several other objectives. It will allow us to re-interpret Hall's material in a different light. As discussed above, Hall became overly concerned by the history of the missing sailors. It is therefore likely that he misinterpreted some of the information passed on to him in an unconscious attempt to further his own interests.

Preliminary research has already brought one such possible instance to light. When Hall interviewed Inuit concerning Kodlunarn Island they told him it was so named because of the *qallunaat* who built a ship there. When he learned that the missing men had built a ship and tried to escape the north he immediately concluded that the ship built on Kodlunarn Island and the ship built by the five lost men were one and the same. However, on the third voyage several ships were damaged. It seems more likely, therefore, that the story of the ship being built on Kodlunarn in fact refers to the refurbishment of a damaged ship. Likewise, the stepping in of the mast at Nepouetiesupbing is more likely to refer to a mast on one of Frobisher's ships rather than a boat built in the north. The data contained in Hall's material can be used to support this interpretation. The few statements we have from the elders of Iqaluit corroborate this earlier testimony and make it even more likely that Hall misinterpreted some of the information that was passed on to him.

There is another important reason to record the oral history of culture contact and of the Frobisher voyages in particular. There is no question that Inuit traditions and oral history are fast disappearing. With the passing of each elder a wealth of information is being lost. Recording memories of the Frobisher voyages while they still exist will permit future generations access to a more balanced interpretation of a crucial moment in history: the first contact in Frobisher Bay between Inuit and Europeans.

Notes

1   "Frobisher Bay" refers to the geographic region surrounding the bay bearing Frobisher's name. The contemporary community at the head of the bay previously known as Frobisher Bay is now Iqaluit.

2   For more information on C.F. Hall, the reader is referred to his biography by Loomis (see references).

3   For a more detailed version of the history of the lost men, see Rowley 1993.

4   Further research on Hall's unpublished data and his massaging of this data prior to publication has led to this additional interpretation.

5   The Hall papers are located in the Department of Naval History, National Museum of American History, Smithsonian Institution, Washington, D.C.

6   The spellings used for geographic locales are those composed by Hall. Where I have been able to document the correct Inuit terms for these locations I have placed them in brackets following Hall's term. The latter name means "place where the mast was stepped in".

ACKNOWLEDGEMENTS: The contemporary oral history research on the Frobisher voyages would have been impossible without the collaboration of the Iqaluit elders. Their generosity and willingness to share information is gratefully acknowledged. In addition, I would like to thank my interpreter and friend Leah Otak for her work on this material. This field work was accomplished through a contract with the Canadian Museum of Civilization. Logistic support while in the field was provided by the Science Institute of the Northwest Territories. I am extremely grateful to both agencies for their assistance.

My research on Hall's unpublished documents has always been encouraged by William Fitzhugh of the Smithsonian Institution. In addition, Harold Ellis, of the Smithsonian's Division of Naval History, has been very helpful in providing access to the Hall papers.

References

Barrow, John
   1818   *A Chronological History of Voyages into the Arctic Regions.* London: John
             Murray.

Hall, Charles F.
   1864   *Life with the Esquimaux.* 2 vols. London: Sampson Low, Son, and Marston.

Loomis, Chauncey C.
   1971   *Weird and Tragic Shores.* New York: Alfred A. Knopf.

Rowley, Susan
   1993   Frobisher *miksanut*: Inuit accounts of the Frobisher voyages. In *Archeology of
             the Frobisher Voyages,* ed. W. Fitzhugh and J. Olin, 27-40. Washington:
             Smithsonian Institution Press.